FLEXIBLE PATTER

FLEXIBLE PATTERNS OF WORK

Edited by

Chris Curson

INSTITUTE OF PERSONNEL MANAGEMENT

First published 1986

Cover design by Anita Ruddell

Phototypeset by Latimer Trend & Company Ltd, Plymouth
and printed in Great Britain by
Dotesios Printers Ltd, Bradford-on-Avon, Wiltshire

British Library Cataloguing in Publication Data

Flexible patterns of work.
  1. Hours of labor—Great Britain
  I. Curson, Chris   II. Institute of Personnel
  Management
  331.25'7'0941   HD5165

ISBN 0–85292–376–7

Contents

Acknowledgements

In the text of the report mention is made of the extensive co-operation that the working party's representatives received from all the companies which they approached, too numerous to mention individually. Without such help so readily given, the entire exercise would have been quite impossible.

The main task of organizing the enquiries, carrying out the case studies and drafting most of the report has fallen equally upon **Stephen Palmer** and **Alastair Evans**, both managers on the Institute's staff. In this they have been ably assisted by a researcher engaged for the exercise, **Jenny Bell**. All three, under the direction of the working party, have carried out these tasks with a very high degree of application and professionalism. Their knowledge of their subject and the readiness with which they have both presented lines of enquiry for consideration and subsequently carried out those enquiries, have greatly assisted the working party and have put us greatly in their debt.

Our thanks are also due to Tracey Palmer, Debbie Roberts and Anne Summun of IPM headquarters staff for typing the manuscript.

Chris Curson, Personnel Manager, South Eastern Electricity Board (Working Party Chairman)

Tony Attew, Functional Personnel Executive, Digital Equipment Co Ltd

Ken Birkett, Chief Manpower Adviser, Anglian Water

Geoff Dobson, Industrial Relations Officer, BOC Transhield Ltd

Paul Massey, Managing Director, Sibson/J&H Ltd

David Redmond, Assistant Managing Director, BOC Transhield Ltd

Les Walker, Company Personnel Manager, Britvic Limited

Introduction

Chris Curson

Over the last few years or so, there have been increasingly clear indications that across most of the developed economies in the world, the notion of a regular working year, based on a five day week, is coming under challenge for many workers. If this is so, and the pattern of at least a generation is now to be modified, then the implications for society may be considerable, even momentous.

Historians may one day determine when this trend first began and what were its causes. Could the first sign be discerned in the late sixties, for example, when relatively full employment conditions and the arrival of a higher proportion of married women in the workforce combined to create job sharing and job splitting ideas? Probably this is too remote, but did the equal pay legislation of the 1970s have any indirect influence? Moving closer to the present, has the rapidly increasing pressure on employers' costs that arose during and after the oil crises been the paramount factor? Has this, by compelling managements to find the most cost effective working patterns and creating higher levels of unemployment, reduced the level of resistance to change from what it might otherwise have been? And, finally, how far has the advent of the so called new technology, with its undoubted potential impact on traditional practices of working patterns in many fields, played the decisive part?

Whatever the relative importance of these and other factors, the recent experience of many personnel managers, concerned as they are with practical problems in industry, has suggested that something of a revolution is now getting under way, and this impression seems to be borne out amply by the opinion of many independent commentators and observers. Furthermore, and perhaps crucially, it may be that the expectations of a whole generation of workers are now being modified to match the changes, in that significant numbers of younger people now no longer expect necessarily to have a working lifetime consisting of such a regular pattern. Increasingly they have come to expect difficulty in obtaining and holding a job and may also increasingly come to expect extended periods away from work to deal with the demands of parenthood, retraining or even 'sabbatical' periods of leave.

Working hours that are less than full time is now the lot of no less than one in five workers. Most, but by no means all, of these workers are women, and they are concentrated in the service industries. An important aspect of their conditions, touched upon again in a later chapter, is that their benefits and legal protection are usually significantly less than those of full time staff. (The same point does not normally apply to shift workers and other 'full time' workers whose hours are nonetheless not the regular '9 to 5' type of pattern). There can often therefore be a conflict between the employer's objective of achieving the most flexible working patterns to meet his type of business, 'and the aspirations of the workforce. This aspect has to be faced by personnel managers and their staffs, who are regularly called upon to advise their managerial colleagues on such issues. But such matters are also, or ought to be, of interest to the community generally because of their relationship with general levels of productivity, their impact on the number and type of job opportunities and their social implications.

It is against this background that the two national committees of the Institute most directly concerned, the Pay and Employment Conditions Committee and the Organization and Manpower Planning Committee, decided in 1985 to set up a joint working party to examine these issues and their implications with the following terms of reference:

> To provide a practical guide describing changing patterns of work and to inform Institute members and others of the practicality of these changes by investigating work patterns in the private and public sectors and considering in particular the methods of and reasons for introducing change, the challenges associated with its introduction and the benefits yielded. The guide would also draw out the implications of change for future employment prospects.

The working party rapidly became aware that over the last few years a considerable amount of work has already been published in this field, and our indebtedness to all those who have produced this (see bibliography) is readily acknowledged. Nonetheless the Institute is able, because of its extensive links with those working in all industrial sectors and at all levels, to gather and analyse information on a scale and in a way not easily achieved elsewhere. For this reason, the results of the working party's enquiries have been a total of over 90 examples of new working patterns, including 16 case studies set out in full, which have been gathered by the Institute's staff and external researcher across a wide range of industrial sectors. The study would obviously not have been possible without the complete co-operation of all those concerned in the organizations that were chosen, and the working party and indeed the Institute, expresses its grateful thanks and appreciation to all who helped in this way.

In addition to the case studies, several other individuals and organizations became aware of the work in progress through publicity in the Institute's journal and they wrote and offered useful information and ideas, so thanks are also due to them.

What follows is in eight chapters and the structure of the book and the main topics covered are as follows:

Chapter 1 sets out the emerging themes in flexible work patterns, summarizing the findings of other researchers in this field and the main findings of the IPM study. This chapter also considers the reported views of trade unions to developments in this field.

Chapter 2 describes the introduction of a variety of patterns of flexible basic hours including flexible daily and weekly hours and annual hours contracts. This chapter also looks at compressed working weeks, including four and $4\frac{1}{2}$ day weeks, and various fortnightly working patterns, including six day, nine day and $9\frac{1}{2}$ day fortnights.

Chapter 3 examines the wide variety of alternatives to conventional paid overtime being introduced by organizations.

Chapter 4 examines new trends in shiftworking, including four, five, six and seven crew operations and the issue of 12 hour daily shifts, with an analysis of the advantages and disadvantages of the various options.

Chapter 5 considers a range of alternatives to the employment of full time permanent staff, including new ways in which temporaries, part timers, job sharers, home workers and teleworkers are being deployed and the costs and benefits of these various alternatives.

Chapter 6 examines sub-contracting involving the replacement of employment contracts and contracts of service by commercial contracts for services. It considers the reasons for these developments, costs and benefits, disadvantages and some of the legal implications of sub-contracting.

Chapter 7 concludes the main body of the study by looking at one aspect of the changing pattern of working lifetimes—sabbaticals, extended leave and career breaks. It considers the reasons for these policies and the nature and types of schemes in operation.

Chapter 8 concludes the study with a consideration of the implications of all the findings for personnel managers and personnel policies, including the possible implications of flexible working patterns for future employment and unemployment.

The last part of the book sets out in full 16 case studies illustrating a variety of different aspects of new work patterns adopted by organizations participating in the study.

1 Emerging themes in flexible work patterns

Alastair Evans and Jenny Bell

By any standards, the economic performance of British industry during the 1970s and into the early 1980s was poor both in relation to its own performance standards of the previous two decades and in relation to competitors. As indicated in figure 1 below, between 1950 and the early 1970s, UK productivity in manufacturing and services rose by around 50 per cent. During most of the 1970s, with the exception of the primary sector (mainly agriculture and mining), the trend in productivity growth flattened out. Similarly, in relation to job creation, during the period from 1950 to the early 1970s, the number of people in employment rose by around two million. Following a period of very little net increase in employment during the 1970s, the number of employees in employment fell by two million between 1979 and 1983, a decline which has recently been offset to a small extent by an upturn in self employment and part time jobs in the service sector.

Against this background, the nature of the labour market has also been changing. In addition to a substantial rise in unemployment, the composition of the employed population has also been undergoing change, as indicated in the table 1 below. Between 1965 and 1985, conventional full time employment has declined from just over four-fifths to just over two-thirds of the employed labour force, with a particular decline in full time males as a proportion of the total. During the same period, part time female employment and self employment have increased significantly as a proportion of the total.

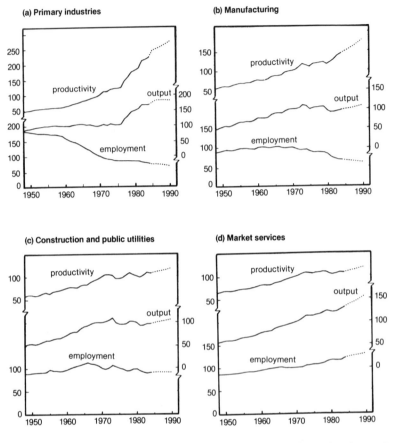

Source: *'Review of the economy and employment',* Vol. 1, Institute of Employment Research, University of Warwick, 1985, p.12.

Figure 1   Productivity, output and employment 1950–90

Table 1   Full time, part time and self employment
1965–1985

	1965	(%)	(000's) 1975	(%)	1985	(%)
Full time male	14,743	(59)	13,144	(55)	11,715	(49)
Full time female	5805	(23)	5448	(23)	4959	(20)
Part time female	2732	(11)	3551	(15)	4449	(19)
Self employment	1617	(6)	1864	(8)	2604	(11)
TOTAL	24,897		24,007		23,727	

(Percentages may not add up to 100 because of rounding)
Source: *Employment Gazettes*

It is, of course, widely argued that the post war period was particularly favourable to economic growth and productivity, but that the period after 1972–73 was characterized by recession induced by the deflationary effects of oil and other energy price rises and uncertainty arising out of volatile currency fluctuations. Whilst these arguments are undoubtedly true, it appears on the basis of international comparisons of economic performance, that the UK's performance was worse than competitors' on a range of measures in these more difficult circumstances, as indicated in figures 2 to 5 below. In relation to labour productivity, unit labour costs and various measures of cost competitiveness, the UK lagged behind most competitors in the period from 1974 to the early 1980s. The figures also indicate that over the last two to three years, there has been a marked improvement in performance, with renewed productivity growth, particularly in manufacturing, and there is a forecast from the University of Warwick that these trends are likely to continue for the remainder of the decade. Internationally, labour productivity in manufacturing has improved in the past five years relative to the USA, France and Italy, and unit labour costs, whilst still higher than many competitors, have also shown a relative improvement. As a result of the depreciation of the sterling exchange rate after 1980, together with improvements in productivity and the slower growth of relative labour costs, the competitive overall position of UK manufacturing has improved since 1980 in comparison with the 1970s.

Whilst many factors, both domestic and international, have influenced this improvement in performance, the concern of this

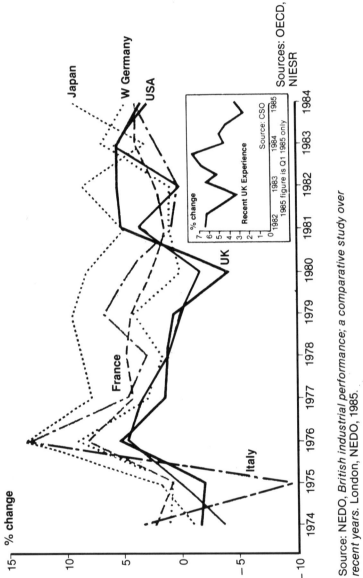

Source: NEDO, *British industrial performance; a comparative study over recent years.* London, NEDO, 1985.

Figure 2 Labour productivity: Annual average growth of output per person hour in manufacturing

Sources: OECD, NIESR

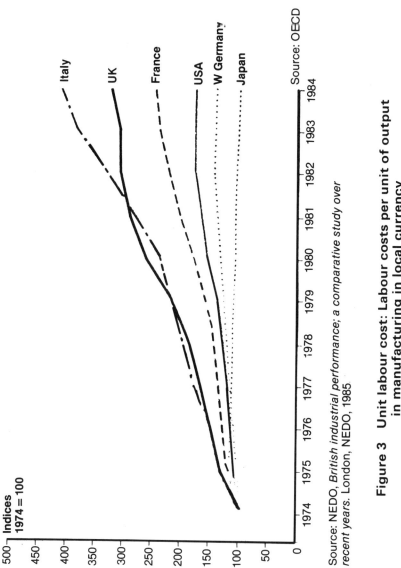

Source: NEDO, *British industrial performance: a comparative study over recent years*. London, NEDO, 1985

Figure 3 Unit labour cost: Labour costs per unit of output in manufacturing in local currency

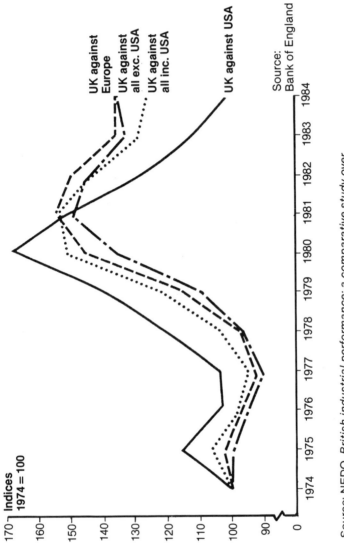

Source: NEDO, *British industrial performance; a comparative study over recent years*. London, NEDO, 1985

Figure 4   Cost competitiveness: In terms of relative unit labour costs in manufacturing

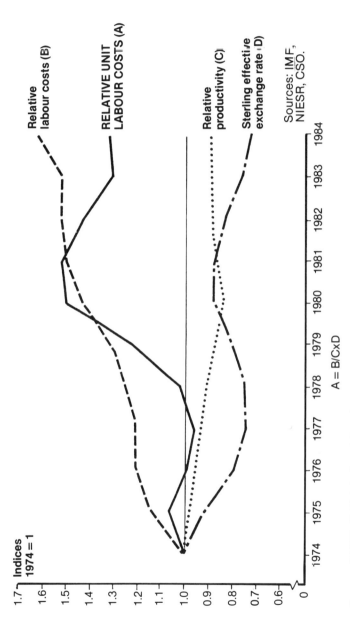

Source: NEDO, *British industrial performance; a comparative study over recent years.* London, NEDO, 1985

Figure 5 Cost contributions: Sources of changes in UK cost competitiveness in manufacturing

book is with the measures taken by employers in all sectors of
the economy to improve the flexibility and productivity of their
workforces through more flexible working patterns.

Employers' strategies for increased flexibility

Against a background of deep international recession, tight
monetary policies, high interest and exchange rates and growing international competition, many UK employers, particularly
in the manufacturing sector, have been faced with a fight for
survival which a considerable number have failed to win. One
major outcome has been demanning on a massive scale with a
resultant increase in unemployment. In the public sector also,
public expenditure constraints and financial targets have similarly led to cutbacks in a sector which had previously been a
growth area of employment.

On the industrial relations front, employers came under
increasing pressure in the late 1970s to reduce standard working
hours which would, without compensating increases in productivity, have further added to unit labour costs. Following the
national agreement in the engineering industry in 1979 to cut
the standard working week of manual workers from 40 to 39
hours with effect from 1981, many other industries followed with
reductions to 39 or 38 hours per week in the early 1980s. Against
a background of recession and other financial constraints, there
were considerable pressures on organizations to introduce productivity improvements to offset the effects of reduced hours on
unit labour costs, including the adoption of new more flexible
work patterns.

Possibly more significant than this, however, has been the
impact of large scale redundancies and the associated costs,
both financial and non-financial, and a growing reluctance of
organizations, in the face of continued market uncertainty, to
commit themselves to the recruitment of full time, permanent
staff even in the event of an upturn. Instead, organizations have
been looking at alternative ways of improving their flexibility
and responsiveness to fluctuations in economic activity with the
leanest possible levels of full time permanent staff. One influen-
tial explanation of the type of employment model increasingly
being adopted has been put forward by John Atkinson of the

Institute of Manpower Studies (IMS) who argues that work-forces are tending to be segmented into two broad categories, the 'core' and the 'periphery', in order to achieve greater flexibility, a model which is illustrated in figure 6.[1]

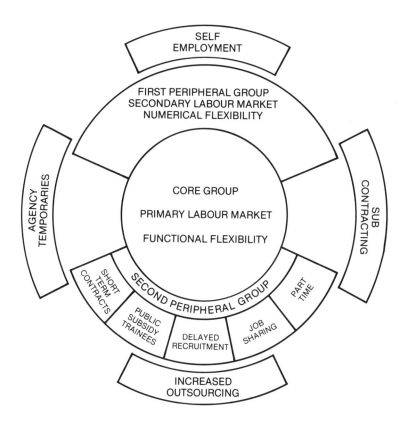

Source: *Flexible Manning: the way ahead,* Brighton, IMS/Manpower Ltd, 1984

Figure 6 The flexible firm

Flexible manning: 'core' and 'peripheral' workforces

As a result of a survey of 72 firms employing 660,000 people in the food and drink, manufacturing, engineering, retailing and financial services sectors, the Institute of Manpower Studies has identified the following characteristics underpinning employers' strategies in the period following the recession of the early 1980s:[2]

- a priority for achieving a permanent reduction in unit labour costs against a background of market uncertainty and growing international competition
- a reluctance of firms to commit themselves to any increase in permanent, full time employees even in the event of an upturn in business
- a need to look for novel patterns of working against a background of pressure for shorter basic hours which would otherwise drive up unit labour costs

The key consideration has been 'flexibility' and firms have, in particular, been looking at three kinds of flexibility:

- *functional flexibility* so that employees, with the appropriate training or retraining, can be redeployed quickly to different activities and crafts. Examples include the multi skilled craftsman or career changes amongst management and professional staff
- *numerical flexibility* which enables the organization to increase or decrease employee numbers quickly in response to short term changes in the demand for labour. Examples include temporary employment, sub-contract and part time staff
- *financial flexibility* which involves the establishment of payment systems which reinforce the organization's greater requirement for flexibility. Thus, for example, there has been a greater emphasis on the market rate for the job rather than 'across the board' increases in pay and a shift towards rewarding performance or rewarding on the basis of the range of skills possessed and individual performance

In order to achieve all these three forms of flexibility, IMS suggests that organizations are beginning to take a radical look at traditional employment patterns and concludes that firms' labour forces are increasingly being segregated into a 'core' group and one or more 'peripheral' groups as illustrated in figure 6.

The core group tends to be characterized by employees with full time, permanent status and is central to the longer term future of the organization. Employees in this group are likely to be highly flexible and adaptable. The training and development resources of the organization are mainly devoted to them and they are more likely to enjoy good career and promotion prospects. Their rewards are closely related to the acquisition and deployment of additional skills and are likely to be more closely related to individual performance. This group also enjoys a higher degree of job security than employees in peripheral groups, in return for the requirement to be more flexible, retrain and relocate. The periphery is characterized by two sub-groups, both more marginal and designed to provide organizations with 'numerical flexibility'. The first group of these consists of full time employees with skills that are more readily available in the labour market, such as clerical, secretarial, routine and lesser skilled manual work. Such employees have less access to career opportunities, little investment in their training by the organization and tend to be characterized by high labour turnover which makes workforce reductions relatively easy by natural wastage. The second peripheral group provides even greater numerical flexibility and includes part timers, casuals, fixed term contract staff, temporaries, sub-contractors and public subsidy trainees, with even less job security than the first peripheral group.

The extent to which these patterns are being adopted by British employers is indicated in a paper entitled *Changing Working Patterns and Practices* produced in 1985 by the National Economic Development Council which summarizes the survey findings as follows:

> A total of 64 of the 72 participating companies had sought to increase the numerical flexibility of their workforces since 1980 and had introduced significant changes in their manning practices to do so. The practices adopted by firms throughout the sectors were diverse, but in general each sought to match labour more accurately to demand. Fluctuations in demand may occur within the working day (peak customer times in shops, banks etc); within the working week (Saturday sales peak in retailing); within the

month (payment of monthly salaries creating peak workload
for banks); or within the working year (seasonal demands
for products, seasonal agricultural production, seasonal
claims peaks in insurance). Demand fluctuations are sometimes predictable but can be very unpredictable: this distinction led to further differences in practices between
firms.

The duration of fluctuations in demand influenced the
form in which numerical flexibility was sought. Short term
fluctuations were more frequently handled through the use
of part time workers or overtime. Longer term fluctuations
were more often met by the use of temporary, casual or fixed
term employees or by increasing shiftwork. The ways in
which each company sought to improve numerical flexibility varied according to circumstances but, overall, four
typical solutions were identified:

- temporary workers
- part time workers
- overtime and shiftworking
- flexible working time

Sixty eight per cent of the respondents had increased their use of
temporary workers, over half of these in the previous five years.
Part time working was almost universally used in retailing and
by about half the respondents in financial services and manufacturing. Seventy one per cent of respondents had increased their
use of sub-contracting in the previous five years, mostly of
ancillary services and almost one-fifth had increased their use of
self employed workers.

In another survey conducted by Manpower Limited in 1984,
employers were asked about the extent to which they had
changed their use of part timers, temporaries and sub-contractors in the previous three years and the answers given by a
sample of nearly 450 employers is set out in table 2.[3]

Table 2   Use of part timers, temporaries and sub-contractors

	Production industries			% of respondents Service industries		
	Incr use	Same	Decr use	Incr use	Same	Decr use
Part timers	18	59	23	24	60	17
Temporaries	49	31	20	40	45	15
Sub-contractors	44	47	9	41	42	17

Source: *Flexible manning in business*, Slough, Manpower Ltd, 1985

The results indicate little change in the use of part timers, but a substantial growth in the trend towards using temporary staff and sub-contractors in the production and service sectors.

Similar views to these have also been put forward by Charles Handy of the London Business School, another leading authority on future work patterns.[4] Handy puts forward the proposals that in the future organizations will increasingly become:

- contractual
- professional
- federal

Charles Handy argues that organizations will concentrate more resources on activities at the core of the business and achieve greater flexibility by contracting out activities at the periphery or by building a category of second class employees on temporary or part time contracts. Organizations will become professional in the sense that they will have at the core a committed, versatile, skilled and knowledgeable group who know the organization's problems and products. These people will benefit from the organization's investment in their training and career development and enjoy greater job security in return for the willingness to try all tasks. Organizations are also increasingly becoming federal, relatively decentralized and made up of small, semi autonomous units in order to keep costs down, maintain flexibility and make the units more manageable.

Similar trends have also been observed in the United States. One study, for example, of 52 employers in California, widely divergent in firm size and industry, found that 49 of these organizations were deliberately fostering a two tier internal labour market.[5] They maintained a core workforce enjoying job security, career ladders, generous fringe benefits and other incentives to stay with the firm. These firms also employed what they termed 'flexible staff', occupying temporary, intermittent, part time or seasonal jobs, with a limited access to fringe benefits and the firms displayed an apparent unconcern about high levels of turnover in this group. The article concludes that many employers are seeking to reduce their reliance on core employees to meet fluctuations in demand because of the higher costs in terms of the reward package applied to this group and the potential damage to their job security in the event of a downturn. Instead, the scarce skills of core employees are augmented by independent consultants or by sub-contracting and routine skills at the periphery are obtained through part

time, temporary or casual working or through short term contracts.

Flexible work patterns—main themes in the IPM study

The IPM study is based upon examples of new working patterns
in 92 organizations, gathered either directly from the organizations concerned or from existing published sources. Twenty
eight of these organizations were visited and interviewed by
the IPM (16 of which are published in full as appendices), a
further 14 organizations sent case material and examples to the
IPM and a further 50 examples were drawn from existing published sources. The final sample illustrates a wide range of
practices from different industrial sectors and breaks down as
follows:

Aircraft manufacture	1
Banking, insurance and finance	6
Cement	1
Chemicals and petroleum products	9
Electrical engineering, office equipment and computer manufacture	8
Food, drink and tobacco	14
Gas, electricity and water	2
Glass	3
Health	1
Local government	10
Mechanical engineering	4
Metal goods manufacture	4
National government	5
Paper, printing and publishing	4
Private services	4
Retailing	7
Textiles	1
Transport	2
Vehicles and parts manufacture	6
TOTAL	92

An analysis of the size of organizations whose flexible work
patterns are described in this study are as follows:

Size	No of organizations	% of total
Less than 500	10	11
500–999	6	7
1000–4999	27	29
5000–9999	13	14
10,000–19,999	14	16
20,000–49,999	15	16
50,000–99,999	3	3
100,000+	4	4
TOTAL	92	

The main feature of the sample is the extent to which smaller and medium sized organizations are represented. Nearly half the companies employ under 5000 and over three quarters under 20,000 people.

Several themes emerge from the IPM study which overlap and are interrelated. As changes have taken place in the business environment, companies have reacted differently, depending on the nature of their business and the pressures upon it, the industrial relations climate and the concerns of particular personnel managers. As pressures for change have built up, some companies have taken a radical approach and tried to rethink their working patterns. Three major and obvious factors underlie most of the pressures for change—the effects of the recession, pressure for reduced working time and the introduction of new technology.

The recession has led to:

- reductions in the size of the workforce, which in turn has led to an examination of how best to make use of the remaining employees' time
- high unemployment, which has meant that employees and trade unions have been more prepared to consider different ways of working to retain jobs
- the creation of a pool of unemployed people prepared to take on more marginal work, such as part time or temporary employment
- a change in company philosophy—concentrating on the 'core' activities and skills and letting others provide

'peripheral' services in order to achieve more flexible ways of meeting upturns in demand without the commitment to employ permanent staff

- increased competition from abroad which has led companies to look at the working patterns of their foreign competitors
- a need to be more flexible in response to the demands of the market, eg by working at weekends, by taking on temporary workers or sub-contractors to deal with fluctuations in activity

Pressures to reduce working time have led to:

- measures, such as the removal of restrictive practices, to avoid the impact of shorter hours on unit labour costs or productivity
- measures to redistribute working time to provide a more cost effective match between the hours available and the pattern of demand for goods and services
- measures to avoid the replacement of shorter basic hours by greater overtime working

The introduction of new technology has also led to reductions in the size of workforces. Other effects have been:

- pressure to use expensive new plant to best advantage
- the opportunity to negotiate new working patterns at greenfield sites or when new technology has been introduced at an existing site
- the opportunity to have a more complex and flexible approach to working hours using computerized monitoring/clocking
- the possibility of more concentrated working hours (eg 12 hour shifts) as work becomes less physically arduous
- more flexibility about the location and timing of work, eg by using computers at home or away from the main workplace

There is also some evidence of changes in attitudes among employers and employees which have led to pressures for changes in working patterns. These include:

- the pressure for harmonization—not only from the unions, but also from some managers who now see the differences between manual and staff employees as no longer possible to justify

- manual workers wanting a more secure guarantee of earnings, eg so they can take out a mortgage
- a desire for time off to be in 'usable' blocks, eg long weekends
- more employees wanting to work less than full time—mainly women who want part time work and job sharing
- more people wanting to be self employed and offering their services as sub-contractors

The changes which have been introduced depend on a number of factors:

- the type of industry—continuous process, distribution etc
- the type of site—traditional, greenfield, office-based
- the type of workforce—young/old, male/female, skilled/unskilled
- the aims of the company—increased productivity/reduced costs/more flexibility
- existing structure/systems
- attitudes of company/employees
- amount of time/effort management is prepared to put into researching, negotiating and selling a new 'package'

Working hours Pressure for the reduction of working hours has been a major catalyst for change. Companies have been under increasing pressure to reduce working hours, both from the unions and because other local employers have reduced the working week.

Because in all the cases reported earnings have been maintained when working hours have been cut, many companies have attempted to get some sort of 'payback' for reducing working hours. They have also taken the opportunity to introduce other changes at the same time as part of a comprehensive productivity deal involving working patterns and practices, pay and terms and conditions of employment.

Although both unions and management have usually started off with the conviction that there should be a genuine reduction in working time—not just an increase in overtime pay—some employers have faced considerable difficulties in achieving this. Others have accepted increased costs and

reduced production. One widespread outcome of shorter working hours has been that many employees now work shorter hours
on Fridays. There are also several examples of the reduction in
working hours leading to radical changes. Among the changes
introduced along with reduced working hours have been:

- harmonization of hours
- changes in shift patterns, eg moving to five crew working
- annual hours contracts
- more flexible working practices
- abolition of overtime
- introduction of variable or compressed working hours

Shift working   The reduction in working hours to 39 or less a
week has had a major impact on continuous process industries
where shift work predominates. Most continuous process companies, until recently, had four crew working with shift workers
working 42 hours a week, including two hours contractual
overtime. Once working hours are further reduced, four crew
systems start to 'creak'. Either overtime is increased or more
'spares' have to be employed. This has led to increased interest
in five crew working and several examples of companies introducing five crew working at no additional cost are described
later. Some companies have been able to create the fifth crew,
without employing extra staff, by combining jobs and increasing
flexibility. Five crew rotas give employees more 'usable' time off
(ie in longer blocks) and can incorporate holidays, enabling
production to be maintained without the need for holiday shutdowns.

    Another way of providing employees with more 'usable' time
off is to move to 12 hour shifts. These seem to be popular with
employees, but some managements are less enthusiastic because
they believe that longer shifts create additional fatigue and that
productivity might fall. The success of 12 hour shifts depends to
some extent on the nature of the work. If it is very arduous then
12 hour shifts may not be possible.

Overtime   Average levels of overtime vary considerably from
company to company, depending partly on the nature of the
business and partly on custom and practice. Nearly all manage-

ments report that they want to reduce and/or abolish overtime. There are several examples of the reduction and abolition of overtime in the study, all of which involved a considerable increase in basic pay, but are said to have been cost effective in the long term.

Some companies have given employees time off in lieu instead of overtime pay, but there are varying reports of its success. Usually a 'banking' system has been necessary and where there has been a peak in activity which requires overtime working, it has sometimes been difficult to give time off immediately. In addition, an efficient monitoring system (usually computerized) is normally needed if alternatives to overtime pay are introduced.

Some companies are finding ways of reducing overtime. Examples are:

- introduction of five crew working
- other changes to shift systems
- not providing automatic cover ie working short crewed
- using 'payback' hours under annual hours agreements
- increased use of temporary workers and sub-contractors
- introducing more flexible working practices to use employees' time to best advantage

Sub-contracting The main reasons why companies are considering sub-contracting may be summarized as follows:

- *a change in company philosophy*: many companies increasingly wish to concentrate on 'core' activities—activities in which they have expertise—and to leave 'peripheral' activities to others. US-owned companies which have established plants in the UK in the last 10 to 15 years seem to have taken this approach for granted
- *economics*: sub-contractors' rates are often extremely competitive and contractors' tenders can be substantially lower than the cost of carrying out an activity directly in house
- *efficiency*: sub-contracting may be used to increase efficiency through the removal of restrictive practices/demarcation, covering for fluctuations in demand and saving the time spent by management on administration and backup

● *at the request of employees*: several examples were found of
   employees approaching the company and offering to provide services as independent contractors which they previously provided as company employees

The main areas where work is being sub-contracted are catering,
cleaning, security and road haulage, but there are examples of
sub-contracting in many other areas, eg secretarial services,
telephonists, drain cleaning, equipment maintenance and painting, decorating, gardening, etc, in several companies.

In effect, as the terms and conditions of manual employees
improve, for example through greater harmonization, it becomes
less attractive for companies to employ them if acceptable
alternatives can be found. Employees may find they have priced
themselves out of a job. If a company has a single status policy
and provides benefits such as pensions and private medical cover
for all employees, it may not be cost effective to employ lesser
skilled employees who have no long term future with the company.

Temporary workers   There is some evidence of an increase
in the use of temporary workers, although a few companies did
report a reduction in their use. The employment of temporary
workers has several functions, including the following:

● to cover for temporary peaks in activity
● to cover for holiday and sickness absence
● to protect the job security of core employees
● to provide a more flexible alternative to full time
   employees

Most temporary workers are employed on short term contracts
of unspecified length, sometimes renewable from week to week.
Most receive the same basic pay and benefits as permanent
employees but are not permitted to enter the pension scheme,
or receive private medical cover, etc.

There is some evidence that the nature of temporary employment is changing away from such traditional uses as holiday
or absence cover towards new reasons such as meeting peak
demand or acting as a buffer providing for greater job security
for core permanent staff.

New technology—homeworking and teleworking A few instances of new technology homeworking and teleworking—working from home via a computer terminal—were found and there was some evidence that productivity levels can be higher and investment in overheads, such as office accommodation, lower through such arrangements. A few organizations are at the stage of experimenting with teleworking and the feeling is that in the longer term it could be expanded from data input work to include field sales staff who do not need to go into their offices on a regular basis.

Part timers and job sharing The major growth area of part time working is in retailing, although there are also examples of part timers replacing full timers in production work. There is also the possibility that the move toward sub-contracting may mean a reduction in the number of part timers employed in traditional areas such as catering and cleaning. Outside retailing, many managers are against the employment of part timers, fearing lack of continuity and less commitment to the job, but in companies where part timers are employed, these problems do not seem to arise. Job sharing is hard to find and where it does exist it has usually come about as a result of an approach from employees (normally women) or has been introduced by employers in both the public and private sectors as a means of providing employment and training for young people. Some of the examples of job sharing encountered were not shared in the real sense. For example, the jobs involved no handover and the work tended to be self contained. As well as advantages for employees, there are some advantages to companies in employing job sharers including:

● the retention of experienced staff
● cover for sickness and holidays
● possibly greater productivity because employees are working shorter hours

Whilst advocates of job sharing see it as applying to all levels of work, a number of managers thought that job sharing could only be used for particular tasks, usually those which did not demand a high level of skill or responsibility.

Sabbaticals, extended leave and career breaks A few examples of these were found, but generally such schemes do not seem to be widespread. Although many personnel managers were aware of such schemes there was no desire to see them introduced. Most managers said that they would not be prepared to take sabbaticals for fear that their jobs would not exist when they returned. Among the organizations which have introduced such schemes, their functions can be broadly categorized as follows:

- sabbaticals as a reward for good service
- extended career breaks and career re-entry
- arrangements for 'banking' extended leave
- extended leave for social, educational and other purposes

Trade union attitudes towards flexible work patterns

During the 1980s, trade unions have been operating in a very different environment from that of the 1960s and 1970s. Since peaking at 13.4 million members in 1979 (55 per cent of the work force), membership has now fallen by over two million to 11.1 million members in 1984 (46 per cent of the workforce). Rising unemployment has reduced trade union bargaining power and the priority of trade union members has tended to focus on the survival of the organizations they work for and the preservation of jobs rather than on forcing issues by means of industrial action.

In its response to the NEDC paper on changing working patterns and practices, referred to above, the TUC rejected the 'core and periphery' model as either what was happening or should happen to work patterns.[6] They expressed doubt whether British management was acting in such a strategic or co-ordinated way but accepted that such measures were being introduced in a piecemeal or 'ad hoc' manner. The TUC was also sceptical about the notion of greater job security at the 'core' and felt that insecurity and worsening conditions were being experienced by all groups of workers. The TUC did, however, acknowledge the growth in use of temporaries, part timers, self employment and sub-contracting and have proposed that union bargaining strategies should ensure that such workers are employed on the same conditions as permanent workers. Wherever possible, contractors should also be unionized.

Another analysis of the trade union position towards flexible work patterns has been prepared by Paul Rathkey, a trade union researcher.[7] He argues that neither the TUC nor individual unions have given very much thought to newly emerging patterns and suffer from a lack of any strategy for reducing working time beyond extolling the virtues of a 35 hour week and the need for early retirement. He argues that the trade union movement as a whole finds it 'hard to think in terms other than a weekly wage for a defined working week on the basis of an eight hour day' and goes on to analyse the positions of trade unions towards the new working patterns which were presented above.

Trade unions generally have no formal policies on such arrangements as flexible daily, weekly or annual hours, but their attitudes may be influenced by the fact that such working patterns may exceed the eight hour day, creating problems of undue fatigue for employees and possibly also doing away with the principle that hours in excess of eight per day should be paid at enhanced overtime rates. A number of new flexible hours arrangements allow for a range of minimum to maximum daily hours to be worked and under such arrangements, rostered days may be as short as six or seven hours or as long as 10 to 12 hours. For example, *British Rail*'s proposals for flexible rostering, involving a day of between seven and nine hours, was strongly opposed by ASLEF who saw it as an attack upon the guaranteed eight hour day achieved in 1919. Equally, a number of new shift arrangements incorporate days of 10 or 12 hours, enabling longer blocks of leisure time to be taken. Despite union objections in principle to such arrangements, they are often preferred by employees. In some instances, unions find themselves opposing systems favoured by employees who end up voting against the official union line for systems which provide more usable chunks of leisure time.

The extension of part time working has also been viewed with some suspicion by the trade union movement. Unionization has traditionally been lower amongst part timers and the employment of them has been seen as a way of fragmenting workforce solidarity and of introducing poor rates of pay, benefits and conditions of employment. With the exception of certain white collar unions, unions have similarly been ambivalent about the development of the concept of job sharing. Traditional hostility to part time working has probably given way to a reluctant acceptance of it, particularly in the face of the reality that it is a growing sector of the labour market and the fact that the vast majority of people working part time have freely chosen to do so for personal or domestic reasons.

Trade union attitudes to overtime reduction have similarly been ambivalent. In 1978, the TUC issued a circular to affiliated members entitled *Overtime Working and Unemployment* which supported the principle of negotiated reductions in systematic overtime as a means of creating new job opportunities. In 1981 and 1982, Congress debated the role of legislation to reduce overtime, but was unable to carry the support of the manual unions whose members would be most affected. Formal policies on this remain unclear, but managements which have been able to secure agreements on the reduction or elimination of over-time, as will be described later, have mostly achieved this through local or company level productivity deals.

Temporary working, short term contracts and sub-contracting potentially pose even greater problems for trade unions since the determination of the pay and conditions of these employees may fall entirely outside the bargaining unit. Trade unions may also see the introduction of such arrangements as a means of weakening trade union organization at the workplace, as a threat to permanent employment or as a means of cutting overtime earnings. In addition, the itinerant nature of such employees makes them difficult to recruit into membership. Formally, the policy of the TUC is that they should be covered by the substantive agreement in operation so that they receive the same terms and conditions as regular employees and should be trade union members. In a number of organizations, the employment of temporary staff has been subject to joint agreement and, in some cases, a maximum number, expressed in terms of a percentage of the total workforce, has been agreed. In some instances, trade unions have openly entered such agreements to provide greater job security for the permanent workforce, with the temporaries at the periphery having much less security of tenure and more likely to be laid off in the event of a downturn in business.

Sub-contracting is also something which trade unions have either opposed or sought to control. In a number of organizations, its use is subject to consultation and in a few industries, for example in the building industry, some agreements lay down that sub-contract staff must be members of a certain specified trade union. In a number of unionized organizations included in the IPM study, however, temporary working and sub-contracting have been introduced by management decisions, without consultation and with little union influence on the outcome.

The evidence of our case studies indicates, at least in the industrial relations environment of the mid 1980s, that traditional trade union postures towards the working patterns described have had little influence on the more flexible arrangements which managements have been seeking to introduce. At the same time, with some notable exceptions, managements have had to invest considerable time and resources in communicating, consulting and negotiating with employees and their representatives in order to achieve the changes desired. Most successful deals have involved a trade off between flexibility of hours and working practices and improved pay and conditions as part of a comprehensive productivity deal.

2 New patterns of flexible dayworking

Alastair Evans and Ken Birkett

For at least the past 200 years working hours have normally been expressed in terms of standard hours in the day and standard working days in the week and throughout most of this period, trade union attention has focussed upon reducing the number of standard hours in the working day. From 14 to 15 hours per day in the eighteenth century, daily hours fell initially to 10 per day in the mid nineteenth century and then to nine per day in the 1870s. The standard eight hour day was established after the First World War. Throughout this period, the number of days in the standard working week remained unchanged at six days. A half day Saturday first emerged when hours were reduced from 48 to 44 between 1945 and 1947. The five day normal week became widespread when basic hours fell from 44 to 40 between 1960 and 1966. A standard pattern of eight hours per day, five days per week, remained the norm for most industrial dayworkers until the early 1980s.

Recently, however, there is evidence that an increasing number of organizations have been departing from this standard pattern. In some instances, organizations have abandoned the long established concept of fixed, standard daily or weekly working hours after which overtime at premium rates becomes payable in favour of fluctuating basic hours on a weekly, monthly or annual basis according to the needs of their business. In other instances, organizations have shifted from the concept of a standard five day working week towards four or $4\frac{1}{2}$ day weeks or, more unusually, 'nine day fortnights' in their search for more effective patterns of work.

No official statistics are gathered on these aspects of work patterns and it is therefore impossible to say with any certainty how widespread new working patterns have become. It is probable, however, that the innovations described have been introduced only in a minority of organizations. However, against a background of further pressures to reduce basic working hours and at the same time reduce costs and increase efficiency, it is likely that increasing numbers of organizations will be considering new options.

This chapter considers some of the main options available for more flexible patterns of work and draws from the experiences of organizations to consider the reasons for introducing particular work patterns, how the changes were implemented and what the effects have been.

Flexible daily and weekly hours

It has been noted that the concept of fixed daily or weekly hours after which overtime becomes payable may not be the most cost effective means of organizing the man hours available to meet demand for goods and services, particularly where levels of demand fluctuate according to a reasonably predictable pattern. One approach to achieving a more flexible and cost effective work schedule is to consider working hours on an annual basis so that working schedules can be altered on a weekly, monthly or seasonal pattern according to business needs. An alternative approach is to incorporate provisions for daily or weekly alterations in working hours into the terms and conditions of employment. Such variations in daily or weekly hours may be fixed in advance according to a cyclical daily, weekly or seasonal pattern. Alternatively, daily or weekly hours may be expressed in terms of a minimum or maximum band of hours which employees may be called upon to work according to the needs of the business. Examples of all these approaches are set out below.

Flexible daily hours   A pattern of variable hours in a week is likely to be appropriate where work loads vary on a regular daily basis. In their book *Industrial relations: cost effective* *strategies*, Brewster and Connock quote an example of an order department in which the number of orders to be processed are high at the beginning of the week and decline during the week in the following pattern[1]:

	Appropriate number of orders to be processed
Monday	1150
Tuesday	1150
Wednesday	1000
Thursday	850
Friday	850

A number of traditional means are available for handling these orders, for example by working overtime or employing part timers on peak days, by employing sufficient staff to cope with peak work loads (but under-utilizing staff on days of lower activity) or by allowing bottlenecks to build up by handling orders later in the week. By using an agreed pattern of flexible daily hours, fluctuating according to typical or expected work loads, the hours of employees can be redistributed across the week without the need for overtime at premium rates, the employment of additional part time staff or the inefficiencies of allowing bottlenecks to build up. In the above example, a basic 37 hour week could be redistributed as follows in order to provide a better match between workloads and hours worked:

	Daily hours
Monday	9
Tuesday	9
Wednesday	7
Thursday	6
Friday	6
Total	37

A highly flexible pattern of daily hours amongst drivers, depot workers and plant operators has been introduced by *Petrofina (UK) Limited* (see p 273 ff) as part of a productivity deal known as 'The New Approach', introduced in September 1984. Prior to the introduction of the agreement, the basic week was 40 hours, on top of which high overtime (averaging about 10 hours per week but reaching nearly 20 hours per week for some workers) was worked. Under 'The New Approach', basic hours were reduced in response to a claim from the TGWU from 40 to 37½ hours. As part of the deal, employees agreed to flexible daily hours, the elimination of overtime, a new pay structure based on an annual salary and complete flexibility such that all employees were required to undertake work for which they were competent. Under the flexible daily hours arrangements, hours may fluctuate from a minimum guarantee of six hours up to a maximum of 11 hours on any one day. Any hours worked in excess of 37½ between Monday and Friday in any one week are deducted from the hours rostered in the following week, instead of paying them as overtime. Despite an increase of £45 in weekly rates to compensate for lost overtime, productivity has risen by around 20 per cent and the scheme has proved to be self financing.

Flexible weekly hours A number of organizations face fluctuations in the nature of their businesses because demand is more buoyant at certain times of the year than others due to the nature of the product or service or, in the case of outside work, longer hours can be worked in the summer than the winter owing to increased daylight hours. Examples of these variations are set out below.

Ranton and Co is a small, private company based in West London, employing around 270 people making electrical accessories from plastic. Its main customers are electrical wholesalers and the company has found that the demand for its product is seasonal, since more electrical work is carried out on the interiors of buildings in the winter than in the summer.[2] Under agreements concluded with the TGWU and AUEW in 1983 and 1984, a combination of shorter and longer weeks was introduced on a fixed rota basis. During the slacker period between May and September each year, employees work a 16 week period of 35 hours per week. A further eight 'flexible' weeks are set aside for 35 hour working at any time during the year, as determined by management, but there is an undertaking to give employees as much notice as possible (normally at least a week) of any change in hours. The remaining weeks in the year are worked at 39 hours. When working 39 hours, normal hours for dayworkers are 8.00am to 4.45pm Monday to Thursday and 8.00am to 3.35pm on Friday. When working 35 hours, hours are 8.00am to 4.15pm Monday to Thursday and 8.00am to 1.00pm on Friday.

Ever Ready's factory in Wolverhampton has also introduced a
flexible working week depending on the time of the year following an agreement concluded with the TGWU and ASTMS. Under
the agreement the working week, averaged over the year, will be
reduced from 39 hours to 36, with weekly hours varying as
follows:

> January and February: 3 days × $25\frac{1}{2}$ hours per week
> March and April: 4 days × 34 hours per week
> May and June: $4\frac{1}{2}$ days × 39 hours per week
> July to November: 5 days × 45 hours per week
> December: mixed pattern of working

Earnings do not vary to the same extent. A standard rate is paid
for non working days and a bonus is added on working days.
Workers have ceased to be paid on an hourly basis. The overall
objective of the agreement is to produce a more cost effective
match between hours worked and seasonal variations in the
demand for the product.

Wold Farm Foods in Grimsby is another company with flexible
hours to meet seasonal peaks.[3] The company produces and
processes vegetables and has a peak season during July, August
and September each year. In the off peak season, employees
work a double day shift system, five days a week. During the
peak season, three crew continuous shiftworking is adopted,
providing cover for up to seven days a week. Permanent staff are
supplemented by temporaries and act in key roles to supervise
and control operations. For permanent employees, the weekly
working patterns during the year are as follows:

> Peak season (July–October): 16 weeks at 40 hours
> Off-peak season (November–June): 18 weeks at 40 hours
> and 18 weeks at 36.5 hours
> Over 52 weeks, average weekly hours of work are 38.8

Under a national agreement for industrial staff, the *CEGB* has
for some years operated a 'staggered hours' scheme.[4] Under this
agreement, employees working light load weeks of less than
normal hours are required to transfer the hours saved to heavy
load weeks involving longer than normal hours. The agreement
also contains provisions for 'winter/summer stagger' under
which an employee may be required to transfer hours worked

below normal hours in the winter to summer weeks of longer than normal hours.

Similar arrangements can be found in the water industry where outdoor work is involved *Wessex Water Authority* (see p 312 ff) has a range of flexible working arrangements amongst its employees, tailored to meet the needs of particular activities. Flexible seasonal hours are worked by some outdoor employees, enabling longer hours to be worked in the summer when more daylight is available and the work demands are higher (eg clearing grass and undergrowth etc). During the winter months, employees work a $4\frac{1}{2}$ day week (7.30am to 4.15pm Monday to Thursday, 7.30am to 12.30pm on Friday). In the summer, they work either Monday to Thursday or Tuesday to Friday on a non rotating basis (7.30am to 5.30pm). The shorter hours worked in the winter are 'banked' to enable longer summer hours to be worked. Over the year, average weekly hours are 39 per week. Prior to these arrangements, employees were under-utilized during the winter and paid overtime to meet peak loads during the summer.

Flexible seasonal hours have also been applied to recreation and planned maintenance staff at the *London Borough of Bromley*. Traditionally, these employees worked long hours during the summer months on overtime rates, whilst they had less to do in the winter months because of bad weather or darkness. The council's aim was to have a pattern of basic hours appropriate to actual requirements as a result of seasonal variations, and the unions agreed to a basic working week of 40 hours in the peak season (April to October) and $37\frac{1}{2}$ hours (November to March), giving a yearly average of 39 hours. The experiment resulted in higher productivity, manpower reductions and reduced overtime costs.

Staggered dayworking rotas are also used by some organizations to increase the use of expensive capital equipment in ways which do not attract the additional cost of shift *premia*. A leading British paper, printing and packaging company uses extended dayworking amongst technicians using expensive CAD/CAM equipment. Fixed shifts of 7.00am to 3.00pm and 11.00am to 7.00pm are used so as to obtain higher utilization of capital equipment and achieve maximum staff cover during the core hours of 11.00am to 3.00pm when working demands are higher. These hours are paid for at standard dayworking rates and do not attract the premium that would be attached to double dayshift working.

Flexible daily and weekly hours This pattern of weekly
flexibility is achieved either by varying daily hours or weekly
hours, or a combination of both, in order to achieve a more cost
effective match between the input of man hours and the output
of goods or services. Unlike the examples quoted immediately
above, rotas do not vary according to a fixed or predetermined
pattern, but vary on a daily or weekly basis, often between
minimum and maximum hours' limits. Three examples of this
approach are given here: 'flexible rostering' at *British Rail*, an
'hours commitment scheme' at the brewers *Whitbread and Company* (see p 321 ff) and contracted hours' options amongst tanker
drivers at a major oil company.

Flexible rostering was introduced by *British Rail* in an
agreement in 1981 as part of a package of productivity proposals
which included a reduction in basic weekly hours from 40 to 39.
Prior to the introduction, most railway crews worked an eight
hour day after which overtime rates became payable, although
some non footplate staff had worked rosters of four 10 hour days
a week in certain circumstances since 1968.[5] Since rail journeys
cannot always be programmed to match eight hour days, crews
either worked a shorter day for a guaranteed eight hours' pay or
worked overtime. Under the flexible rostering scheme, which
was introduced in 1982, the length of daily shift can vary within
the range of seven to nine hours and the length of the working
week can normally vary between 37 and 41 hours for most
employees, although for some (as in the example of freight
guards given in figure 7 below) the variation in weekly hours
can be greater than these lower and upper limits. Over the 16
week period of the roster cycle, the working week will average
39 hours.[6]

For payment purposes, the 39 hour week is paid for, irrespective
of hours worked, providing rostered turns are worked. Hours
actually worked in a week above or below 39 are recorded and
either a plus or minus is carried forward. Over the 16 week cycle,
the plus and minus amounts balance out. Overtime is calculated
on a daily basis and is linked to daily rostered hours, not the
basic 39 hour week. Any time worked over daily rostered hours
is paid at overtime rates. Thus, for example, if $7\frac{1}{2}$ hours have
been rostered, but $8\frac{1}{2}$ hours actually worked, an additional
hour's overtime would be paid.[7]

The main difficulty encountered in introducing flexible
rostering concerned the attitude of the train drivers' union
ASLEF. ASLEF had achieved the guaranteed eight hour day

Average 39 hours

Week No.	Monday Time on duty	Monday Total time	Tuesday Time on duty	Tuesday Total time	Wednesday Time on duty	Wednesday Total time	Thursday Time on duty	Thursday Total time	Friday Time on duty	Friday Total time	Saturday Time on duty	Saturday Total time	Total time for week
1	0300	7.19	0455	7.00	0410	7.15	0615	7.00	0540	7.35	Rest day		36.09
2	1740	8.40	1740	8.40	1740	8.40	1740	8.40	1740	8.40	Rest day		43.20
3	1101	7.45	1110	7.45	1110	7.45	1110	7.45	1110	7.45	Rest day		37.45
4	Rest day		2200	8.00	2200	8.00	2200	8.00	2105	8.45	2000	8.00	40.45
5	0455	7.00	Rest day		0455	7.00	0455	7.00	0455	7.00	0515	8.00	36.00
6	1400	9.00	1400	9.00	1400	9.00	Rest day		1400	9.00	1400	9.00	45.00
7	1957	7.53	1957	7.53	1957	7.53	1957	7.53	Rest day		Rest day		39.25
8	0540	7.35	0540	7.35	0540	7.35	0540	7.35	Rest day		Rest day		30.20
9	Rest day		Rest day		1725	8.20	1725	8.20	1725	8.20	2000	8.00	33.00
10	0410	7.15	0410	7.15	Rest day		0410	7.15	0410	7.15	0330	7.12	36.12
11	2033	7.00	2033	7.00	Rest day		2033	7.00	2300	8.06	2300	9.00	38.06
12	1000	7.20	1000	7.20	1000	7.20	1000	7.20	1000	7.20	Rest day		36.40
13	Rest day		2355	9.00	2033	9.00	2355	8.18	2315	7.00	2200	8.00	41.18
14	0515	8.00	0515	8.00	0515	8.00	0515	8.00	0515	8.00	Rest day		40.00
15	1700	9.00	1700	9.00	1700	9.00	1700	9.00	Rest day		1700	9.00	45.00
16	0001	9.00	0007	9.00	0007	9.00	0007	9.00	0007	9.00	Rest day		45.00

Source: *Industrial Relations Review and Report*, No 267, March 1982, p 12

Figure 7   The 16 week roster cycle for a freight guard on the Western Region

under an agreement concluded in 1919 and the concession of a longer basic working day for their members was a major point of principle. In the event, ASLEF was defeated after a two week strike and was forced to accept flexible rostering and an end to the guaranteed eight hour day.[8]

The costs and benefits of flexible rostering are more difficult to assess because it formed part of a wider package of changes in working practices, including administrative reorganization, unmanned stations, the easing of restrictions on the movement and flexibility of staff and single manning of locomotives. *British Rail's* published figures indicate an estimated saving of over £12 million in the period 1982 to 1985 as a result of flexible rostering.[9]

An 'hours commitment scheme' was introduced by *Whitbread* at their packaging and distribution depot in Romsey, Hampshire in 1983 as part of a comprehensive package aimed at harmonizing terms and conditions of all staff, reducing high overtime levels and establishing more flexible working patterns and practices. The agreement covers all 225 blue collar and white collar employees (other than senior management) represented by the TGWU and ACTSS at the location.

The basis of the scheme is a requirement for individuals and sections to commit themselves to being available to work a number of average weekly hours over a 12 month period as determined by the needs of the business. The nature of the product market for beer involves fluctuations in activity which are fairly predictable throughout the year. Peaks occur in the period before Christmas, over Easter and the summer holiday months, with lower activities at other times, particularly in the early months of the year. Flexibility was therefore required to work longer weekly hours during these peak periods, compensated by shorter weekly hours during the periods of lower activity. Under the previously fixed working week of 40 hours, manpower tended to be under-utilized during slacker periods, whilst high levels of overtime (in some cases of up to 30 hours per person per week) were worked during busy periods.

Under the hours commitment scheme, the daily or weekly attendance hours of individuals may vary by up to 20 per cent either side of the daily and weekly average or 40 per cent above the minimum. The range of daily and weekly hours which may be worked is set out in the agreement and reproduced in table 3. One of these hours' bands is allocated by occupation and department on the basis of past and expected work load commitments, examples of which are set out in table 4.

Table 3 Daily/weekly commitment hours

Daily hours			Weekly hours	
Min	Max	Av	Min	Max
7	7	35	35	35
7	8	$37\frac{1}{2}$	35	40
7	9	40	35	45
$7\frac{1}{2}$	$9\frac{1}{2}$	$42\frac{1}{2}$	$37\frac{1}{2}$	$47\frac{1}{2}$
8	11	$47\frac{1}{2}$	40	55
8	12	50	40	60

Table 4 Departmental committed working hours

Department	Av hours	Min hours	Max hours
Senior secretary (Production)	35	35	35
Laboratory assistant	$37\frac{1}{2}$	35	40
Stock clerk	40	35	45
Vehicle fitters	$42\frac{1}{2}$	$37\frac{1}{2}$	$47\frac{1}{2}$
Engineering fitters	45	$37\frac{1}{2}$	$52\frac{1}{2}$
Porter/yard cleaner	$47\frac{1}{2}$	40	55
Delivery driver	50	40	60

In addition to daily and weekly committed hours, separate provisions are made committing individuals, where appropriate, to a certain number of Saturdays and, in some cases, Sundays during the year. Examples of these provisions are set out in table 5 on page 36.

Employees are paid monthly salaries, calculated on a matrix according to grade, in equal instalments by credit transfer on the basis of the average daily and weekend committed hours. Daily or weekend hours worked in excess of their maximum hours' commitment are compensated by time off in lieu. Time off in lieu is accumulated at a flat rate from Monday to Friday (eg one hour off for each excess hour worked), at 1.25 rate at weekends and 1.75 rate on bank holidays.

Table 5 Weekend working

Job group	No of committed Saturdays per year	Committed total Saturday hours per year	No of committed Sundays per year	Committed total Sunday hours per year
Stock control clerk	8	32	—	—
Delivery driver	6	44	—	—
Maintenance fitters	17	100	6	36
Maintenance electricians	25	74	4	22
Plant service operator	21	124	8	44

Three years on from the commencement of the scheme, the company cites a range of benefits arising from it for both management and employees. For management, benefits have included:

● an improved industrial relations climate
● reduced overtime working to the extent that the time off in lieu provisions have hardly been used
● higher productivity and flexibility
● reduced overheads as a result of shorter working hours
● more accurate predictions of labour costs
● less need to use sub-contractors

For employees, the scheme has provided:

● single status terms and conditions
● stable incomes
● shorter working hours
● better sick and holiday pay and higher pensions
● greater job security

A third example of flexible weekly hours may be taken from the 'contracted hours' options' which operate amongst tanker drivers at a major oil company. These arrangements were introduced under two productivity deals made in 1982 and 1985. Prior to these agreements, drivers worked a basic 40 hour week, were paid for the hours spent driving and worked high levels of overtime. Under the agreements, working hours were reduced to 37½ and overtime was reduced in return for substantial increases in basic pay. Under the new arrangements, work measurement has been introduced to provide operating standards for deliveries and payments are related to measured 'schedule hours' rather than for the actual time worked. Work schedules are planned every six months by management in consultation with TGWU representatives. At least one month before the six monthly schedule comes into operation, drivers have the option of working one of two contracts:

- *contract 1*: To work only the basic working week of 37½ schedule hours over four duty periods. Each duty period may fluctuate between eight and 11 hours and 37½ hours' pay is guaranteed

- *contract 2*: To work a fifth duty period and so work up to a maximum of 55 schedule hours a week if required by management. Contract 2 employees receive an additional contractual payment equivalent to three hours on the basic rate of contract 1 in return for undertaking to work up to 55 schedule hours if required. Although no overtime rates are paid, all additional hours worked are paid at the scheduled hourly rate

Under both contracts, additional unsocial hours payments are made where work periods commence outside 6.00am to 9.00am (Monday to Saturday) to reflect the degree of inconvenience involved.

The package as a whole has enabled management, with the aid of computerized scheduling, to allocate work so as to make the best possible use of drivers' time, reduce overtime, increase flexibility and enhance productivity.

Compressed working weeks

A compressed working week is one in which the working time for dayworkers has been reorganized in such a way that less than five standard days are worked. Typically, working time is reorganized so that the same basic hours are worked in four or 4½ days in a week, or nine or $9\frac{1}{2}$ days out of the ten full working days available in a fortnight. A feature of a number of these schemes is a longer working day during four days of the week, enabling employers to extend the use of capital equipment on these days and reduce overhead costs on the non working day. Other benefits of the schemes are greater leisure time for employees and, where four days only are worked, reductions in the weekly time spent by employees travelling to work.

Compressed working hours have probably been used more in the United States and Canada than in Britain or the rest of Europe, although in the absence of any statistics about this working pattern in the UK, this cannot be fully substantiated. One American survey has indicated that around three per cent of all employees in the United States have compressed working hours arrangements.[10]

Experiments with compressed working hours in the UK have demonstrated cost savings through reduced overheads, increased productivity and greater flexibility to carry out maintenance without disrupting production.[11] The benefits claimed by American studies of the four day week include:[12]

- improvements in recruitment
- reductions in labour turnover
- less in absenteeism
- better time keeping
- higher morale
- increases in output
- reductions in production costs
- increases in productivity

These benefits have not, however, always been evident in subsequent evaluations, and problems can be encountered where the work is too tiring because long days are involved.[13] One American survey, for example, revealed that about 30 per cent of the organizations that had adopted compressed working hours had subsequently abandoned them.[14] Companies in the UK have also been unwilling to adopt four day working because of the problems arising out of loss of contact with customers and suppliers.[15]

The most common form of compressed working hours in Britain is the $4\frac{1}{2}$ day week involving a half day Friday. Less common is the nine or $9\frac{1}{2}$ day fortnight and the four day week, but examples of organizations using these patterns are set out below. In the IPM study, one example was found of a six day fortnight in which the workers involved completed two weeks work in six days by working long daily shifts and then had the next week off, being replaced by a second crew working the same pattern. This example is also described below.

4½ day week One major effect of the general reduction of manual workers' hours during the early 1980s has been the widespread adoption of a 'short Friday'. One survey by the Department of Employment investigating the patterns of hours' reductions in the engineering, pharmaceutical, printing and construction industries revealed that almost 70 per cent of firms applied the whole of the weekly hours' reduction to Friday afternoon.[16] Many employers selected this option rather than cutting a few minutes off each working day because it was preferred by employees and provided them with a more usable chunk of leisure time. A number of employers also felt that production levels could be better maintained by applying the whole reduction on Friday rather than by deducting a certain number of minutes off each working day.

One possible extension of the principle of a short Friday is a move towards half day working on Friday. The 4½ day working week normally involves the lengthening of each working day from Monday to Thursday so that total weekly hours remain the same but are spread over 4½ days rather than five. Apart from being popular with employees, a number of other cost benefits may accrue to an employer adopting this pattern of working. Where overtime is regularly worked at weekends, the cost of overtime can fall. Overtime can be worked during Friday afternoons at lower premium rates than might otherwise be payable for Saturday working. Where Sundays have been worked, for example for repair or maintenance of machinery when not in use for production, this work may be carried out on Saturdays at lower premium rates than would apply on Sundays. A further cost benefit from the half day Friday is that canteens can be closed, providing a further saving on overheads.

One example of a 4½ day week is *Bronx Engineering*, a Stourbridge based machine tool manufacturer which adopted this pattern following an agreement with the AUEW to move to a 39 hour week in 1979.[17] Prior to this, the company had operated a full five day working week of eight hours per day, with 4½ hours' voluntary overtime on Saturday morning (which was worked by about 50 per cent of manual employees). Under the revised system, employees work nine hours per day Monday to Thursday (8.00am to 5.30pm, with a 30 minute's meal break) and three hours on Friday morning (8.00am to 11.00am). A further $5\frac{1}{2}$ hours on Friday can be worked voluntarily as overtime, paid at time and a half. The company points to a number of benefits of the new system. For employees, it provides an additional chunk of leisure time on Friday afternoon or, alternatively, an opportunity to enhance weekly earnings significantly by opting to work overtime. There have also been benefits to the company. The first is that more workers are willing to work overtime on Friday afternoon than on Saturday morning. About 80 per cent opt to work the Friday afternoon overtime against 50 per cent previously working overtime on Saturday morning. A second advantage to the employer is that technical staff, previously unavailable during overtime hours, are now present during the Friday afternoon overtime period. As a result, the overtime period is generally more productive. A third benefit to the company is that routine maintenance work is cheaper. It previously took place on Sunday and was paid at double time. It now takes place on Saturday morning and is paid at time and a half.

Another company with long experience of the $4\frac{1}{2}$ day week is the *Imperial Tobacco Company* which first adopted a shorter Friday when it reduced basic hours for manual day workers from 40 to 38 in 1974. Double day shift workers have worked a 35 hour, 5 day week pattern since 1972.

When entering into further negotiations on hours' reductions in the early 1980s (which eventually led to a staged reduction of basic hours for all categories of non shift employees to 35 in 1985) the company made clear its intention to maintain $4\frac{1}{2}$ day working in those areas where it was already a feature. Whilst in theory, parts of their operation could have fitted into a four day, 35 hour week, in practice it would not have been possible in the majority of other areas. In manufacturing, a five day week was necessary for the double day shift working pattern which already covered half of the production employees. In distribution, maintenance and administration, a five day operation was still required and the company resisted a claim for a move from $4\frac{1}{2}$ to four days for any group of workers on the grounds of equity and because, with an increasingly integrated multi site operation, five day cover remained an overall operational necessity.

The agreement on further hours' reductions was in the context of major technological change and a major restructuring within the company. As part of that agreement, the company insisted that a minimum of four hours must be worked in manufacturing on the half day Friday period so that a reasonable period of productive time could be maintained. In distribution, agreement was obtained to move to a pattern of five equal work days in order to meet operational requirements. Two further issues arising out of the half day Friday at *Imperial Tobacco* are worthy of note. First, the company obtained agreement that any holiday taken on Friday would count as a whole day for holiday purpose, even though Friday was only half a working day. Secondly, it is important to be aware that a Friday afternoon closure was likely to result in a loss of earnings for some part time workers, eg canteen workers or afternoon only production workers. At *Imperial Tobacco*, on the insistence of the trade unions, steps were taken partly to offset this by bringing forward lunch times during the period Monday to Thursday. This increased the hours of afternoon part time employees from Monday to Thursday and thus minimized the loss of the Friday afternoon shift.

Overall, the company regards its experience of reducing basic hours by five over a 10 year period as a success. Against a background of declining demand for its products, productivity has improved significantly, overtime has fallen and the labour force has been reduced by over 50 per cent. During this time, the company has adopted a 'high wage, high productivity' policy which has enabled hours' reductions to take place concurrently with investment in highly advanced machinery, in addition to agreements on flexible working practices. The hours of all employee groups are now harmonized at 35 hours.

The extent to which a $4\frac{1}{2}$ day working week has been adopted in Britain is not known but indications are that it may have become quite widespread, whether as a result of reduced working hours or for some other reason. Elsewhere in the engineering industry, *Mather and Platt* in Manchester operate an $8\frac{1}{2}$ hour day Monday to Thursday, with five hours on Friday; *May and Baker* in Norwich, with a basic $37\frac{1}{2}$ hour week, work $8\frac{1}{4}$ hours Monday to Thursday, with $4\frac{1}{2}$ hours on Friday; and *Rolls-Royce Motors*, on a 39 hour week, work $8\frac{1}{2}$ hours Monday to Thursday (7.55am to 5.10pm with a 45 minute break for lunch) and five hours on Friday (7.55am to 12.55pm).[18]

In the clothing industry, the $4\frac{1}{2}$ day week, involving a half day on Friday, has become increasingly common during the past 10 years. A survey carried out by the *British Clothing Industry Association* in 1981 indicated that 60 per cent of firms in the industry worked this pattern and it is thought that it could now have become universal. The 4½ day week did not emerge as a result of hours' reductions, but rather because it proved popular with the industry's largely female workforce, most of whom work a standard week of 37 or 38 hours.

A recent survey of employers in the box and packaging industry indicates that almost all operate a shorter Friday, varying from four to seven hours in length. A further reduction from 39 to 38 hours is being applied by a majority of companies reducing hours on the Friday, although some are reducing hours on other days of the week to avoid reducing Friday hours still further.

The 4½ day week, involving a short Friday, was also introduced amongst manual dayworkers at some plants of the *Ford Motor Company* as part of an agreement in 1982 to reduce basic hours from 40 to 39. The company believes that the move to a short Friday has produced benefits in the form of improvements in employee relations and morale. The company notes, however, the 'knock on' effect of short Fridays on other bargaining groups. A major result of the change for manual workers at *Ford* was its effect on the aspirations of salaried staff, some of whom demanded a similar change in their patterns of work. Despite concern about the loss of flexibility and availability of staff, management agreed to apply a 4½ day week to staff at plants where this pattern had been negotiated by hourly paid employees. At main offices, however, the 5 day week continues because of the need to maintain cover, liaise with customers and with suppliers.

One last example of the 4½ day week may be quoted where it has been introduced by a company as a staff benefit during the summer months. Office staff at *McDonalds Hamburgers* work a standard five day week, 9.00am to 5.00pm in the winter, but during the summer (from May to the end of September), they work from 8.30am to 5.00pm Monday to Thursday and a half day on Fridays (8.30am to 1.00pm). The summer 4½ day week pattern was brought from the US where it operates throughout the company.

Evidence on the impact of 4½ day working on productivity and unit costs is inconclusive. Potential benefits include:

● overtime working at lower premium rates
● greater willingness on the part of employees to work overtime
● reduced overheads through the closing of canteens on Fridays

● its attractiveness to employees which may help in the recruitment and retention of staff

The main concern amongst employers is that the 4½ day week might eventually lead to a four day working week. In particular, where a firm cannot offer overtime opportunities on a Friday afternoon, it may find that the short Friday will increase the incidence of absenteeism and lead to the abandonment of Friday as a normal working day.

A further potential problem was illustrated by the *Ford* example. The establishment of a 4½ day week amongst some workers may lead to pressures for its introduction from others. Where work involves contact with customers or suppliers, a half day Friday could potentially lead to lost business opportunities and reduced services to the customer.

The four day working week A more unusual working pattern amongst dayworkers is the four day working week, although four nights per week among shiftworkers have been quite common for a number of years. One example of a company in the UK with many years of experience of a four day week is *Steloy Foundry Machines* which manufactures core-making and shell-moulding machines for the foundry industry. The four day week was adopted in the mid 1970s. Previously, a conventional five day, 40 hour week had been worked with additional overtime working on Saturday and Sunday.

The stimulus for change at *Steloy* came after the three day week as a result of the miners' strike in 1973. The firm was able to maintain its five day level of output in three days and management concluded that in the future it ought at least to be possible to maintain these levels of output in four days. Following a series of meetings with the workforce, the company agreed to introduce, initially for a one month trial period, a four day, 10 hours per day work pattern. The new pattern operated from Monday to Thursday, 7.30am to 6.00pm. After an extended trial period of three months, the system was adopted on a permanent basis for all shop floor employees. As a result of the four day working week, four main financial benefits have accrued to the company: a reduction in overhead costs, improved output, the virtual elimination of overtime and improved recruitment and labour retention. The company saved 20 per cent on its heating, lighting and fuel bills because of not having to open the workshops on Fridays. Output has increased about 50 per cent, partly through reductions in start up and shutdown times and partly through negotiation of more efficient working practices. In addition, these levels of productivity have enabled the company largely to dispense with overtime working. Finally, the company has found that the four day week acts as an added attraction to potential recruits and, moreover, as a result of the change, labour turnover fell substantially. For employees, the four day week brought the benefits of more leisure in the form of a longer weekend, saved time and money spent travelling (through one fewer journey per week) and provided employees with a free day on which to attend to domestic and personal arrangements.[19]

Another company with long experience of a four day working week is *Everest Double Glazing* which has operated this pattern amongst most of its factory employees for the last 15 years. The original move to a four day week came about because of the large volume of overtime being worked when the company's business was expanding rapidly in the 1970s. A 10 hour day was introduced and the basic working week became four days, Monday to Thursday. This enabled some of the high overtime levels to be worked on Friday which was felt to be preferable to Saturday overtime working when there were competing leisure activities. More recently, against a background of falling demand for double glazed products and shorter hours amongst comparable workers, the basic week was reduced to 38 hours as a result of a management initiative in 1985. Each factory was left free to decide how to implement the hours' reduction. Most now work three 10 hour days Monday to Wednesday (7.00am to 5.30pm), with eight hours on Thursday to give an early finish; the remainder have chosen four $9\frac{1}{2}$ hour days (7.00am to 5.00pm). The management reports that the four day pattern is attractive to the company and its employees. The company is able to achieve savings on heating and other overheads, particularly through not operating factories on Fridays, since much less overtime is now worked.

Daybrook Linen Services, a laundry company employing 180 people and based in Nottingham, has adopted a flexible four day week in order to increase the production time available. Previously the company had worked a conventional 39 hour, five day week (8.00am to 4.45pm on Mondays, 8.00am to 4.30pm, Tuesdays to Fridays, with a total of one hour's unpaid break each day). Under the new pattern, the factory continues to work five days, but each employee works for four days out of five, with a fifth day off on a rota basis. The length of each working day has been increased and now runs from 7.30am to 6.00pm. The main advantage of the system is that production time has increased from 42 to 47½ hours per week without the payment of shift *premia* or the need to increase investment in capital. In addition, if the level of business requires it, employees can work overtime on their rostered weekly day off at standard rather than weekend rates of overtime.

Four day working has also been introduced by *Winn and Coales*, a south London based engineering company employing 200 people. Under an agreement concluded in 1985 with the TGWU, the basic hours of work of the company's 65 manual employees were reduced from 38 to 35, worked over four days rather than the previous 4½. Management found that the short Friday, combined with a number of restrictive practices, was proving costly. A four day week, 7.45am to 5.00pm, was agreed as part of a productivity package involving the removal of paid tea breaks, provisions to keep production flowing by means of staggered lunch breaks in certain areas and the elimination of a daily late starting allowance. The company's objective is to raise output by 8½ per cent, despite the three hour cut in basic hours, as a result of the new arrangements.[20]

Amongst white collar employees, the Solihull office of the *Inland Revenue* has introduced a four day week on an experimental basis. Under the scheme, which is optional, employees can complete their contractual 37 hours in four days of 9¼ hours, with the proviso that counter service and telephone cover must be maintained for a full five days by means of rostering arrangements.[21]

The nine or 9½ day fortnight   A further alternative to four or 4½ day working is a working pattern termed the 'nine day fortnight'. Rather than enabling all employees to have a half or whole day off per week, this system enables employees, on a rotating basis, to have one full day off per fortnight. In order to achieve this, employees work a slightly longer working day for nine of the 10 working days in a fortnight. Thus, for example, a 39 hour week would require employees to work eight hours 40 minutes per day; in a fortnight 78 hours' work would be achieved by the employee working nine days of eight hours 40 minutes, with one day off. A 37 hour week, for example, would entail a working day of nearly 8¼ hours. Fred Dickenson, writing in *Personnel Management*, has argued that the nine day fortnight has considerable advantages for an expanding company, especially if it is heavily capitalized.[22] Since the working day is increased by 10 per cent, it achieves a 10 per cent greater use of its capital equipment. Thus, output can be increased by 10 per cent without additional space and equipment or increased overheads. In addition, absenteeism is likely to decrease, since employees will no longer need to take as much time off to attend to personal matters.

In terms of implementation, the nine day fortnight could easily vary according to the circumstances of the company. In those situations where the ability of employees to do their work is very dependent on the presence of other employees, the day off per fortnight would have to be on a strict rota basis. This might have to be as rigid as 10 per cent of the workforce taking any one day off in the fortnight, perhaps rotating so that the more popular Fridays and Mondays off are shared evenly amongst employees. In other companies it may prove workable to allow 25 per cent of employees to take off the first Monday in the fortnight, 25 per cent the first Friday, 25 per cent the second Monday and 25 per cent the second Friday. In this way all employees will be at work on Tuesdays, Wednesdays and Thursdays and 75 per cent on Mondays and Fridays. The advantage of this over the stricter rota is that all employees take their free day immediately before or after a weekend.[23]

Only a small number of organizations are thought to work this pattern. One such organization is *Wrekin District Council* which introduced a nine day fortnight following local government reorganization in 1974 as a benefit for employees and as a means of attracting and retaining staff. The scheme involves a 72 hour working fortnight, spread over nine days of eight hours. The tenth day off is agreed with the supervisor and is granted according to the workload commitments of the department. The scheme applies to all non manual staff (manual and craft employees are outside the scheme) except:

● shiftworkers
● certain supervisors with direct responsibility for manual and craft employees
● employees who wish for domestic or personal reasons to work a normal five day week

The scheme provides a limited choice of start and finish times, as follows, with 45 minutes being taken for lunch:

● 8.30am to 5.15pm (the most popular choice)

- 8.45am to 5.30pm
- 9.00am to 5.45pm

Some of the benefits of the scheme include the following:

- it helps to build the Council's image as a good employer
- it is attractive to potential applicants
- it contributes to a reduction in occasional absenteeism (for example, because there is a free working day to attend to domestic chores)
- it may help to counter demands for additional paid holiday entitlement
- the tenth day is useful and cost effective as a training day (for example, certain employees pursuing further qualifications take their free day on the day they attend college)
- it affords employees the opportunity to arrange appointments with doctors, dentists, etc on the tenth day rather than taking time off work
- it is valued by employees and has probably contributed to a lower labour turnover

Some of the problems arising include the following:

- providing adequate cover (Fridays and Mondays are popular days to take off and this needs careful managing)
- in an authority which has a strong commitment to single status policies, the nine day fortnight is perceived as a significant difference between staff and manual/craft conditions of service
- senior staff with heavy work loads frequently do not take the tenth day off to which they are entitled
- there is some political sensitivity about the working pattern in the light of the continuing need to provide better services

A similar scheme operates amongst administrative, professional, technical and clerical staff at *Strathkelvin District Council* in Glasgow where a $9\frac{1}{2}$ day fortnight has been introduced, enabling staff to work a half day every alternate Friday. This pattern was introduced as part of a new technology agreement concluded with NALGO which also provided for a reduction in the basic week from $36\frac{1}{4}$ to 35 hours. The trade union side were anxious to achieve an early finish to the week rather than have a later start or earlier finish to each day. The union initially proposed that

all staff should finish 1¼ hours earlier on a Friday, but the
Council was concerned that this would result in a reduction of
services to ratepayers. Instead, it was agreed that the working
fortnight would be cut by 2½ hours. Staff operate on two rotas
and each week half the staff are entitled to finish at 2.30pm, or
1.30pm if they did not take their lunch break. Each Friday
afternoon, therefore, half the staff are available to maintain the
service to the public. Generally, the system has proved to be
acceptable to staff and management, although there is some
concern that the lower staffing levels on Friday afternoons can,
in certain circumstances, reduce the efficiency of the operation.
However, staff welcome the opportunity of the early finish and
management believes that the scheme has made a positive
contribution to morale.

In another organization, a chemical company manufacturing at several plants in the UK and Europe, the experience of
introducing a 9½ day fortnight was less favourable. When considering the implementation of a reduction of basic hours of
dayworkers from 40 to 38 in 1983, management looked at three
options—daily reductions of 24 minutes, finishing two hours
early on Friday afternoon or finishing at midday every second
Friday. The unions pressed for the latter option, the 9½ day
fortnight, on the grounds that it provided a usable chunk of
leisure time. Reluctantly, management eventually acceded to
this following reassurances from departments that it was possible to maintain production levels. In retrospect, management
have been dissatisfied with the arrangement which has led to
proportionately lower productivity on the half day Friday and
an increase in the already high levels of overtime working.
There has also been a 'knock on' effect on staff employees who
subsequently pressed for and obtained a 9½ day fortnight for
themselves. With hindsight, management believe that a 24
minute reduction in the working day would have been a less
costly and complicated alternative.

The six day fortnight   This pattern, referred to by the firm
operating it as '75 hour team working', is currently used at two
production locations of a major British paper, printing and
packaging company and involves employees working for 12½
hours per day, six days a week, with Sunday off. Shift A works
Thursday, Friday, Saturday, Monday, Tuesday and Wednesday
and then has a full week off, being replaced by shift B which

again works the same weekly pattern. Each working day runs from 7.00am to 7.30pm and, with a basic week of 37½ hours, each shift does the equivalent of two weeks' work (75 hours) in one week. Since the pattern involves extended dayworking, rather than conventional shiftworking, it does not attract the premium that might be paid to late shift or night shift workers. In addition to this pattern of working hours, 'team working' has been introduced to reduce demarcation. Each team consists of a mix of printers, engineers and general workers and the only lines of demarcation are based on real skills and not on traditional union boundaries. The work patterns prior to these changes involved a mix of day work plus overtime and double day shifts, and the new patterns required considerable negotiation with the trade unions. Trade union officials were opposed in principle to the long daily and weekly hours which were proposed. Employees, however, were highly attracted to the idea of a week's work and a week off and this enabled the agreement to be concluded.

Advantages of '75 hour team working' include the following:

- more cost effective than conventional shift patterns
- more popular with employees, since it avoids the problems eg transport problems, of very early morning starts and late night finishes sometimes found with conventional shiftwork. For these reasons, the patterns are also popular with women
- increased productivity by reducing the time lost through shift handovers and by enabling tasks to be completed by one shift rather than split between two

Disadvantages include the following:

- little scope for working overtime, since long daily hours have been worked
- risk of employees taking a second job during the week off
- problems in communicating with employees during their week off where urgent information needs to be conveyed; this sometimes necessitates communicating directly with them at home

The gains in productivity achieved are a result of a combination of changes: technology, working methods, patterns of hours and small factory units. New technology brought faster throughput and smaller units brought a number of spin off benefits: more effective use of space, tighter stock control because of lack of space, fewer staff in stock handling and, generally, a more tightly managed operation. As an indication of these combined effects, four years ago 4500 employees were employed at three sites in paper converting. Now, under the new work patterns, 1350 employees are employed at four sites to produce considerably more output, a three to fourfold increase in productivity. The company would not necessarily apply the 75 hour pattern generally, but believes that it is particularly appropriate for fast moving, high volume production.

Annual hours

For many organizations, the demand for their goods and services fluctuates according to readily identifiable cycles throughout the year. In retailing, peaks occur before Christmas and during the winter and summer sales. In the energy industries output is highest during the winter months and lowest during the summer period. Peaks and troughs of activity can also be identified within particular functions of organizations. Staff in accounts departments, for example, tend to work longer hours during the six monthly and annual audits. In other sectors, such as local government or the water industry, peak levels of activity occur when rates bills are sent out at annual or six monthly intervals. Most firms have to cope with certain fluctuations throughout the year which either affect the organization as a whole or parts of it in differing ways. Many organizations tend to establish manning levels sufficient to cope with normal levels of demand. During periods of low activity, inefficiencies may arise since there are likely to be more people employed than the workload demands. Alternatively, employees may continue to work at normal levels of performance producing for stock which adversely affects cash flow and adds to the costs of stockholding. Periods of peak demand, on the other hand, are usually met by working overtime at premium rates or by employing additional temporary staff. These inefficiencies are illustrated in figure 8.

In the example, peak periods of activity occur during the spring and autumn months. During periods of lower activity (January to March and June to September), man hours available from the

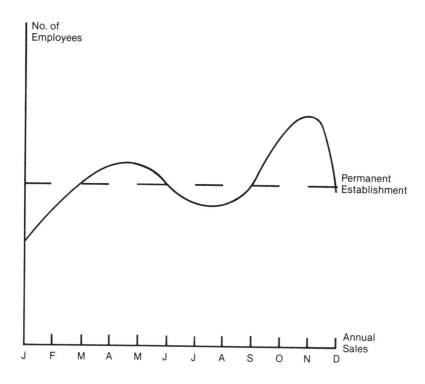

Figure 8 Fluctuations in staffing requirements

permanent establishment exceed output requirements and labour is under-utilized. During the peak periods (April to June and November/December), additional hours are bought by means of overtime working.

The major objective of scheduling employee hours in terms of annual working time is to obtain a better match between output requirements and the hours actually worked by employees. Employment contracts based on standard weekly hours are rigid and divorced from output requirements. Annual hours contracts provide employers with flexibility to increase or reduce hours worked in a given period, according to the demand for goods or services. In order to achieve a better match between hours and output in the above example, the weekly hours of employees based on an average working week of 39 hours, might, for example, be re-scheduled as follows:

Month	Basic Weekly Hours
January	34
February	37
March	39
April	41
May	41
June	39
July	35
August	35
September	40
October	44
November	44
December	39

Over the year these variable hours work out at an average of 39 hours per week on an annual basis. During the months when hours below 39 are being worked, the company is able to 'bank' spare hours which are then worked during periods of peak activity without premium overtime payments.

Origins of annual hours   The concept of annual working hours is generally considered to have originated simultaneously in France, West Germany and Scandinavia during the mid 1970s, although seasonal fluctuations in working hours can be found in Britain before this time. Parts of the building industry had agreements to work longer hours in the summer than the winter as far back as the last century[24] and seasonal variations in summer and winter hours were included in an agreement concluded by the *CEGB* in the 1960s.[25] The French employers' organization became interested in the concept of annual hours in 1975 on the grounds that weekly hours were 'too rigid for efficient production processes in private enterprises'[26] and subsequently included it as part of their response to a trade union claim for shorter working hours in 1978.[27] The concept of 'flexi-years' has been introduced by about a dozen smaller companies in West Germany since the mid 1970s, particularly in the retailing sector. Under this scheme, employees are asked to contract at the beginning of the year the number of hours each wishes to work and rosters are prepared on the basis of this response. Probably of most significance to the UK have been the developments in the use of annual hours in the Swedish and Finnish pulp and paper industries, to which developments in the growing use of annual hours in the UK can be directly linked. The Swedish pulp and paper industry introduced the concept by industry level agreement over the three years 1975 to 1977 when shift workers' hours were reduced in stages from 40 to 36. The adoption of annual hours has enabled capital intensive pulp and paper plants to achieve improved operating efficiencies, despite additional manning for five (and sometimes six) crew operations.[28] In Sweden, annual hours are calculated as follows:

> Annual length of the year: 52.18 weeks
> Deduct (a) statutory and
> collective agreement
> holidays − 2.24 weeks
> (b) annual holidays − 5.00 weeks
>
> 44.94 weeks

Annual hours = 44.94 weeks × 36 hours per week
= 1617.85

NB: by counting a year as 52.18 weeks, provision is made for leap years. Each year is counted as 365.25 days and the average number of weeks is derived by the formula $\frac{365.25}{7} = 52.18$ weeks per year.

Finland followed the Swedish example and continuous shift workers (mostly working five crew rotas) work 1692 hours per year. In Finland, the employers' federation has developed a computerized rota planning and wage administration system for member companies, over 80 per cent of which use the system and are provided with yearly printed rotas for their workforces.[29]

The introduction of annual hours in these two countries is said to have led to more intensive use of capital and plant, and improved unit costs at the same time as hours were considerably reduced. In Finland, the annual hours system has been extended outside the paper industry to the chemical and metal manufacturing sectors.

It was the threat from Scandinavian competition which led the British paper industry to examine the annual hours concept. In 1978, a management study group of the *British Paper and Board Industry Federation* (BPBIF) produced a report on the economics of work and leisure in the paper industry which recommended the introduction of annual hours. This was fol-

lowed by the establishment of a joint management/union working party to work out the details. Rather than establish a
compulsory agreement for the whole industry, an enabling
agreement came into effect in January 1983 which permitted
individual companies to introduce annual hours if the conditions were right. Certain conditions have been attached to the
agreement and mills are not allowed to proceed with the introduction of annual hours unless either:

(a)   the mill is operating profitably (or is likely to become
      profitable as a result of introducing annual hours) with
      an acceptable return on capital employed; *or*
(b)   the company is satisfied that the changes would meet a
      number of conditions, which include the following:
   ● there must be an actual reduction in working hours
   ● production levels must be maintained or increased
   ● there must be no increase in unit labour costs
   ● overtime should be reduced or eliminated

The 1983 agreement was part of the *BPBIF*'s response to a claim
for a reduced working week of 39 hours. For those mills which
were not ready to introduce annual hours, the agreement contained fallback arrangements whereby these firms would reduce
hours by 47 per year without loss of pay in order to achieve a 39
hour week. This fallback arrangement meant that there was no
apparent or obvious advantage to the unions at company level to
negotiate annual hours, since hours' reductions had been
achieved without loss of pay. The result has been that only 16
mills have so far introduced annual hours out of the 100 or so
covered by the agreement. A further six have tried and failed to
introduce local agreements. The most significant obstacle to
introducing annual hours from a trade union point of view has
been the problem of reduced earnings as a result of lower
overtime. Very high levels of overtime had become usual and
successful negotiations required compensation for lost overtime
to be built in to annual hours agreements. Other problems
arising out of unsuccessful attempts to introduce annual hours
included disagreements over rostered holidays, new manning
levels and new shift rotas.

During 1984, the *BPBIF* carried out a follow up survey of
the results of the annual hours, receiving responses from 12 of
the 16 companies which had adopted the annual hours concept.
Some of the benefits reported by these companies included the
following:[30]

- lower overtime costs
- more production (and less shut time)
- changed working practices
- more efficient rotas
- improved productivity
- improved versatility

Annual hours in the paper industry have tended to be applied mainly in the continuous process plants, but are also to be found amongst dayworkers. In one British paper company, 10 different annual hours rotas are in operation covering production, maintenance, quality control, ancillary and white collar staff.[31] The current formula based on the 39 hour week, is as follows:

Number of weeks per year:	52.18 weeks
Deduct (a) holiday weeks	−5.0 weeks
(b) bank holidays	−1.6 weeks
Total working weeks	45.58

Annual hours = 45.58 weeks × 39 hours per week
= 1778

NB: The annual hours are reduced to 1776 in normal years and increased to 1784 in leap years.

At present it is thought that between 30 and 40 organizations in the private sector in Britain are using annual hours, including companies in the glass, chemicals, oil refining, cement, food, drink, can-making and paper sectors.

Blue Circle Industries (see p 205 ff) introduced the annual hours concept as part of a major package of changes amongst unionized manual workers at two of its cement plants. Against a background of recession, reduced manning and increased overseas competition, the company introduced an agreement known as 'The Stable Income Plan for Integrated Working' which incorporated the following elements:

- *flexible working*: this involved multiskills training and the reduction of demarcation to enable any employee to carry out any duty, as required by management, within their competency
- *new continuous shift patterns*: a novel seven crew shift system was introduced in order to overcome the problems

of lack of cover or high overtime levels in the light of
reduced basic hours or time lost through absence and
holidays. This pattern will be described in more detail in
Chapter 4.

● *a new stable income plan*: this established a guaranteed,
regular level of earnings, providing manual employees
with payment by credit transfer every four weeks in place
of weekly payments mainly by cash.

Focussing specifically on the company's annual hours scheme,
its main aims are to reduce the reliance on high overtime levels,
whilst retaining flexibility to cope with peaks and troughs in
production demands. The annual hours contract which was
agreed is as follows:

	Hours
45.8 working weeks and 4 days at 39 hours per week	1786
23 days annual holiday plus 8 public holidays at 39 hours a week	242
Built in flexible time at 12½% of 1786 hours	223
Annual contract hours (maximum)	2251

The annual hours contract which was agreed includes a built in
'flexible hours' provision allowing the company to call upon
employees to work limited extra hours above basic hours when
necessary. Flexible hours replace overtime and constitute an
additional 12½ per cent on basic hours. These are included in the
annual hours calculation on which salaries are based and are
therefore paid for whether they are worked or not.

Under the rules of the scheme, each employee accumulates
attendance hours towards the annual contract from 1 April.
Hours may be accumulated when at work, according to defined
start and finish times, or when working additional flexible hours
authorized by the supervisor. Time lost through lateness is not
credited and must be made up. Holidays, certified sickness,
training courses and other authorized leave accumulate at the
rate of the defined work pattern hours on the days concerned.
Unauthorized absence results in the loss of pay for each day
concerned, but the defined work pattern hours for each day are
credited.

The operation of the annual hours scheme is overseen by a
joint planning committee involving management and employee
representatives, meeting at quarterly intervals. This group reviews the scheduling of additional, flexible time in the previous

quarter and may recommend where improvements in the methods of scheduling workloads need to be made.

The administration of the scheme is highly dependent on computer technology, without which the system could have been impossible to operate. The hours worked are monitored by a computerized clocking system and printouts are available to each employee to show how many annual hours have been accumulated as the year progresses. The scheme also incorporates mandatory limits to the flexible hours which employees may be asked to work in specified periods in order to prevent the working of excessive hours; the computerized system is also used by management to ensure that flexible hours working is evenly spread among employees.

After six months' operation of the annual hours agreement, management has made a comparison between traditional arrangements and the package of new measures, including annual hours, associated with the new working arrangements. The resulting indices are as follows:

	Traditional arrangements	New arrangements
Manning	100	71
Labour costs	100	85
Output per employee	100	136
Hours worked	100	82 (min)–93 (max)

Another company using the annual hours concept is *Pedigree Petfoods* (see p 269 ff), which employs 1800 people at three locations in England. Prior to the introduction of annual hours for all employees (manual and non-manual) in 1981, basic hours ranged from 37½ for office workers and some shift workers to 39½ for four crew shiftworkers. In 1980, management committed the company to a principle of harmonization of basic hours of all staff at 37½ per week and adopted the annual hours concept as the means of comparing the hours worked by different groups of employees. Using 37½ hours as the base for harmonizing working hours, the annual hours calculation works out as follows:

	Hours
Gross annual hours (52 × 37.5)	1950
LESS annual holidays	150
LESS statutory holidays	60
LESS 4-year effect (for non leap years)	1
Annual hours	1739

Under the annual hours scheme at *Pedigree Petfoods*, overtime hours are excluded from the arrangement. Thus, if an employee is scheduled to work a $7\frac{1}{2}$ hour day, overtime *premia* apply for daily hours worked above this and employees have the option of taking this in the form of premium payments or time off in lieu.

Whilst mainly aimed at achieving harmonization, the company has subsequently recognized that a range of further benefits can be achieved from this pattern of working. In particular they see annual hours as an 'enabling' concept which allows for the easier implementation of more flexible working patterns, for example, by varying the patterns of hours to meet peaks at certain times in the month.

Prior to introducing the new scheme, management spent six months explaining the annual hours concept to employees and implementing the changes. In retrospect, management underestimated the amount of preparation involved in this and with the benefit of hindsight they highlight the following main factors in the successful introduction of annual hours:

- careful and lengthy preparation
- tight control over the project
- an efficient time keeping system
- minimum of other changes to shift systems
- harmonization of pay systems in advance

3 Overtime and its alternatives

Alastair Evans and Chris Curson

Overtime working has for the past two to three decades been a subject of considerable controversy amongst participants and observers of the British industrial relations system. Despite reductions in basic working hours over the last 40 years from 45 to 39 per week, overtime amongst male manual workers has tended to rise and has in consequence reduced the real impact of shorter working time as indicated in table 6 below. From an average of two hours overtime per man per week in the mid to late 1940s, it increased to over $3\frac{1}{2}$ hours per week in the 1950s and to around $5\frac{1}{2}$ hours per week in the 1970s where it remains at the present time after declining slightly in the early 1980s.[1] Innumerable epithets have been used to describe the phenomenon, including 'the curse of the male manual worker', 'a strange scandal' and an 'institution that will not die'.[2] Apparently despised by both sides of industry, overtime has come to be viewed as both necessary and unavoidable, and possibly also cost ineffective. Whatever the reasons for overtime working, a view has long been held that much of it is 'institutionalized' and a number of studies have shown that levels of overtime working have been considerably more stable in many industries than economic fluctuations might have led one to expect.[3]

Attempts to tackle the issue of overtime have regularly been made over the past 25 years, the best known example being the productivity agreements concluded at *Esso's* Fawley refinery in the late 1950s.[4] Here, overtime was reduced significantly over a three year period as a result of changes in working practices. In the maintenance and construction departments, for example,

Flexible patterns of work

Table 6
Normal and actual hours of manual men: 1945–1985

	Normal hours	Average weekly overtime per worker	Actual weekly hours
1945	47.2	2.2	49.4
1946	(n/a)	(n/a)	47.6
1947	45.3	1.0	46.3
1948	44.6	1.9	46.5
1949	44.4	2.2	46.6
1950	44.4	2.6	47.0
1951	44.4	3.5	47.9
1952	44.4	2.9	47.3
1953	44.3	3.5	47.8
1954	44.3	4.0	48.3
1955	44.3	4.6	48.9
1956	44.3	4.3	48.6
1957	44.3	4.1	48.4
1958	44.2	3.8	48.0
1959	44.2	3.8	48.0
1960	43.3	4.7	48.0
1961	42.5	5.4	47.9
1962	42.1	5.2	47.3
1963	42.0	4.9	46.9
1964	41.9	5.9	47.8
1965	41.2	6.3	47.5
1966	40.3	6.1	46.4
1967	40.2	5.9	46.1
1968	40.1	6.1	46.2
1969	40.1	6.3	46.4
1970	40.1	5.6	45.7
1971	40.0	4.7	44.7
1972	40.0	5.0	45.0
1973	40.0	5.6	45.6
1974	40.0	5.1	45.1
1975	40.0	3.6	43.6
1976	40.0	4.0	44.0
1977	39.9	5.8	45.7
1978	39.9	6.1	46.0
1979	39.9	6.3	46.2
1980	39.7	5.7	45.4
1981	39.7	4.5	44.2
1982	39.4	4.9	44.3
1983	39.2	4.7	43.9
1984	39.2	5.1	44.3
1985	39.1	5.4	44.5

SOURCES *British Labour Statistics Historical Abstract 1886–1968* (HMSO, 1971), p 160; *British Labour Statistics Yearbook, 1975* (HMSO, 1977), p 109; Department of Employment, *New Earnings Survey*, annual results; EG Whybrew, *Overtime Working in Britain* (HMSO, 1968), p 11 overtime was reduced from 18 per cent to six per cent of all hours worked and in process departments from 15.5 per cent to 10.5 per cent. Numerous other examples of similar productivity agreements concluded during the 1960s may also bo found, yet the experience has been that custom and practice and informal practices at workplaces have tended to erode such agreements. Interestingly, *Esso* has again been negotiating productivity deals amongst craft and process workers at Fawley in the early 1980s, one objective of which was the reduction in institutionalized overtime.[5]. Two other companies, *Petrofina* and *Mobil*, which abolished overtime in the 1960s, have also recently been negotiating agreements to eliminate it once again. At *Petrofina*, overtime was reintroduced after pressure from drivers for overtime earnings and subsequently grew, especially in the winter, when there was a high demand for heating oils.[6] The reintroduction of paid overtime probably further added to inefficiencies and restrictive practices which crept back in order to enhance overtime working at premium rates.

Despite unsuccessful attempts in the past to deal with the overtime issue, the problem appears to be as live in the mid 1980s as it was two or three decades ago and new solutions are being sought. The current position is summed up in the words of one recent commentator as follows:

> Overtime is, in my view, both a neglected area for management and an avoidable cost in most organizations. But it is one which is so embedded in the British industrial system that it is hard to break. The best approach may be to undertake a complete review and reorganization of working time as part of a new wage-working time agreement.[7]

This concern is reflected by the managements participating in our study, most of whom reported that they wanted to reduce or abolish overtime. Similar moves to reduce systematic overtime were also observed in a recent NEDC study of working patterns and practices covering 72 firms in food and drink, engineering, retailing and financial services.[8] Although traditional productivity bargaining remains the main vehicle for change, a number of the organizations included in our case studies were also utilizing many of the concepts of flexible work patterns, as described in this chapter and elsewhere in this book, as an important part of a new dimension being brought to the overtime question. The remainder of this section provides an overview, with company examples, of how these various concepts are being applied in practice. The main methods adopted are:

- productivity agreements
- flexible hours arrangements
- additional shift crews
- time off in lieu
- overtime limitation agreements
- other methods

In a number of the examples quoted, more than one of these has been incorporated as part of the package for reducing overtime.

Productivity agreements

Against a background of greater competitiveness in the airline industry, in part brought about by increasing deregulation, *British Caledonian Airways* (see p 226ff) initiated an extensive policy review of its operations in 1983, with the objectives of enhancing quality and service, achieving high productivity and high pay and creating a climate of greater mutual trust in industrial relations. As part of a productivity deal known as 'The Way Ahead', the company was able to accommodate a claim from the unions in its engineering and maintenance bargaining unit to reduce basic hours from 39 to 37½ and virtually eliminate high levels of overtime working which had, in some cases, been as high as nine hours per man per week, without any increase in staffing levels or unit labour costs. It was agreed that overtime could only be worked in an emergency, but that it would be compensated only by time off in lieu. As part of the deal, demarcation was removed, with the provisos that individuals would only be required to carry out tasks for which they were trained and competent to perform within safety regulations; grading structures were rationalized and virtually all pay elements were consolidated into annual salaries, paid on a weekly basis.

Flexible hours arrangements

A variety of floxiblo hourз зchemeѕ haѕ Leeи iиlroduced, aѕ described earlier, with hours fluctuating on a daily, weekly, monthly or seasonal basis, or during the course of a year, according to the needs of the business. The essence of such schemes is that they enable longer hours to be worked during periods of peak demand without the need for overtime working at premium rates, while shorter hours may be worked during periods of slacker trading.

At *Whitbread's* distribution depot in Romsey, the 'Hours Commitment Scheme' resulted in the abolition of paid overtime which had previously been averaging 15 to 20 hours per employee per week, with some working up to 30 hours overtime weekly. Instead, employees are committed to working a range of minimum and maximum daily and weekly hours, fixed according to estimates of their likely workload on an annual basis, and are paid a salary calculated on the hours committed. Any excess hours worked above this commitment are compensated by time off in lieu: one hour off for each additional hour worked Monday to Friday, $1\frac{1}{2}$ hours off for each extra hour on Saturday and Sunday and $1\frac{3}{4}$ hours off for each hour worked on a bank holiday.

Flexible weekly hours amongst drivers at *Petrofina* have also been used to eliminate overtime. At *Petrofina*, drivers may be rostered to work between six and 11 hours per day for which an annual salary is paid. Against a background of average weekly overtime of 10 hours per man, nearer 20 hours per week in some cases, overtime has been abolished and the basic working week cut from 40 to $37\frac{1}{2}$ hours without increases in unit costs. Any additional hours that are worked are compensated by time off in lieu. Under a similar scheme amongst tanker drivers at another major oil company, truck operators work four basic duty periods per week of eight to 11 hours ($37\frac{1}{2}$ hours per week), but may opt for an alternative contract to work up to 55 hours per week. Remuneration is paid according to the contractual options selected. The new system replaces previous arrangements involving high levels of overtime working.

Additional shift crews

As will be discussed further in Chapter 4, falling basic hours of
work tend to change the economics of continuous shift working.
Continuous shift systems need to cover all the available 168
hours in the week and this is typically achieved by employing
four shift crews, each working 42 hours per week, 40 hours at
basic time and two hours' built in overtime. On top of this,
further overtime is likely to be worked to provide cover for
holidays and absence. As the basic working week falls below 40
hours, so further overtime has to be built in to provide the
necessary cover. As will be explained in the next chapter, a
number of organizations have found it more economic to recruit
an additional shift crew in order to operate a five crew pattern,
with a consequential reduction on the amount of overtime hours
worked.

At *Pedigree Petfoods* (see p 269 ff), the move from four to five
crew working amongst security staff cut overtime from 38 per
cent of total hours to almost zero, in this case without any
additional manning because of changes in working practices. At
Kimberly-Clark (see p 259 ff), where five crew working is
planned, the company reckons that where overtime has reached
15 per cent under four crew systems, it becomes more cost
effective to recruit a fifth crew. As a result of five crew working,
Don and Low (see p 238 ff) in the textile industry were able to cut
overtime by half and achieve total cost savings of around 18 per
cent; *Continental Can* (see p 232 ff) reduced overtime from 16 to
eight per cent, with a 12 per cent saving in payroll costs; *Thames
Board* (see p 293 ff) cut overtime by a half from previous levels of
20 to 30 per cent; and a major oil company cut overtime from 13
to eight per cent amongst process workers, with a target of five
per cent once initial retraining is complete. At *Blue Circle* (see
p 205 ff), overtime was running at about 30 per cent under a
conventional four crew system. Under a radical agreement
involving flexible manning, annual hours and a new seven crew
shift working system, this was replaced by built in flexible time
at $12\frac{1}{2}$ per cent of basic hours. These additional hours were
incorporated into an annual hours contract for which an annual
salary was paid and may be worked flexibly according to the
needs of the business. As a result of all the changes introduced,
labour costs have been reduced by 15 per cent and output per
employee has risen 36 per cent.

Time off in lieu

Although there is no strong evidence that employers are generally moving away from overtime at premium rates to time off in lieu, the latter was becoming quite usual amongst the companies in our study anxious to tackle the overtime issue. Reference has already been made above to the abolition of paid overtime, with excess hours being compensated only by time off in lieu at *British Caledonian Airways* (see p 226 ff), *Whitbread* (see p 321 ff) and *Petrofina* (see p 273 ff). At *Pilkington's* Greengate works (see p 279 ff), all employees receive time off in lieu for working above the basic 39 hours. Any additional hours worked, referred to by the company as 'alternative hours', attract time off on the basis of one hour off for each additional hour worked, even for weekend working. Employees are entitled to bank their alternative hours and take time off as agreed with their supervisor. A minimum of half an hour's additional work must be done to count towards time off and no restrictions are placed on the number of hours which may be banked and taken as time off.

At *Pedigree Petfoods* (see p 269 ff), day workers have the option to take time off in lieu instead of overtime pay, up to a maximum of 15 hours, the equivalent of two days off in a monthly period. At *Kimberly-Clark* (see p 259 ff), all employees also have the option of taking time off in lieu instead of paid overtime. The agreement states that this option will only be available when the workload permits and no more than 24 hours per month may be accrued for time off purposes, with any hours in excess of this being paid at overtime rates. Lieu time must also be taken in minimum periods of four hours. The company reports, however, that in practice very few employees have taken advantage of this facility and most have preferred overtime pay.

Overtime limitation agreements

In recent years, there has been a growth in interest in some parts of the trade union movement for measures to reduce overtime working in order to create new job opportunities for the unemployed. Since the mid 1970s, the Brussels based European Trade Union Confederation has campaigned for a 10 per cent reduction

in working time throughout Europe, including reductions in
overtime. In 1978, the TUC issued a circular to affiliated members entitled 'Overtime Working and Unemployment' which
recommended that unions should take action where overtime
was systematically worked or where it exceeded 20 hours a
month per worker. In 1981, a special conference of the TUC
debated whether the UK should introduce some legislative
control of overtime, along the lines found in most other European countries. Although a few white collar unions supported
control by legislation, many of the manual unions, whose members would be most affected, did not and the conference concluded with a recommendation that unions should seek voluntary reductions in overtime by collective agreement. Although
the TUC did consider again the role of legislation in reducing
overtime in 1982, the main thrust of its present policy is a
voluntarist one, favouring overtime reduction by agreement, but
little more has been said on this subject in the last few years.[9]

One review of overtime control through collective agreements by *Industrial Relations Review and Report* appeared in
1982 and it concluded that few such agreements had been signed
at either national or company level.[10] Where agreements did
exist, they varied from general exhortations to minimize overtime to placing very high limits on permitted levels. In the
engineering industry national agreement, concluded in 1981,
overtime limits were reduced from 30 to 26 hours per worker per
month, with exemptions applying in the case of breakdowns,
repairs, deadlines and other contingencies. In the textile industry, the national agreement for textile finishing limits weekly
hours to 55, and company level agreements at *Alcan Sheet Metal*
and *Tucker Fasteners* restrict overtime to 20 hours and 30 hours
respectively per month.[11]

In a subsequent review of overtime restrictions in 1984,
Industrial Relations Review and Report concluded that the
problem of overtime remained difficult to control and that a
concerted effort from industry had yet to emerge, but that the
way ahead might lie in the introduction of flexible work patterns.[12] Such a view would be confirmed by the organizations
taking part in our study. Few organizations reported any attempt to control overtime by collective agreement, but rather
the focus was upon productivity agreements to change working
practices, linked to more flexible patterns of work associated
with variable weekly or annual hours contracts and five crew
shiftworking.

Other methods

A variety of other approaches involving alternative working patterns are also used by organizations to obviate or reduce their reliance upon overtime working. Most notably, these involve the use of part time workers, temporary workers or subcontractors, all of which are described in more detail elsewhere in this book, but examples are set out below to illustrate how they may be used as alternatives to overtime.

Part time workers may be employed on evening or 'twilight' production shifts in preference to employing full timers for longer hours on overtime rates. Where work is routine or repetitive, there is some evidence that levels of productivity can be higher through the employment of additional twilight shift-workers than through additional overtime working amongst full timers. Part timers are also widely used in retailing to provide cover for longer opening hours or weekend working rather than employ full timers at premium overtime rates.

Again in retailing, temporary or short term contract staff are employed to meet trading peaks rather than having to resort to overtime. Temporaries are also used in a wide range of industrial contexts to cover for prolonged sickness absence or short term upturns in business, in preference to using full timers working longer hours at premium overtime rates. Because casual or temporary staff do not usually attract the full range of benefits applicable to permanent employees, they are less expensive in employment costs than the overtime they replace.[13]

It would appear that sub-contractors are also increasingly used in preference to additional overtime working amongst full timers, particularly in the fields of plant maintenance and driving. At *Petrofina*, for example, an agreement to reduce long weekly hours and eliminate high overtime working makes provision for the use of outside contractors to meet peak workloads or cover for sickness.

4 New forms of shiftworking

Stephen Palmer and David Redmond

This chapter considers the economics of shiftworking, the kinds of traditional patterns of shiftworking adopted and how the trend towards shorter basic hours and the reduction of overtime is increasingly leading organizations to seek new, more cost effective alternatives to continuous four crew shiftwork. A newly emerging pattern is the adoption of five crew shiftwork systems, but examples of six and seven crew systems are also to be found and are described later in the chapter.

The economics of shiftworking

The economic factors which influence the suitability or otherwise of a shiftworking arrangement contain within them many of the reasons for the changes that we have noted in the traditional systems. Economic logic is not, of course, in itself the sole determinant of whether shiftwork is, or is not, adopted within any particular enterprise. Much of the public sector and the chemical industry must work round the clock for reasons either of safety or to provide a service for which there may be a 24 hour demand. In those circumstances, management must start with the assumption that a high level of cover will be required and work backwards, as it were, in order to find the most cost efficient way of providing it within the safety and other constraints that exist. Indeed, one could argue, that if economic considerations were the sole determinant of shiftworking there could be arguments for closing ambulance services or electricity supply systems for part of the night.

These considerations apart, for most employers the decisions about shiftwork must be based on some economic analysis of the implications. Generally four considerations will be taken into account:

- demand requirements
- capital utilization
- technical necessity
- productivity.

Indeed, according to the National Board for Prices and Incomes' excellent survey in 1970[1] the first two factors were the reasons given for introducing shiftwork in over half of the establishments surveyed, whilst a third also gave technical necessity as the reason.

In the case of *demand requirements*, the decision to work shifts is to a large extent consumer led. The *London Underground*, for instance, has a high demand for its services at various stages of a day lasting from 5.00am to midnight. It can only meet this demand via a shiftworking system. On the other hand, the *British Sugar Corporation* must use its plant to full capacity during the annual 'campaign' season of about six months. *BOC Transhield*, which supplies a food delivery service to a major retail chain, needs to be able not only to deliver the goods to the various stores during the night and early morning, but also be able to accept deliveries to its warehouses during the day and get the loads ready.

So demand requirements need not just be based on the daily service provision, but can also be influenced by seasonal aspects.

Capital utilization as an influence on the adoption of shiftwork speaks for itself. Many organizations need to get the most out of expensive machinery if they are to achieve satisfactory levels of return to capital employed. This is particularly so if the speed of obsolescence is also high. This factor may well account for the increasing levels of white collar, generally computer, staff and female employees who now work shifts. As capital costs are generally fixed, one way of reducing unit costs and increasing competitiveness is via the more intensive use of machinery.

We have already touched upon some of the implications that *technical necessity* has on shiftworking. Steelworks are one example of a process that does not allow for easy shutdowns and where the costs of so doing can be prohibitive. It could be said in these instances that economic rationale takes second place to production needs, but there are costs in closing down plant and machinery of this kind.

Finally, the expected levels of *productivity* under various shift systems will have an effect. There is, in fact, no evidence that suggests that shiftworkers are any more or less productive than dayworkers. Even night shiftworkers, whose productivity may have been expected to be the lowest, are often a self selecting group who prefer to work nights and are not affected by it.

However, despite what employers say, these factors on their own are not sufficient grounds for introducing shifts. For instance, reducing the capital element of unit costs by using machinery over longer periods will not increase profits if the variable cost elements, particularly labour costs, are allowed to rise. And since shiftworking can carry a premium of between 15 and 35 per cent, depending on shift, not to mention substantial overtime payments and the costs of providing ancillary services, it is very easy for increases in variable costs to outweigh any savings in fixed costs.

Before taking the shiftwork road or extending shiftworking, employers will therefore have to look at the factors which affect the variable cost side of the equation. According to Evans and Palmer,[2] consideration must be given to the impact on costs of:

- legislation
- the availability of suitable labour
- trade union attitudes
- organizational problems
- labour costs.

These are interrelated influences. Labour costs will themselves be influenced by the availability of suitable labour, trade union attitudes, custom and practice within the industry, and comparability considerations. Nor must employers neglect taking account of employees' attitudes to shiftwork and the psychological, domestic and social factors that affect their willingness to do it and therefore the premium that they will demand.

'Traditional' shiftwork systems

Despite the impact of reduced working time the 'traditional' concepts of providing cover via shiftwork have changed little. Generally, there remain three distinct groups of shiftwork systems providing different degrees of cover. These are known as double day, three shift discontinuous and three shift continuous systems. Between the first two methods there is now a blurring of the lines of demarcation caused by the move in some companies away from eight hour shift units towards 10 or even 12 hour units. Delineation between them should therefore be based on the total amount of weekly cover provided and the crews needed.

In this way a *double day* shift system will be expected to use two crews to provide a total weekly cover of up to 78 hours (ie 2×39 hours) usually between Monday and Friday inclusive. Before the advent of the shorter working week the system generally operated as follows:

		M	T	W	Th	F
6.00am–2.00pm	Crew	A	A	A	A	A
2.00pm–10.00pm	Crew	B	B	B	B	B

The two crews would work alternate shifts of mornings and afternoons over a two week cycle.

Three shift discontinuous systems extend double shiftworking with the addition of a night shift so that three crews provide 117 hours cover per week (ie 3×39 hours), again usually between Mondays and Fridays. The following pattern is generally used:

		M	T	W	Th	F
6.00am–2.00pm	Crew	A	A	A	A	A
2.00pm–10.00pm	Crew	B	B	B	B	B
10.00pm–6.00am	Crew	C	C	C	C	C

The three crews would work five straight shifts of mornings, afternoons and nights over a three week cycle.

With the addition of a further crew, *seven day continuous* shiftwork uses four crews to provide 168 hours per week (ie 4×39 plus 12 hours overtime). Despite the move from basic hours of 40 to 39, many organizations have chosen to stay with the traditional four crew system meeting the excess 12 hours required either out of overtime or equivalent time off in lieu.

Adapting the shift system above to four crew working would give the following type of rota:

Crew A	M	T	W	Th	F	S	Sun
	M	M	M	M	M	M	M
	R	R	A	A	A	A	A
	A	A	R	R	N	N	N
	N	N	N	N	R	R	R

The system gives seven consecutive shifts of mornings, afternoons, rest days and nights. The system operates over a four week cycle.

Often used in four crew systems, and occasionally with three crew discontinuous systems, is a refinement called the *continental shift system*. This comes in many forms but frequently takes the following shape:

Crew A	M	T	W	Th	F	S	Sun
	M	M	A	A	N	N	N
	R	R	M	M	A	A	A
	N	N	R	R	R	M	M
	A	A	N	N	N	R	R

Although seven shifts are still worked in any one run they are broken up so that there is no requirement to work seven consecutive nights. This particular rota is *forward rolling*, so called because the pattern is mornings, afternoons, nights and rest days. A refinement is *backward rolling* which reverses the order and gives a greater rest period either side of the night shift.

There are, as mentioned, any number of variations in these rotas taking account of shift units longer than eight hours, the introduction of day shifts running concurrently with mornings and afternoon, twilight shifts and so on. Indeed, in its last survey of shiftworking arrangements in 1979 the Industrial Society[3] found over 250 variations on the traditional themes.

'Traditional' systems under review

In recent years, changes in working methods and employment conditions have led many organizations to review their traditional shiftworking arrangements.

A major influence has been the reduction in working hours,

particularly the move from a 40 to 39 hour week. The impact of this change was felt primarily in the areas of continuous shift-working where there were already some logistical problems in meeting a 168 hour week with only four crews. The answer to this conundrum has been met in many ways, ranging from increased overtime payments to the introduction of five crew working. At the more simple level of dealing with reduced working time in a double day shift system, organizations have reduced working time by a number of means such as agreeing the removal of tea breaks or reducing the working day by 12 minutes, but more radical approaches have adopted a nine shift fortnight or reduced shift on Friday afternoons. A reconsideration of the shift week sometimes leads to a reassessment of the shift unit and a move towards 10 hour and 12 hour shifts to compress the working week yet further.

The most startling change occasioned by reduced hours however, has been in thinking. Attempts to jiggle with a 39 hour week and traditional shift systems have led many managements to rethink completely the philosophy behind their existing systems and move towards concepts of annual or monthly hours arrangements. This reassessment has been assisted by the move towards greater flexibility in the labour resource, partly as a means of 'paying' for reduced time and partly as a result of the introduction of new technology. In many cases the old shift-working methods appeared inappropriate in this new environment.

Nowhere is this more clear than in organizations whose output or service is subject to seasonal fluctuations. Here the annual hours concept has particular advantages in helping management meet changes in demand without recourse to over-time payments via a system of 'banking' hours. The concepts of annual hours and compressed working weeks have been discussed in Chapter 2, but they have also had a considerable impact on shiftwork arrangements as well as on dayworking generally.

Discontinuous systems

The term 'discontinuous' is usually generic and applies to two main types of shift systems. These are double days and three shift, Monday to Friday arrangements. Their characteristics have been explained on page 71.

The impact of reduced working time has perhaps been less disruptive for discontinuous than for continuous systems. This is largely because the reduction can easily be taken at the beginning or end of the week (with double days the reduction can, of course, be taken on a daily basis) and has no necessary impact on either manning levels or overtime working.

Thus an organization operating *double days* can give, for instance, two hours off by reducing the Friday afternoon shift to six hours so that over the two week cycle average hours are 39 and employees have free time on Friday evening. By extending shifts, using a 39 hour week, it is possible to introduce a nine day fortnight also for double dayworkers. One week a crew would work five 9 hour morning shifts and the following week four $8\frac{1}{4}$ hour afternoon shifts to give an average working week of 39 hours.

The longer the shift unit hours, the greater the amount of time off that can be generated. Some organizations have introduced 10 and even 12 hour double day shifts to generate extra time off at the beginning and end of the week. Others have chosen to work a mix of eight, 10 and 12 hour units with the same effect of compressing the working week.

The white collar employment areas, where the working week tends towards 35 hours or fewer, have been most affected by these changes, particularly the jobs of draughtsmen and computer operators.

According to an IDS Study[4], computer operators at *Refuge Assurance* have a $4\frac{1}{2}$ day week worked as 8.00am to 1.00pm (Monday to Thursday) and 8.00am to 3.00pm (Friday) during week one; followed by 12.45pm to 8.45pm (Monday to Thursday) in week two. Average hours work out at $29\frac{1}{2}$ gross or $27\frac{5}{8}$ exclusive of meal breaks.

At *Westland Helicopters*, those computer and technical staff required to work shifts are offered two (and in some individual cases, three) choices. These choices are as follows:

System A/Crew A

	M	T	W	Th	F
Week 1	—	A	A	A	A
2	A	—	M	M	M
3	M	M	—	A	A
4	A	A	A	—	M
5	M	M	M	M	—

Start times are 6.00am to 2.45pm (mornings) and 2.45pm to 11.15pm (afternoons) both inclusive of a 30 minute teabreak. This system gives a 'four day' weekend every five weeks for its five half crews.

A second system, which uses the same times and crewing as system A, brings all the rest days together to give one full week off in every five as follows:

System B/Crew A

	M	T	W	Th	F
Week 1	M	M	M	M	M
2	A	A	A	A	A
3	M	M	M	M	M
4	A	A	A	A	A
5	—	—	—	—	—

There is a third system which is to be used by specialist individuals where system B would provide insufficient cover, based effectively on six crews working a combination of mornings and short and long afternoons. The system operates over a six week cycle to give a range of long weekends:

System C/Crew A

	M	T	W	Th	F
Week 1	M	M	M	M	—
2	A	A	A	A	SA
3	—	M	M	M	M
4	A	A	A	A	—
5	M	M	M	M	M
6	—	A	A	A	SA

Some of the principles that have been discussed elsewhere: annual hours, compressed working weeks etc, can be applied to double day shiftworking as, indeed, they can also be applied to *three shift discontinuous systems*. The approaches to new working patterns for three shift systems, caused by reductions in working time, have either been to reduce the length of one particular shift, so that, for example, the Monday morning shift starts at 10.00am rather than 6.00am, or, more commonly, to dispense with one complete shift. In this case, the Friday night shift is usually abolished:

Crew A

	M	T	W	Th	F
Week 1	M	M	M	M	M
2	A	A	A	A	A
3	N	N	N	N	—

This was close to the system adopted at *May and Baker* where the Friday night shift was indeed abolished but an extra half an hour was worked on that day's afternoon shift (eg to 10.30pm).

The pursuit of 'usable free time' has again made some organizations look at extending the basic shift unit to 10 or 12 hours. Such an approach works as follows:

Crew A

	M	T	W	Th	F
Week 1	D	D	—	N	N
2	—	—	D	D	D
3	N	N	N	—	—

This gives quite substantial periods of time off especially for two weekends out of three.

There is, of course, no particular reason why crews should rotate over days, afternoons and nights. The textile industry, it appears, quite often operates a permanent night shift, with a double day system to cover for mornings and afternoons. Evidence does exist to suggest that nightwork appeals specifically to some individuals and by keeping them on this shift all the time could raise productivity.

Conclusion: although there have been some interesting changes in the discontinuous shiftworking areas, in general, patterns have been changed to improve on the length of rest periods. Many organizations consulted did say that they had found that this approach had increased productivity and morale, however measured.

Continuous systems

Four crew shiftworking The continuous operation of

plant and machinery seven days, 168 hours a week, has traditionally been carried out using four crews each working 42 hours per week. As already noted, this approach, which involved quite substantial levels of overtime to ensure cover even when the working week was 40 hours, started to 'creak' even further as contractual hours fell to 39. Indeed, at the 38 hour per week level many employers started to toy with new concepts like annual hours and five crew shiftworking.

However, it would be an overstatement to suggest that all employers have abandoned the traditional four crew approach as basic hours have fallen. Some have retained their existing system and taken account of reductions by building extra rest days into their rotas, meeting the extra cover so required either out of overtime payments or by carrying extra crew members on each shift. According to IDS[5] *CPC* provide cover on the basis of four people to every three jobs, increasing to three to two in important areas. At *British Nuclear Fuels Ltd* (BNFL) the ratio is $4\frac{1}{2}$ to 3. It is at this marginal point, ie whether to build in extra cover and at what level, that the attractions of a five crew rota become self evident.

The retention of four crew systems will therefore be influenced by the size of the crew. Obviously, if there is only one person on the shift, ensuring full cover could require a ratio of two people to one job—there being no other choice—if four people are employed in the crew—and absence is 25 per cent—the ratio falls to 4:1 and so on. Thus, the lower the crew number the higher the cost of providing full cover by incorporating extra manning actually into the crew. Another approach employs a pool of labour, outside the rota system, from which extra manning can be drawn. However, this is an expensive option and, when this stage is reached, is so similar to a five crew operation (except with one crew permanently on relief) that the five crew operation might as well be adopted.

One impact of reduced working time, and indeed of the moves towards harmonization and staff status that have often gone hand in hand with increased employee flexibility, has been to raise employees' desire for their rostered free time to be in usable slices. Even the four crew system has not been immune from pressure to move to 12 hour shifts which allow longer periods of rest.

After a great deal of experimentation, such a system was ultimately agreed for four crew continuous workers at *Kimberly-Clark's* Flint plant. The system was actually introduced at the request of employees despite some management misgivings that such long shift hours could lead to fatigue and a reduction in productivity. In fact, this fear appears to have been largely groundless. The rota works as follows:

Crew A

	M	T	W	Th	F	S	Sun
Week 1	N	N·	—	—	D	D	D
2	—	—	N	N	—	—	—
3	D	D	—	—	N	N	N
4	—	—	D	D	—	—	—

Initially there were also fears that it would be impossible to provide absence cover under a 12 hour system. The usual way of providing such cover in the past involved half shift working at overtime rates by the preceding and following crews. This was considered problematic because such a system could involve crews working 18 hours at a stretch. Again this has not been a problem and absence has been met either by running light or by bringing in employees on their rest days. There is no need to rota in holidays as the plant shuts down completely for periods of annual leave four times a year.

Conclusion: where four crew shiftworking has been retained there has not generally been a major change in the pattern of work. The impact of meeting the extra overtime and/or manning caused by reduced hours can be offset to some extent by improved flexibility, demanning and so on. Sooner or later, however, a continued fall in weekly hours will make the old four crew systems increasingly inefficient and costly. Some employers have chosen to make changes now, as we shall see in the next section, rather than wait for further reductions.

Five crew shiftworking The failings of traditional four crew working in continuous process organizations have already been explained above. Indeed, these failings existed even when the basic week was 40 hours, as on average at least two hours per crew per week had been met either from extra manning or in-built overtime or some combination of the two. With the reduction to 39 hours and, in some cases, to $37\frac{1}{2}$ hours, some organizations felt that these costs were prohibitive and began to search around for a new shift system which would provide full cover in a flexible and cost efficient manner.

In arriving at these new rotas, the annual hours concept was an important analytical tool. The old method of merely considering the total of weekly cover needed in order to establish crewing levels gave way to a look at needs over a full year. This was an important step because it allowed holidays and absenteeism to be taken into account and thus provide a real figure for crews needed.

A typical calculation would be carried out as follows. It assumes an absence level of 10 per cent per annum, five weeks' annual leave and eight public holidays and a basic working week of 39 hours.

The total hours required on a particular process (168 hours per week × 52) are 8735 hours per year.

Time available per employee per year	2028
less— annual leave	198
— statutory holiday	62.4
— absence	177
Total working time	1590.6 hrs

The total number of crews needed (but not the total number of employees as this will depend on crew size) is $8735 \div 1590 = 5.5$ crews. It is not always the case that any particular machine runs non stop for the year and an annual maintenance shutdown reduces the crewing requirement as does a decision to retain overtime for at least part of the cycle.

Not all companies have moved over to five crew working, however, and it is worth noting that at *BNFL* employees voted to retain the four crew system. Similarly, process workers at *Pedigree Petfoods* work a four crew system over a four year cycle which evens out the number and type of shifts used. One rota builds in a Saturday morning shift of $5\frac{1}{2}$ hours compensated for by an afternoon shift of 10 hours. At its Peterborough plant employees work 12 hour shifts at weekends thus increasing the length and frequency of weekend breaks.

The reduction of 'institutionalized' overtime is, of course, quite an important factor in looking at five crew working. *Pedigree Petfoods* already has a five set system for its security guards, which, when it was introduced around three years ago, reduced the level of overtime worked from 20 per cent to virtually nil. The scheme is based on an annual hours contract by which the actual rota hours are some 60 per annum less than the individual's annual contractual hours. The hours that each employee owes the company are used for training and to provide absence cover, the former being actually written into the rota. Other advantages to the employee include longer breaks in the summer and a number of 10 day breaks written into the rota; the company also found savings by converting to this system using existing staff and without increasing employment.

According to IDS[6], *American Can Company* also found quite distinct advantages in moving from four crew to five crew working. Certain traditional problems were identified with the old four crew system, notably:

● the high levels of overtime necessary to provide cover
● the instability of shift teams caused by cover arrangements
● the waste of management time in ensuring adequate manning levels during absence periods
● the longer hours raised fatigue levels
● the shortness of the leisure periods allowed by the rota

Again using the annual hours concept, the company proposed a move to five crew working which was ultimately accepted by the workforce. Although the scheme increased employment by a quarter, these costs were offset by the advantages that five crew working gave in saving management time, lessening employee fatigue, and ensuring cover and predictability.

In the same line of business *Continental Can* also moved from a four crew to a five crew system under the impetus of a cut in the working week to 39 hours and management's insistence that the cut should give 'real' time off. The old system was based on 12 hour shifts worked by four crews on a two shifts on, one shift off, two on, four off basis to provide cover for the entire working week as follows:

Crew A

	M	T	W	Th	F	S	Sun
Week 1	D	D	R	N	N	R	R
2	R	R	D	D	R	N	N
3	R	R	R	R	D	D	R
4	N	N	R	R	R	R	D

The system was based on an average week of 42 hours with the extra two hours per week required by the rota paid as overtime. The added costs of providing this level of cover, including absence, amounted to around 15 per cent of payroll.

The influence of already high cost levels and the agreement to reduce hours to 39, compelled management to seek a new shift system. Eventually they decided on a five crew system which, after a ballot of employees, was based on eight hour shifts. Average hours are 33 per week. The inclusion of holidays into the rota brings the average up to 36 hours per week and extra maintenance shifts increase it to 39. Maintenance shifts last 12 hours and the opportunity is taken to carry out tasks that are impossible whilst the production line is running.

In this case the change created five new jobs as the fifth crew was established by reducing the other crews. This reduction goes some way to explaining the decision of employees to revert to eight hour sets because the 12 hour shifts became more tiring for the substantially reduced crews.

A final example of the sort of pressures that companies experienced from reduced working hours is that of *Thames Board* at Workington. When hours were reduced to 39 in 1982, the initial reaction was to meet this reduction for shiftworkers by granting a further six days' annual leave per year. This only added to the already high overtime levels, pushing them to over 30 per cent in some areas. By 1983 management had set itself a number of objectives of which achieving a minimum dependence on overtime and ensuring continuity of manning figured high on the list. After considerable internal debate they chose to look at five crew working and annual hours agreements as a means of reaching their objectives.

During negotiations with the unions in 1984, agreement was finally reached on an annual hours contract and five crew shiftworking with no increase in employees. The rota allows for blocks of 10 rest days, nine times per year, with a summer break of 20 days. A further 48 floating hours may be taken off at any time. In the end, the benefits accruing to the company are:

- there is no annual shutdown
- overtime has been halved and should be reduced further
- competitive manning levels
- a stabilized holiday system
- greater flexibility

It is quite clear that there are quite substantial advantages to working five crew shift systems, these have been summarized by TURU[7] as follows:

- it is possible to provide some cover for absenteeism and reduce the need for increased manning or overtime

- a degree of overlap between successive shifts can be incorporated into the shift rota
- future reductions in normal basic hours towards 34 hours per week can be managed without generating major distortions in the shift system
- the availability of more weekends and longer rest periods in each shift cycle may prove more socially acceptable
- where four team shift systems have degenerated a five team rota will give a less complex shift rota
- where four team rotas entail substantial amounts of institutional overtime, five shift rotas can be more cost effective

However, there may be disadvantages with five crew working, particularly if it reduces earnings from overtime, although earnings are often maintained owing to the higher productivity allowed by the extra flexibility of five crew working. Another problem is the building of holiday periods into the rota which may be said to reduce employee choice. Indeed this is believed to be the major reason why employees at *BNFL* rejected five crew shifts, and some employees also object to the long periods of free time that tend to fall during the winter months. There is some scope for reintroducing choice into the rota by adopting a 'modular approach' (see p 86).

Types of five crew working

The concept behind most five crew systems is rooted in the means employed under four crewing methods to provide cover. In many of these more traditional systems cover for absence is provided either by building in extra manning into each of the four crews, or holding the additional manning in a central pool from where it can be allocated on a rota basis (to meet foreseen absence) or otherwise as the need arises.

Generally, five crew systems move away from the idea of spare manning being held within the pool or as a central resource, by introducing a fifth crew which can operate as a relief crew every so often, in order to provide holiday cover. Because actual shift hour requirements are 33.6, well below the contractual average week of 39 hours, the difference can be used by management to provide cover without recourse to overtime. Indeed the number of such relief hours available per annum are around 250 per person (about eight shift weeks) assuming holidays of five weeks and eight public holidays.

In IDS Study 335[8], an example of this approach is drawn from *Associated Octel* where each crew in turn works the relief shift to the following five week pattern:

Crew A

	M	T	W	Th	F	S	Sun
Week 1	A	N	N	—	—	M	M
2	M	A	A	N	N	R	R
3	R	R	R	R	R	—	—
4	—	M	M	A	A	N	N
5	N	—	—	M	M	A	A
							etc

With the exception of the seven relief shifts, the progression through the rota is based on the $2 \times 2 \times 3$ continental shift pattern. The arrangement at *Sevalco*, where five crew shiftworking has been in operation for some time, gives time off in seven day blocks and makes relief days part of a continental roster as follows:

Crew A

	M	T	W	Th	F	S	Sun
Week 1	—	—	—	—	—	—	—
2	R	M	M	A	A	N	N
3	N	R	R	M	M	A	A
4	A	N	N	R	R	M	M
5	M	A	A	N	N	R	R

The *Sevalco* arrangement obviously gives usable time off in that a crew receives a full seven free days every five weeks arising from the lumping together of the free days that would otherwise occur during the rota; a possible disadvantage, however, is that there are then four weeks of work without a break.

At a more basic level and eschewing the continental shift systems, there is no reason why a five crew system should not operate as seven days of mornings, afternoons, nights, rest days and relief rotating in turn. This system is comparatively rare.

Not all organizations operate the relief shift concept in the sense of not actually building relief into the roster. At *Don and Low*, for example, the agreed system carries a requirement on employees to work five 'payback' shifts as required (based on the

difference between rostered shift hours and contractual hours)
to provide cover in emergencies. Because of the added disturbance involved in this approach, these payback shifts are paid at
time and a half. A further two payback shifts are used for
training and paid at normal rates. The 'payback system' would
allow for a working week of 35 hours without causing major
disruption to the system.

Working days are based on a continental system but allowing for an extended period of rest days as follows:

Crew A

		M	T	W	Th	F	S	Sun
Week	1	M	M	A	A	N	N	N
	2	—	—	—	—	M	M	M
	3	A	A	N	N	—	—	—
	4	—	—	M	M	A	A	A
	5	N	N	—	—	M	M	M
	6	A	A	N	N	—	—	—
	7	—	—	—	—	—	—	—
	8	M	M	A	A	N	N	N
	9	—	—	M	M	A	A	A
	10	N	N	—	—	—	—	—
	11	M	M	A	A	N	N	N
	12	—	—	—	—	M	M	M

During the holiday period when each crew receives a 17 day
break, the rota changes so that fewer rest days are received by
the other four crews. In July/August, for example, when crews
A, B, C and E receive either all or part of their annual holiday,
Crew A would work:

July/August 1986

		M	T	W	Th	F	S	Sun
w/b	30 June	—	—	—	—	—	—	—
	7 July	—	—	—	—	—	—	—
	14 July	M	M	M	M	A	A	A
	21 July	N	N	—	—	M	M	M
	28 July	A	A	N	N	—	—	—
	4 August	M	M	A	A	N	N	N
	11 August	—	—	A	A	N	N	N
	18 August	—	—	M	M	A	A	A
	25 August	N	N	—	—	—	—	—

In essence, the system amounts to a five crew rota during most of the year with the holiday period being covered by a traditional continental style four crew operation.

So far, our examples have assumed that a basic eight hour shift unit is in operation and, indeed, that the five crews work a seven day rota. In some cases the changes occasioned by five crew shiftworking have not followed this pattern.

The textile company *Vantona Viyella* is practically unique in this country in respect of its approach to five crew continuous shiftworking. Under cost pressures to make the most effective use of expensive capital equipment, the company looked to extending its three shift discontinuous cover to give full seven day working. At the Fold Mill in Bolton, the approach adopted was one of avoiding the disruption of existing three crew working, Monday to Friday, by introducing two crews working solely at weekends by means of two, 12 hour shifts each. Taking account of all the various *premia* that had to be paid (shifts, unsocial hours etc), the weekend workers receive the equivalent of five days' pay. So successful has this approach been that the company has extended it to other units.

The moves towards five crew working as a means of reducing costs, at least from the employer's point of view, also allow considerable scope for providing longer and longer periods of 'usable time off'. We have already seen that, even with 8 hour shift units, a five crew system can allow up to one week of rest days at any time to be taken by each crew during the five week cycle. If the basic unit is increased to 10 or even 12 hours, the amount of 'usable' time off is similarly increased. For example, by working 16×12 hour shifts over a five week cycle, some 19 rest days are generated as follows:

Crew A

	M	T	W	Th	F	S	Sun
Week 1	—	—	—	—	N	N	N
2	N	—	—	—	—	—	—
3	M	M	M	M	—	—	—
4	N	N	N	N	—	—	—
5	—	—	—	M	M	M	M

This arrangement gives an average working week of 38 hours. Although management often opposes such arrangements on the grounds of possible harmful impact on productivity, they are very popular with employees. In fact, little evidence has been found to suggest that productivity suffers.

The 'modular' approach to five crew working

Both management and employees alike have been keen to ensure that the new five crew rotas are equitable in terms of the apportioning of weekends off, nightwork and annual leave amongst the crews. Whilst some organizations have chosen to go to consultants with their specifications and have rotas prepared for them, others have decided to design their own.

A great help for those designing shift systems is the 'Pentagram' modular approach invented by D R Wilson and reported quite fully in the Chemical Industries Association (CIA) report, *Introduction of the shorter working week*[9].

Under a five crew system, each crew works 219 eight hour shifts per calendar year or 21 working shifts in a five week period. It is possible to compile shift rotas based upon five weeks or multiples thereof which even out the apportionment of time off etc mentioned above. These modules can be slotted into the general rota to take account, for example, of annual leave arrangements without disrupting the overall equity of the system. Naturally, the use of five as the basic building block requires that the year for roster purposes should be either 50 or 55 weeks long.

The approach also allows the basic shift units themselves to be varied. Thus eight hour shifts could be worked for most of the year, with 12 hour shifts being introduced during the summer months to maximize 'usable' time. Certainly, the rostering of holidays that five crew working entails, is often their least attractive aspect, but using holiday modules allows employees a sizeable element of choice. As the CIA concludes:

> (*But even*) with the current range, it is possible to alternate periods of eight hour and twelve hour shifts; to work stints of two, three, five, six or seven days in either uniform or irregular patterns; to arrange for blocks of aggregated time off varying from five to twenty days at a time; to stagger annual holidays over periods of six to fifteen weeks; or to allow all five crews to take seven or fifteen days off simultaneously.

One such holiday module has already been discussed in respect of the *Don and Low* example above. A further example, which allows each crew a 10 day break in five weeks, and could be used, say, at the spring or autumn break, is as follows:

Crew A

	M	T	W	Th	F	S	Sun
Week 1	M	M	A	A	N	N	N
2	—	—	M	M	A	A	A
3	N	N	—	—	M	M	M
4	A	A	N	N	—	—	—
5	—	—	—	—	—	—	—

It will be noticed that the maximum break period always follows the nightshift.

Conclusion: there can be no doubt about the high level of interest shown in five crew working, in continuous shiftworking industries in particular, and also in other industries where the cost of new machinery makes continuous working increasingly attractive. Five crew working enjoys considerable cost advantages over more traditional methods, but these advantages are themselves largely reliant upon how far custom and practice overtime, inherent in the four set systems, can be reduced or contained, and by how little extra employment is created. Even so, increased productivity from shorter hours can easily pay for increased manning, but there are few examples of five crew working creating 25 per cent extra manning (which is what one would expect) and a great many where the impact on total manning was negligible or even zero. Introducing an extra crew, effectively made up of the previously existing cover crewmen, costs nothing and is the approach that many have taken. Even where relief workers were not built into the system, with shifts operated short manned or by overtime during absence, the reductions in these costs by moving to five crew working can easily pay for themselves.

Six crew shiftworking It would require a dramatic reduction of basic weekly hours, to well below 35 per week, before employers would look to six crew working to minimize costs. However, some employers are already considering the aspects of six crew shiftworking albeit, as yet, for very small groups of employees.

At its Greengate Works, where the basic week for all employees is 39 hours, *Pilkington Glass* has introduced such a system for its 24 engineering shiftworkers and six quality control technicians. The system is used where only one person works at a time and where the job must always be covered. However, the use of additional day and make up shifts, to bring hours up to the contractual level, means that more than one person works those shifts.

The shift cycle operates over 24 days and there are five make up days in every 84 days. The rota is as follows:

DAY	1	2	3	4	5	6	7	8	9	10	11	12	13	14	15	16	17	18	19	20	21	22	23	24	25	26	27
Days	A	A											A	A										A	A		A etc
6–2			A	A											A	A										A	
2–10					A	A											A	A									
10–6							A	A											A	A							
Make up																A											
Rest									A	A	A	A									A	A	A				

According to the company there are considerable advantages from this approach in these areas:

- pressure on individuals and team to operate efficiently
- operates without supervisory involvement
- flexibility to use dayturns and make up days to provide extra manpower (if workload is appropriate) otherwise cover spread evenly
- will cater for the shorter working week in future
- gives employees considerable flexibility

There are some perceived disadvantages of which the most important might be the need for supervisory intervention if all individuals do not contribute equally. Otherwise there could be a need to intervene in the event of long term sickness or the scheme could, if not monitored, lead to three employees being present when only one is required. In any event, an absence level of around 1.5 per cent probably speaks for itself.

The impetus to the Greengate approach came from management's desire, in the face of a world recession in the glass making industry, to break away from traditional working practices in what was a greenfield site. Part of this desire was to increase worker flexibility.

Seven crew shiftworking   Seven crew shift systems are extremely rare, indeed we could find only one example in operation—in parts of the Cauldon and Dunbar plants of *Blue Circle Industries*. Original shift patterns at the plant were based on four crew continuous shiftworking processes and included all the inherent problems of overtime working such systems entail and which were exacerbated by reduced working hours and/or increased holidays.

As part of their massive investment programme at the plants, management considered, amongst many other things, introducing new shift systems. Eventually, the conclusion was reached to go for seven crew working. Although seven crew working implies a basic working week of only 24 hours, the use of relief shifts brings the average week up to the contractual 39 hours. The new shift pattern is based on a new 7 × 3 shift pattern over a seven week cycle as follows:

Crew A

	M	T	W	Th	F	S	Sun
Week 1	M	M	M	M	M	—	—
2	—	A	A	A	A	A	A
3	A	—	—	N	N	N	N
4	N	N	N	—	—	S	S
5	S+	S+	S+	S	S	—	—
6	—	—	—	S+	S+	S	S
7	S	S+	S+	—	—	M	M

NB: S = Spare day used to cover shift absence or to undertake other integrated duties. Days indicated S+ are to be of seven hours duration to yield an average working week of 39 hours over the seven week cycle. The basic shift unit is eight hours.

On any day for each position, there will be one person each on mornings, afternoons and nights, two people resting and two on spare duties. The characteristics of the system, apart from spare days, are: five weeks out of seven are worked under daytime conditions in normal circumstances; two weekends off in seven weeks, one of which forms part of five consecutive days off; rest periods in all other weeks.

Part of the cost saving of moving to this system is the reduced overtime arising from having two standby shifts to cover for absence. In addition, a yard gang employed on day shift was abolished and shiftworkers are expected to carry out clearing and simple maintenance work done previously by the gang. It is worth noting that, like the six crew system, this new crewing arrangement is currently restricted to a small group of employees in an area where cover is essential and there is scope for individual arrangements of this kind.

5 Alternatives to full time permanent staff

Alastair Evans and Tony Attew

This chapter considers a range of alternative options to full time permanent staff which are increasingly being considered and implemented by organizations. The various alternatives considered are:

- temporary working
- part time working
- job sharing
- new technology homeworking and teleworking

Temporary working

It is probable that recent years have seen a growth in employers' use of temporary workers in order to reduce their commitment to the costs of employing people on a permanent basis and to achieve greater numerical flexibility to increase or reduce numbers to match fluctuations in the level of business activity. In addition, temporary workers are widely used for a number of 'traditional' reasons, such as cover for permanent staff who are off sick or away on holiday. Temporary workers may either be directly employed by an organization, be the employees of a temporary staff agency or be self employed and may be employed either on fixed term contracts or for a specified period. Recent survey evidence indicates that over 80 per cent of temporary work involves direct employment by the employing organization, the majority involving contracts of unspecified length rather than fixed term periods.[1]

Recent survey evidence also indicates that about seven per cent of all employees are in temporary jobs and that two-thirds of temporary employees are women. Whilst there is some debate about whether temporary work has been increasing in recent years, the indications are that temporary working probably declined to about five per cent of employment as a result of the recession in the early 1980s but has recently increased again. A survey by *Manpower Limited*, for example, found that between 1982 and 1985, 49 per cent of production firms and 40 per cent of service firms increased their use of temporary staff.[2] Around three-quarters of all organizations use temporary workers, with the extent of their use being proportionately higher in larger organizations and in growing sectors of the economy.[3]

As regards the occupations of temporary workers, there has been increasing speculation in recent years that the range of jobs involved has been widening from the traditional fields of catering, cleaning, clerical and secretarial work to management and professional occupations. For example, a joint venture has been established by the *CBI* and *Inbucon* to provide top level executives on a temporary basis, including managing directors, sales and technology specialists,[4] and some companies covered in our case studies reported the employment of engineering, technical and professional specialists on a temporary or sub-contracted basis. Overall, however, survey evidence indicates that temporary working is still concentrated in the occupations traditionally associated with temporary work. In a recent survey by the *Institute of Manpower Studies*, for example, the occupations involved in temporary working break down as follows:[5]

Personal services (catering, cleaning, etc)	53%
Clerical, secretarial and office machine operators	14%
Semi skilled and unskilled manual	17%
Sales	6%
Managerial, technical and professional	5%
Other	5%

Employers' reasons for using temporary workers A number of surveys have been carried out over the years examining employers' use of temporary workers. A survey by the

Institute of Manpower Studies in 1975 revealed seven principal reasons for temporary working:

- to cover for absence due to sickness or holidays
- seasonal factors affecting the workload
- fluctuating workloads
- to cover shortages while recruiting regular staff
- to cover 'long term' shortages where skills were in short supply
- to ease reorganizational problems by employing temporary staff during build ups or run downs
- special 'one off' events, such as the launch of a new product or the introduction of new computer systems

In a survey of 446 managers responsible for the recruitment of temporary staff conducted by the *Alfred Marks Bureau* in 1982, the traditional reasons for using temporaries—holidays and sickness cover and unexpected additions to workloads—predominate, as indicated in the table below.[7]

Table 7   Employers' reasons for using temporary staff

Reason	Percentage of respondents giving reason
When a permanent member of staff is ill	73
When a permanent member of staff is on holiday	73
When there is unexpected additional work	65
When there is a special project of limited duration	44
During recruitment of permanent staff	42
During maternity leave of permanent staff	33
During seasonal peak periods of work	27
Because of uncertainty about future staffing requirements	21
To 'try out' a worker before offering permanent employment	15
Because there is a fluctuating workload	14

More recent surveys indicate that a change may have been taking place in the past two or three years in employers' uses of temporary working from 'ad hoc', traditional reasons to a more strategic approach. An IPM study published in 1983 noted the possibility that more employers might be reducing their numbers of permanent staff and meeting fluctuations in demand through temporary staff.[8] A report by *Incomes Data Services* in the same year found that tighter manning amongst permanent staff and the avoidance of redundancy were important reasons for turning to the employment of temporary staff.[9] The most recent analysis of employers' use of temporary workers was published in 1985 by the *Institute of Manpower Studies* and it provides further evidence of new rationales amongst employers for using temporary workers, as indicated in table 8 below.[10] The

Table 8   Reasons for use of temporary workers

Reason	Percentage of employers giving reason
TRADITIONAL REASONS	
To provide cover for holidays, sickness, maternity leave etc	69.0
Because of irregular or unforeseen fluctuations in the activity of the establishment	44.2
Because of seasonal variations in the workload	40.3
To cover some special 'one off' event	32.6
To provide specialist expertise in areas where the workload would not justify recruitment of permanent staff	19.4
Because of a shortage of suitable candidates for permanent posts in the jobs concerned	17.1
To provide staff for the early stages of a new development, product, service etc	16.3
NEW REASONS	
To avoid recruitment of permanent employees at a time of uncertainty about future employment levels	30.2
To avoid future costs of making permanent employees redundant	13.2
To avoid the costs associated with the recruitment and employment of permanent staff (advertising, training, pensions, holidays, etc)	3.9

(n=129)

Note: column totals to more than 100 as employers could list more than one reason

Source: MEAGER N, *Temporary work in Britain: its growth and changing rationales*, Brighton, Institute of Manpower Studies, 1985, p40

reasons given are divided into 'traditional' and 'new' and the report argues that, while traditional reasons predominate, a number of significant new reasons have recently emerged for the use of temporary workers. In particular, employers are using temporary staff to avoid recruiting permanent employees in the light of future uncertainties and also out of a wish to avoid the future costs of declaring employees redundant. Amongst the traditional reasons for using temporary staff, seasonal or other fluctuations were more widely quoted by employers than in previous surveys, providing further evidence that employers may be keeping permanent staffing to a minimum and meeting peaks through temporary working. This use of temporary workers provides further evidence that employers are seeking to establish a core group of employees with greater job security, with the risks and uncertainties of fluctuating demand being borne by temporary staff at the periphery.

New trends in temporary working Amongst our case study organizations, traditional reasons for temporary workers were frequently stated, including holiday or absence cover and temporary employment as a form of recruitment. In addition, however, two further reasons emerged as significant influences on their use of temporary working:

- first, to establish permanent staffing levels to meet minimum or normal levels of demand and rely on temporary staff (or sub-contractors) to cover peaks
- secondly, to establish a 'two tier' workforce in order to provide greater job security for permanent employees at the core by employing a certain percentage of temporary staff at the periphery. Various examples of these approaches are set out below

Manning for minimum or normal cover

In one retail department store group in our study, 'zero base' analysis is used to establish core staffing levels of permanent full and part time employees during the low trade season. This establishes the permanent staff complement which cannot be exceeded and, as trade increases during 'sales' or the pre-Christmas period, the permanent core is augmented by temporary staff engaged for a period of less than 13 weeks or short term contract staff for a period of 13 weeks or more. Short term contract staff may be drawn from a pool of trained and experienced employees who remain 'on call' throughout the year. The company's distribution centre also operates an 'on call register' of staff who are prepared to work at short notice in order to meet peak workloads at particular times of the year. These employees have no fixed, contracted hours of work nor are they guaranteed a specific number of hours of work during a year. They can be requested to work at 24 hours' notice or less on short daywork hours (usually 9.30am to 3.15pm) and the majority of employees in this category are married women with children, since the basic patterns of hours have been chosen to fit in with normal school hours. The 'on call register' system enables workload peaks to be met without a commitment to additional permanent staff and without the costs of additional overtime working amongst existing employees.

The *Ford Motor Company* also reports an increase in the use of temporary workers on short term contracts in recent years. Employment has been contracting in recent years against a background of pressures to reduce costs and avoiding the carrying of surplus labour. In an industry which is also cyclical in its pattern of demand, temporary workers are brought in to meet peak periods. Temporary workers are mainly hourly paid and are normally employed on fixed contracts lasting between two and nine months. For the company, the advantage of the fixed contract is that it establishes a fair reason for dismissal and compels management to reconsider its manpower needs when contracts come up for renewal.

An interesting arrangement covering temporary employment has been introduced by the *Bank of Ireland* in order to achieve a more flexible and cost effective workforce in the face of seasonal requirements to cover for annual or maternity leave. Under an agreement concluded with the Irish Bank Officials Association in 1982, there has been a phased increase in the previously agreed proportion of temporary staff that may be employed at any one time, as follows:

> 1982: up to 4 per cent of total staff
> 1983: up to 5 per cent of total staff
> 1984: up to 6 per cent of total staff
> 1985: up to $7\frac{1}{2}$ per cent of total staff

The Bank reports that this increased use of temporary staff has provided the benefits of greater flexibility to meet seasonal peaks and has reduced the on-costs that would otherwise be associated with the employment of permanent staff.

Enhancing the job security of permanent staff

A number of organizations specifically referred to the development of 'two tier workforces' or core and peripheral workforces as the main means by which the job security of permanent staff is enhanced by means of a buffer of temporary workers. In some of these organizations, the maximum number of temporary employees has been expressed as a percentage of total employment in agreements with the relevant trade unions.

GR-Stein Refractories in Sheffield has been moving towards a two-tier workforce involving permanent and temporary employees over the last four years. Prior to this, when there was a downturn in orders, the company's most frequent response was to institute short time working. In order to avoid the necessity of short time working in the future and enhance the security of longer serving employees, agreement was reached between the company and the unions (TGWU and ASTMS) that up to 15 per cent of production operatives could be employed on temporary contracts. Under these arrangements, temporary contracts are terminated first in the event of a downturn in work, but once temporaries have been employed on a continual basis up to two years, they automatically become classed as part of the permanent workforce. Within the group of employees on temporary contracts, two further categories of employee exist: 'category 1', with up to 26 weeks' continuous service and 'category 2', with more than 26 weeks' service, which enjoys enhanced terms and conditions, slightly higher job security than 'category 1' employees and priority when opportunities arise to transfer to permanent employment. A copy of the agreement setting out the terms and conditions involved in these arrangements is set out in the box below.

GR-STEIN REFRACTORIES LIMITED

TERMS AND CONDITIONS FOR STAFF EMPLOYEES ENGAGED ON TEMPORARY CONTRACT

As and when Management determines there is a need to recruit employees for a temporary period, ASTMS will be consulted prior to recruitment.

Such employees will be engaged on a contract which clearly stipulates this is for a TEMPORARY period of employment.

Payment

Rates of basic pay will be determined by the appropriate Company/Union Agreements.

This Agreement covers:

Temporary Employee

Category 1 — Up to 26 weeks continuous service

Category 2 — From 26 weeks continuous service till cessation of this Agreement.

Service for the purpose of defining categories 1 and 2 will exclude any previous temporary service accrued in a 'non-staff' capacity.

Any continuous 'non-staff' temporary service will however be taken into consideration for all other purposes.

Category 1 Agreement

Holidays

1. Payment will be made for any *Public Statutory* holiday during the employee's period of temporary contract.

2. Payment will be made for any *Fixed* holiday during the employee's period of temporary contract, in the appropriate week's pay *BUT* the corresponding amount will be *deducted* from any *accrued holiday pay* due upon the individual's termination unless the employee is transferred from a temporary contract to a Category 2 or normal contract, in which case no deduction shall be made.

3. Holiday pay will be accrued as normal during the temporary period of employment.

4. Accrued sum will be transferred as part of ongoing conditions in the event of the temporary employee gaining a Category 2 or normal contract status.

5. There will be no guarantee of employment over recognised holiday periods, although every effort will be made to effectively utilise temporary employees at such times.

   A period of unpaid holiday will not break continuity of service and will count towards the 26 weeks.

Attendance and Discipline

As the requirement for temporary employees is to cater for urgent needs, absence for any reason will be closely scrutinised and the Company will terminate the contract of any temporary employee whose attendance and/or timekeeping is not acceptable but not without loss of union representation or appeal.

Requests for time off, for any reason, will be subject to consideration by the appropriate manager or his deputy and, if granted will be unpaid. Unpaid leave granted will not break continuity and will count towards the 26 weeks.

Time off will not be granted in excess of 2 weeks.

Lay-Off

48 hours notice will be given by the Company of intent to Lay-off Category 1 employees, unless the Trade Union covering the employees is in dispute with the Company, in which case no notice will be required.

After 4 weeks continuous service, the statutory Guarantee Payment will be made in *appropriate* lay-off situations, bearing in mind the foregoing paragraph.

Recruitment

In the event of recruitment for normal contract not met from Category 2 employees, consideration will be given to suitably qualified and experienced Category 1 employees *within the specified recruiting area*.

N.B. This does not mean automatic selection of temporary employees, as other permanent employees may wish to be considered for such vacancies.

Vacancies in areas where there are no temporary employees will, in the first instance, be advertised internally.

The Company reserve the right to advertise externally if they consider it necessary to do so.

Termination of Employment

During the first 4 weeks of Category 1 employment the contract may be terminated by either party at 1 day's notice. Thereafter, 1 week's notice will be necessary, except in instances of breach of rules or safety regulations, in which case employment may be terminated without prior warning.

All things being equal, if necessary to reduce the number of temporary contract employees, this will be achieved by termination of appropriate Category 1 employees.

Severance pay for Category 1 employees will be 1 week Tax Free, after 13 weeks continuous employment and after 26 weeks continuous employment 2 weeks Tax Free.

In the event of transfer to Category 2, length of service will be determined by date of engagement as temporary, or if transferred from a temporary non-staff area, from the date of acceptance into temporary staff.

In the event of transfer to normal contract, length of service will be determined by date of engagement as temporary, regardless of initial area engaged as temporary, providing service is unbroken from that date.

Pension and Life Assurance
Temporary employees will be required to join the Superannuation and Life Assurance Scheme in the same way as normal contract employees and will be subject equally to the Pension Scheme rules.

Category 2 Agreement

On completion of 26 continuous weeks on a Staff Category 1 contract such employees will be given the same terms and conditions of employment as all other normal contract employees, e.g. Sick Pay, Holidays, with the undernoted exceptions.

1. On transfer to this category, length of service will be determined by date of engagement as Category 1 providing service is unbroken from that date.

2. The established "Permanent" Manning Budget will be maintained. Any shortfall to be achieved by transfer wherever possible, of suitable Category 2 employees.

3. In the event of the Company needing to reduce the Manual manning levels, the initial reductions will be achieved (all other things being equal) by termination of employment of Category 1 employees.

4. Should the necessary reduction not be achieved by the above step (3) then automatically the next redundancies will be achieved by termination of Category 2 employees, i.e. before implementation of the Company Redundancy Agreement.

5. Severance Pay for Category 2 employees will, from the date of this Agreement be:

After 26 weeks continuous employment – 2 weeks Tax Free
„ 39 „ „ „ – 3 weeks Tax Free
„ 52 „ „ „ – 4 weeks Tax Free

Maximizing the job security of core production workers is also one of the main objectives of personnel policy of *Xidex UK* (see p 333 ff), an American owned manufacturer of computer disks and microfilm based in South Wales. Against a background of unemployment of around 30 per cent in the locality and volatile market conditions for the company's products, one of the company's main concerns has been to provide stability of employment for its long serving employees. The company has therefore instituted a system of 'supplemental' or temporary employment up to a maximum of 20 per cent of the total labour force. It has been agreed with the union (EETPU) that after the 20 per cent level is reached, permanent staff will be engaged from amongst the supplementals. Initially, supplemental employees were employed on 10 month fixed term contracts, either 30 or 37½ hours per week, but in the light of further downturns in the market, the policy now is to employ supplementals on contracts of varying lengths, depending on market requirements, and to move towards the employment of part time supplementals only, working 30 hours per week, in order to maximize employment opportunities.

As part of its agreement on flexible working practices at the Aintree biscuit factory, *Nabisco* (see p 264 ff) has an agreement with the unions (GMBATU, AUEW, EETPU and UCATT) enabling management to employ up to 25 per cent of total employees on temporary contracts before trade union representatives are notified, up to an absolute maximum of 30 per cent. A list of people prepared to do temporary work is kept and the people concerned are called in, as required, according to season or to meet demand during special promotions. The three year agreement, which is designed to achieve substantial increases in productivity and basic pay, also contains undertakings on the avoidance of compulsory redundancy. This use of temporary working may therefore be seen as a means of enhancing the job security of core employees in return for greater flexibility and higher productivity in the working patterns adopted.

Elsewhere in manufacturing industry, similar arrangements have also been reported at *Caterpillar Tractor* and *Perkins Engines*.[11] At *Caterpillar Tractor* in Leicester, the company has an agreement enabling it to employ up to 10 per cent of the hourly paid workforce on temporary contracts. The contracts run for a minimum period of six months up to a maximum of 12 months, after which temporary employees become eligible for consideration as permanents, with service backdated to the original date of commencement. Once the level of temporary employment reaches 10 per cent, temporaries are also eligible to be considered for permanent employment on the basis of seniority. A maximum of 10 per cent of temporary workers also applies at *Perkins Engines* and the agreement specifically states that 'no permanent employee will be made compulsorily redundant whilst temporary labour is employed on site and is performing duties which the permanent employee is willing and competent to perform'.[12]

Costs of temporary working

No strong evidence emerges from the information that a major reason for the use of temporary workers is to achieve immediate cost savings. Where temporary employees were being used instead of permanent staff, generally long term considerations relating to cost and flexibility seemed to be more important. Thus employers are choosing the temporary work option in order to avoid the future costs and implications of laying off staff.

It was noted at the beginning of the chapter that most temporaries are directly employed and the actual savings to be derived in the short term depend on the extent to which the employer applies the same package of benefits to temporary as to permanent staff. Evidence suggests that it is unusual for all benefits to apply, particularly in relation to occupational pension and sick pay schemes,[13] with the result that the direct employment of temporaries could also prove cost effective in the short as well as the long term.

The cost of hiring temporary staff through private employment agencies compared with employing their equivalents on a permanent basis also depends on the cost of the employment package offered to permanent staff over and above basic salary. This has been estimated at around 80 per cent on average on basic salary for senior staff, around 60 per cent for semi skilled operatives and around 50 per cent for clerical staff.[14] In order to establish whether it is more cost effective to hire agency temporaries, it is necessary to compare the real cost, including on-costs, of employing a permanent employee against the rates being charged by the agency. One study has concluded that, outside central London where agency fees tend to be higher, the real cost of employing temporary staff is frequently less. The same study points out that where the costs of a firm's employment package are relatively high and the workload is highly variable, temporary agency staff are likely to be more cost effective. In the converse situation, with a relatively lower cost employment package and stage workloads, the use of permanent staff is likely to be a more cost effective solution.[15]

Part time working

As indicated in table 9, part time working, which is defined by the Department of Employment for statistical purposes as working 30 hours per week or less, has grown significantly during the past 35 years. Accounting for only 2.7 per cent of total employment in 1951, part time working now accounts for over a fifth of all employment in Britain. Whilst there has been some small growth agmongst men working part time, the most significant growth has been amongst female part timers who now account for 46.5 per cent of total female employment.

Whilst employment overall has been decreasing in recent years, part time employment has been increasing, particularly in the sectors of the economy which have been experiencing employment growth—insurance, banking, professional, scientific and miscellaneous services and retail distribution. In retailing, there has been a decline in full time employment whilst part time working has continued to grow substantially.

In comparison with other countries, part time working is generally more significant in the UK. Whilst it accounts for around 20 per cent of total employment in Britain, the equivalent figure in France, West Germany and Italy is between seven and nine per cent of total employment, 10 per cent in Japan and 14 per cent in the United States. Similar levels of part time working to the UK are found in Denmark and Holland and only in Sweden (25 per cent) and Norway (36 per cent) is part time working more widespread.[16]

Part time working offers employers a flexible alternative to full time working and has been increasingly adopted in recent years as a cost effective pattern of work appropriate to their needs. In the longer term, it is likely that the distinction between full and part time working will become increasingly blurred as the hours of full time workers, particularly in the light of the shorter hours already worked by white collar employees, continue to fall.

Table 9 Trends in part time working, 1951–1985

	1951	1961	1971	1975	1980	1985
Number of male part timers	139,000	148,690	584,000	697,000	705,000	n/a
Male part timers as % of all male employees	1.9	1.0	4.4	5.3	5.5	n/a
Number of female part timers	416,880	2,060,500	2,757,500	3,551,000	3,765,000	4,339,500
Female part timers as % of all female employees	6.0	25.8	33.6	39.4	40.9	46.5
Total part timers (male & female)	555,940	2,209,190	3,341,000	4,248,000	4,489,000	n/a
Total part timers as % of all employees	2.7	9.8	15.5	19.1	20.3	n/a

Sources: Department of Employment, *British Labour Statistics Historical Abstract* (HMSO, 1971). Manpower Services Commission, *Working Patterns: Part-Time Work, Job Sharing and Self-Employment*, (1982); *Employment Gazette*

Advantages and disadvantages to employers   Some of
the *advantages* to employers of employing part time workers
include the following:[17]

- the hours of part timers can be varied more readily to meet
  fluctuations in business activity, to cover for planned
  contingencies such as annual holidays or to meet unexpected contingencies such as increases in absence
  through sickness
- part timers may be more productive than full timers when
  carrying out repetitive work, since they can give closer
  attention to their work because they are employed for
  fewer hours per day
- part timers can be used to cover for full time employees
  during their break periods
- absenteeism may be lower among part timers because they
  have free time during the normal working day to accommodate domestic or other arrangements
- using part timers can extend the period over which machinery and equipment is used (eg through the introduction
  of a 'twilight' shift) or the period over which business
  premises can be kept open (eg in the retail trade)
- part time working can cut down the need for overtime or
  unsocial hours payments to full time workers and may
  therefore be more cost-effective
- part time working does not normally attract premium
  rates of overtime until the standard weekly hours of full
  timers have been worked
- the earnings of many part timers fall below National
  Insurance and PAYE threshold levels, leading to savings
  in employers' contributions and a reduction in the administration overheads involved in gathering income tax
- the unit labour cost of employing part timers may be less
  than for full timers because their benefits and conditions
  of service may be less favourable (for example, part timers
  may not be eligible to join an occupational pension
  scheme or enjoy other benefits, such as holidays, on a pro-
  rata basis with full timers)

Some of the potential *disadvantages* to employers of part time
working include the following:[18]

- there may be problems in recruiting the required numbers
  of morning and afternoon part timers, since morning
  hours tend to be preferred by many part time workers

- part timers may be unwilling or unable, because of domestic or other arrangements, to vary their hours of work
- part timers may be less committed than full timers to their employers or may feel less a part of the organization
- the administrative costs of employing two part timers are likely to be higher than those involved in employing one full timer because of a more casual attachment to the job
- rates of labour turnover may be higher amongst part timers
- part timers may be relatively immobile, with a reluctance to travel to other locations or branches when the need arises.

Reasons for part time working The *Institute of Manpower Studies* has identified three broad categories of part time employee, as follows:[19]

- classical
- supplementary
- substitution

Each of these is examined in more detail below and is illustrated by examples of company practice.

Classical

This category covers part time posts where the nature of the job itself requires that only a few hours a day need to be worked, usually on a fixed basis, and is a traditional reason for employing part time workers. Typical part time jobs in this category include cleaners, employed for a few hours in the early morning or in the evening, security workers who again work a pattern of morning and evening hours and canteen workers working a pattern of hours around the middle of the day to provide a lunchtime catering service.

Supplementary

This category covers posts where part time working is used in addition to full time posts in order to increase the flexibility and effectiveness of an operation. A wide variety of patterns of supplementary part time working are found, some typical ones being as follows:

Short days and half shifts: these may be worked where additional cover is needed during a peak period (for example lunchtimes in retailing and banking), where the workload does not require full time cover (for example some clerical or secretarial jobs), or to provide relief cover for full time employees during their break times.

Barclays Bank, for example, employs around 13 per cent of its total staff as part time auxiliaries to provide additional lunchtime cover during this peak business period, averaging about $22\frac{1}{2}$ hours per week.[20] At *W H Smith*, where over half the total staff are part time, a typical pattern of part time hours would be 8.30am to 12.30pm, 1.00pm to 3.00pm and 1.30pm to 5.30pm, with hours overlapping during the peak lunchtime period to provide maximum cover.[21]

Half shifts are used amongst production workers to provide relief cover and maintain production during breaks. At the Bermondsey biscuit factory of the *Nabisco Group*, a part time relief shift manned at a rate of one relief to five permanent operators and running from 8.30am to 1.30pm, provides cover for full time early shift operating from 7.30am to 3.10pm. An evening shift (discussed further below) runs from 5.30pm to 10.00pm to provide cover in the same ratio for the late 3.00pm to 10.00pm shift. A similar approach has been adopted by *J S Fry*, who employ a small number of part timers on fixed morning or afternoon shifts, each totalling $19\frac{1}{2}$ hours per week.[22]

Evening or twilight shifts: these may be used either to extend opening times, as in retailing, to extend production time and utilization of capital or provide relief cover in a manufacturing environment. Where evening shifts are used to extend productive capacity, they are used in preference to additional overtime working at premium rates by full time staff. A twilight shift running from 6.00pm to 10.00pm is used at the Enfield factory of *Thorn EMI Ferguson* where overall, 20 per cent of the labour force is part time.[23] Five evening shifts are also used by *Findus*, a company employing a large number of part timers on processing work, by *Reed Executive* for computer key punch operatives and by publishers, *Morgan Grampian*, for VDU operators.[24] In the retail sector, *Fine Fare* supermarkets have a 6.00pm to 10.00pm evening shift for stocking shelves and *Claude Gill Books*, a medium sized retailer which has profited from the growth in extended shopping hours, operates an evening shift from 6.00pm to 8.00pm, four nights a week, to facilitate evening trading.[26]

Other patterns: a variety of other patterns of supplementary part time working are also found, including one day per week (typically Saturday staff in retailing) or patterns of two, three or four part days. At *Claude Gill Books*, for example, a variety of one or two day shifts are used, including Saturdays from 9.30am to 6.00pm or 11.30am to 8.00pm (to provide additional lunchtime and evening cover).[27] Some retailers also bring in Saturday staff to work additional evening hours on late night trading. This has the advantage that Saturday staff are already trained and familiar with the business and may work several additional evening hours at flat time rather than overtime rates before any National Insurance costs are incurred. *SGS Inspection Services* operate a mix of three, four or five part days or alternatively three full days amongst clerical workers. The main reason for this is to retain the services of experienced employees when their domestic circumstances have changed.[28]

Substitution

This third category of part time posts is used to describe a situation in which an employer has intentionally decided to replace full timers with part timers. This is a more recent development in the use of part time staff and is potentially of greatest interest in this review of the changing role of part time work. The reasons for this development relate mainly to the cost savings on employment overheads and the greater flexibility which can be achieved, reflecting the benefits of part time working to employers, as described above.

The substitution of full timers by part timers has probably gone furthest in the retailing sector in recent years, as part of a strategy for cost reduction in a sector where staffing and associated on-costs represent a relatively high proportion of total costs. The trend began around 1979/1980 against a background of recession and the effects on trading of a doubling of VAT which led firms to look at ways of cutting staffing costs in order to remain competitive. In addition, this period was associated with a rise in unemployment, which brought about changes in the nature of the labour supply to the extent that more people were willing to accept part time work. Part time employment has generally been introduced gradually, for example by using the relatively high wastage rates in retailing to replace full timers by part timers or by introducing part time working on a widespread basis at new stores. For many firms in the industry, the last five or six years have seen a shift from a part time/full time

ratio of 30:70 to a reverse situation in which many now employ
around 70 per cent of total employees on a part time basis.
Typically, part time staff are engaged to work up to 16 or 17
hours a week, since this normally yields earnings below the
threshold for National Insurance contributions. Whilst a pattern of four hours per day, four days per week is often worked,
part time workers are employed on the basis of total flexibility of
hours and days worked which may fluctuate according to the
needs of the business and the availability of staff as a result of
absence or holidays. Apart from achieving greater flexibility in
the deployment of staff, one department store chain calculates
that the real hourly cost of employing part timers is about 12 per
cent less than the equivalent full timer as a result of the
following:

●   savings on the employer's occupational pension contribu-
    tions, since part timers are ineligible to join
●   savings on the employer's National Insurance contribu-
    tions where part timers' earnings fall below the lower
    earnings threshold
●   savings on the costs of paid morning and afternoon breaks
    of 15 minutes each for which part timers are generally
    ineligible.

Outside retailing, there are a number of examples of part time
working being used in place of full time to achieve the same
number of production hours, sometimes referred to as 'mini
shifts'. *United Biscuits* have adopted this approach at their
plants at Rotherham and on Teesside. In place of a full time day
shift of eight hours, the company has introduced two part time
shifts of around five hours each to extend daily productive time
to 10 hours. The recruitment of full timers has been frozen and
part timers have been recruited to work 25 to 27 hours per week.
Savings have been made in shift *premia* and overtime payments
and the changes have resulted in a two per cent reduction in unit
labour costs, an overall reduction in employment of one per cent
and an estimated cut in hours worked, including overtime, of
around 30 per cent.[29]

   The *Lyons Tetley* factory at Eaglescliffe employs 76 per cent
of its production workforce as part timers working three overlapping mini shifts, running from 7.20am to 12.20pm, 12.15pm to
5.15pm and 5.10pm to 10.00pm on a rotating basis, after which a
full night shift takes over. The company has found that productivity is higher on a five hour shift than a full time one and has

introduced this pattern as part of a positive policy for achieving flexibility, and not because full timers could not be recruited. Part timers are also felt to be more productive where the work involved is routine and repetitive. No shift premiu are paid and productive time during the day is increased since the part timers only have two 12 minute breaks in the five hour period which are staggered so as to maintain production. The short shifts can be extended to meet higher production demands and overtime at time and a half is paid on hours worked in excess of five.[30]

Xidex (UK), formerly *Control Data*, produce computer tapes and disks at their plant in Brynmawr, South Wales. Around 20 per cent of the company's 775 production workers are termed 'supplemental' employees working part time weekly hours of 30 per week (Monday to Thursday or Tuesday to Friday). These employees are engaged on a range of short term contracts of varying length, depending on market requirements. As described in more detail in the case study in the appendix, the aim of the company's policy is to maximize the job security of full time production workers as members of the core labour force by employing part time supplemental workers on short term contracts at the periphery with less job security. These arrangements are embodied in agreements with the EETPU which is the only recognized union and has full negotiating rights for production workers.

Other companies using mini shifts include *Cadbury Typhoo*, where three overlapping part time shifts run from 6.00am to 9.30pm and *Findus*, where two thirds of process workers are part timers. *Findus* find that machinery can be more fully utilized without breaks for meals and that productivity is higher during part time than full time shifts.[31]

Job sharing

Job sharing has been defined as an arrangement whereby *two* employees share the responsibilities of *one* full time position, with the salary, paid leave, pension rights and fringe benefits divided between them, according to the time each works.[32] Unlike much traditional part time working, job sharing starts from the premise that there is a full time job to be done, but that it could, for a variety of reasons which will be considered later, be performed by two people on a shared basis.

Job sharing came to prominence in the UK about five or six years ago for a variety of reasons. The main stimulus came from people, particularly women, who wanted to continue in work and combine this with a family role. Further stimulus has come from employers, mainly in the public but also in the private sector, who have viewed job sharing as a means of reducing unemployment, particularly amongst young people, or as part of their equal opportunities policy. Some of the principles underlying job sharing became part of official public policy when, in 1982, the Government introduced its Job Splitting Scheme providing grants to employers offering part time work to unemployed people on a shared basis. Subsequently in 1983, the Government introduced a Part Time Job Release Scheme providing allowances to individuals approaching retirement to encourage them to work part time and create a part time job opportunity for an unemployed person. Neither scheme has been successful, probably because they provided insufficient financial incentives to employers and the Part Time Job Release Scheme has since been abolished.

Although interest in job sharing has grown in recent years, the concept has a history going back some time before this. *Barclays Bank*, for example, has employed secretarial and administrative staff on a system of alternate weeks known as 'twinning' since the early 1940s in response to problems of skill shortage and about 7500 of its total of 62,000 staff now work on this basis.[33] The system involves splitting a job between two part timers, each of whom works a full week on alternate weeks, a system which was subsequently adopted by the other major clearing banks. In 1969, the *Department of Health and Social Security* adopted a policy of urging health authorities to seek ways to encourage the return of married women to employment through job sharing. In 1975 a scheme was introduced by the *Lothian Health Board* allowing two people to apply jointly for any grade of medical post, from house officer to consultant.[34] Recently, job sharing has expanded into a range of sectors of the economy, notably local and national government, health, education and community service. Leading employers of job sharers in the public sector include the *City of Sheffield* where 160 posts are shared and the *London Boroughs of Camden* and *Hackney*. *Camden* has 75 posts shared, 40 per cent of which are at senior and principal officer grade. In the *DHSS*, existing employees have the right to opt for job sharing (providing operational requirements permit) and the *Irish Civil Service*, which launched its scheme in 1984, has 345 job shared posts, with a further number of employees waiting to join the scheme. Job sharing also exists in a small number of private sector organizations, including *GEC Telecommunications, Fox's Biscuits, The Stock Exchange, Pedigree Petfoods* and others.

A wide range of jobs have been split for job sharing purposes, although the majority are clerical or secretarial in nature, since it is relatively straightforward to divide the tasks involved. Some professional jobs are also carried out on a shared basis, including such occupations as librarians, teachers, social workers, personnel and training officers, doctors, lecturers and community workers.

Outside the UK, job sharing has also been introduced into a number of organizations in the United States over the last 10 years. About 60 per cent of these jobs are in public sector and educational institutions. In California, for example, about one-third of all the State's school districts have introduced job sharing programmes for teachers, amounting to a total of 1500 teachers working under this arrangement. Employers using job sharing in the private sector include *Xidex (UK), Hewlett-Packard* and *Levi Strauss.*[35]

Working patterns of job sharers As with conventional part time working, the hours and patterns of job sharing can be highly variable, but the following are quite commonly found:

- *split day*: one job sharer works in the morning while the other works in the afternoon, possibly with some overlap during a handover period. From the limited evidence available, it would appear that this is the least used pattern of job sharing, since travelling time and cost may be disproportionate to the time spent at work and the wage or salary earned
- *split week*: one job sharer works the first half of the week (eg Monday, Tuesday, Wednesday morning) while the other works the second half. A survey by the *Equal Opportunities Commission* (EOC) found this to be the single most popular working pattern[37]
- *alternate week*: under this pattern, one job sharer works one full week, while the other job sharer works the next full week. This pattern may be particularly appropriate where the time and cost of travel are significant and employees can benefit from buying a weekly season ticket for the week they are working

- *no fixed schedule*: the EOC also reported that a number of job sharing arrangements were highly flexible and operated to no fixed schedule. Rather, patterns of work were changed according to the needs of the organization or the personal needs of the individuals concerned. Clearly such an approach would require close co-operation between supervisor and job sharers, but could provide organizations with considerable scope for flexibility

Potential benefits of job sharing Some reports have suggested that employers may find a number of advantages in adopting job sharing which may enhance flexibility and productivity. It should be stressed however that these potential benefits are largely based upon a relatively limited experience of job sharing, rather than on any extensive or systematic survey, and need to be treated accordingly. One notable exception is a German study of 35 medium sized companies using job sharing, published in 1981, which indicated productivity gains averaging 33 per cent where job sharers replaced full timers.[38]

The benefits of job sharing, some of which might also apply to conventional part time working, include the following:[39]

- *reduced labour turnover*: for a variety of reasons, job sharing may contribute to a reduction in labour turnover. Because some jobs are tedious or highly pressurized, turnover rates amongst full time staff may be high. Turnover may be reduced by opening up such jobs to job sharing. Employers may also lose valued employees because full time work does not suit personal needs. Job sharing can be one way of retaining highly capable staff who might otherwise have left. For example, employers may be able to retain trained female staff who may wish to combine a family role with part time working
- *reduced absenteeism*: a job sharer, unlike a full timer, has more free time during the week to attend to family or personal business, such as visits to the doctor or dentist or staying at home to supervise builders, gas or electricity people, etc
- *greater continuity*: when one job sharer goes sick or on holiday, at least half the job will be done by the other sharer. There is also the possibility that the other sharer may be able to work more hours on a temporary basis

- *greater effort*: because a job sharer's day or week is shorter than a full timer's, there is the possibility that he or she will be able to put greater effort and energy into a job, particularly where a job is tedious, repetitive or physically tiring
- *availability of a wider range of skills*: job sharing enables employers to utilize the skills and knowledge of two people for the price of one. Except in the most routine work, most people have their respective strengths and weaknesses. Job sharers may be able to organize the workload so that the particular strengths or capabilities of each sharer are used to the full
- *tapping a wider employment pool*: job sharing enables employers to recruit capable people who might otherwise not be considered because they are not available for full time work
- *better training for young people*: some employers may wish to increase the number of young people being trained in order to meet future skill requirements, but feel constrained by the cost because of current financial circumstances. Job sharing is a way of doubling the number of young people being trained without doubling the cost
- *easing older workers into retirement*: a number of potential benefits may arise from the introduction of job sharing amongst people approaching retirement. Reduced hours for older workers may assist the transition between full time work and full time leisure. It may also provide a method of training young people where a job is shared between an older worker and a young trainee

Possible disadvantages Against these potential advantages of job sharing, there are also a number of possible disadvantages which employers will need to consider, including the following:[40]

- *administrative costs*: employing two people in place of one adds to the cost of payroll administration, although this need not be very significant where payroll systems are computerized. In addition, job sharing will increase the workload of the personnel function, since recruitment, selection, other procedures related to engagement (medical checks, references, employment contracts etc), induction, job training and employee record keeping, will all be doubled

- *communication*: extra care will be needed to ensure that all communications are received by both job sharers and to ensure that further time is allowed for job sharers to communicate adequately with each other during any handover period
- *supervision*: job sharing calls for additional efforts on the part of managers or supervisors when allocating work, co-ordinating the work of the sharers and communicating with them
- *division of responsibility*: problems may arise out of a division of the tasks performed, for example, where the job sharers perform at different levels of competence. Should one job sharer bear the responsibility for the errors or shortcomings of the other? Should one job sharer be responsible for putting right the errors of the other?
- *delay*: where one job sharer has particular skills not possessed by the other or has not communicated properly with the other, delays may occur because a matter may remain unresolved until the other job sharer returns to work

The practicalities of job sharing This section considers the practicalities of introducing job sharing into organizations by reference to a number of case examples. The introduction of job sharing is examined under two broad headings, reflecting the reasons for its adoption:

- youth training
- employment policy

Youth training

A number of organizations in both the public and private sectors have introduced schemes of youth job sharing, combining work experience and periods of study, as a means of combatting youth unemployment in their localities and also of providing a flow of skilled employees to fill future vacancies.

A scheme of this type was introduced at *GEC Telecommunications* in Coventry in 1981 and involves about 100 school leavers who are recruited into the job sharing programme for a minimum of 18 months.[41] Trainees share a single trainee post on a split $2\frac{1}{2}$ day week basis, working either from Monday to

Wednesday morning or Wednesday afternoon to Friday. On at least one of their free days in the week, they are required to attend a course of further education at the local technical college which is unpaid. *Fox's Biscuits* in Batley, West York-shire, run two job sharing schemes for school leavers.[42] Under one of these, about 20 school leavers are recruited to fill 10 trainee vacancies in the factory. Trainees work on alternate days, three days in one week (Monday, Wednesday and Friday) and two days in the next (Tuesday and Thursday). They are paid at the same hourly and overtime rates as full time employees and receive, pro-rata, half the annual entitlement to holidays and sick pay. Another smaller scheme operates for 'A' level school leavers wishing to train in various production skills and incorporates a course of higher education. Further details of the first of these schemes are set out in the box below.

FOX'S BISCUITS LIMITED

Job Sharing Scheme For School Leavers

1. The Scheme is aimed at the large group of unqualified School Leavers required for tasks that can be taught by the Company.

2. Objectives of the Scheme
2.1 To assist in easing the problem of Youth Unemployment by inviting two first time Employees to share one full time vacancy.
2.2 To enable more young people to be gainfully employed and become proficient at an actual and ongoing job.
2.3 To maintain a reserve of skilled labour readily available for relief work as necessary.
2.4 To ease the significant mental and physical transitional period between schooling and full time employment.

3. Scheme Outline
3.1 Each year half the vacancies for School Leavers to be filled with Job Sharers.
3.2 The other half to be filled by the previous year's Job Sharers becoming Full Time Workers.
3.3 Casualties during the year to be replaced with Job Sharers (they will benefit by working a shorter period before becoming Full Time Workers).

4. Example
4.1 Assume 20 Annual Vacancies for School Leavers

	1982	*1983*	*1984*	*1985*	*1986*
Required Full Time Intake	20	20	20	20	20
Work Share Intake	20	20	20	20	20
Transferred to Full Time		10	10	10	10

5. Terms and Conditions of Employment (Appendix A)
5.1 Equally shared between the two Employees for each job.

6. Benefit to Job Sharers based on current Fox Rates

7. Cost to Employer
7.1 By halving all administrative tasks   NIL
     e.g. Pay fortnightly instead of weekly
         Change overalls at half frequency of Full Time Workers
7.2 Recruitment and Training   NIL
     e.g. As all Starters eventually become Full Time Workers no increase in Work Load.

Appendix A

Terms and Conditions of Employment

1 To be equally shared between the two Employees for each job.

2 Days of Work

Employee 'A'	Week 1	Monday, Wednesday, Friday
	Week 2	Tuesday, Thursday
Employee 'B'	Week 1	Tuesday, Thursday
	Week 2	Monday, Wednesday, Friday

3 Rates of Pay
Normal hourly rate.
Overtime paid on a daily basis.
Wages to be paid each fortnight.

4 Statutory Holidays
In a full year each Employee will receive 4 Statutory Holidays. Where necessary, days of work adjacent to each holiday will be interchanged to make this possible.

5 Annual Holidays
Each Employee will receive half the full entitlement. Where necessary, days of work will be interchanged to enable each Employee to have two complete weeks of annual holiday.

6 Sickness
Qualification and payments to be half the full time entitlement.

7 Period of Employment
One year Job Sharing employment from the August of the School Leaving Year.

Automatic transfer to Full Time Employment from the following August.

Source: SYRETT M, *Employing Job Sharers, Part-Timers and Temporary Staff*, London, Institute of Personnel Management, 1982, pp 103–105.

In the public sector, *Staffordshire County Council* introduced a youth job sharing scheme for trainee entrants in 1982.[43] The scheme had its origins in the desire of council members to provide more work experience, training and employment opportunities for the rising number of young unemployed. Job sharing was felt to be a useful means of achieving this objective and, as a result, up to 50 young people are recruited each year from amongst school and further education leavers who have not previously held a job. They spend 2½ days a week at work and one day at college following an approved course of study, such as BTEC national or higher certificate or other courses in typing and word processing skills. All 3½ days are paid for (a total of 27 hours per week) and trainees are encouraged to participate in voluntary work in the community on their free 1½ days. Whilst no guarantees of employment at the end of the two year course can be made, *Staffordshire* finds that, with careful selection, fall out rates are low and success rates in finding full time permanent jobs are high.

A similar scheme has operated at the *Greater Manchester Council* since 1982. Eight supernumerary trainee posts have been established, six junior clerical assistants and two secretarial assistants, and these are allocated to departments according to their wishes. Job sharers are required to study for an appropriate qualification (eg BEC) and the period of their appointment is limited to the length of the course of study (usually three or four years). There is no guarantee of continued employment beyond this time. Job sharers work two days per week and attend college on one day. Out of term time, they work $2\frac{1}{2}$ days per week and are paid as if they worked $2\frac{1}{2}$ days per week throughout the year.[44]

Employment policy

Job sharing generally may be introduced for a variety of reasons which have been gathered here under the umbrella of employment policy. Organizations have introduced job sharing for policy reasons in order to achieve one or more of the following objectives:

- to be seen to be creating new employment opportunities in their communities
- to aid the retention of experienced staff under flexible arrangements enabling employees to combine work and other roles in the light of changed personal circumstances
- to achieve more effective work patterns of benefit to the organization
- as part of a package of equal opportunities policies providing a new option for women to return to their former posts after maternity leave under more flexible arrangements.

The creation of employment opportunities is a major consideration underlying the introduction of job sharing in the *Irish Civil Service*. Along with a career break scheme (see p 166 ff), the job sharing scheme arose from the recommendations of the Cabinet Task Force on Employment and was introduced on a pilot basis in early 1984. The scheme is open to all full time officers, whether established or unestablished, who are entitled to a pro rata 50 per cent of salary and benefits in return for a commitment to attend for 50 per cent of the time. For superannuation purposes, each year's service in a job sharing capacity is reckoned as six months' pensionable service. Actual times of attendance are agreed with management in the employing department and may not necessarily follow a half day on/half day off pattern. Participants in the scheme are required to work in a job sharing capacity for at least three years, although exceptional circumstances will be considered, and are entitled to return to full time working after this period. All vacancies arising as a result of job sharing are filled.

The *Irish Civil Service* has put considerable efforts into the promotion of the scheme which is monitored through a sub-committee comprising management and union interests. Shortly after the launch of the scheme, all major departments were visited and briefed on how the scheme would work. Promotional posters were displayed and leaflets describing the scheme and explaining its impact on earnings were circulated with pay cheques to all staff. Applications to job share are made through the local personnel units and for those without a partner, a central register of applicants is held for matching purposes. As of 30 April 1986, a total of 328 existing staff had opted to participate in the scheme from the Clerical Assistant, Clerical Officer, Executive Officer, Higher Executive Officer and departmental grades. In addition a further 150 staff had been recruited on a job sharing basis at Clerical Assistant, Clerical Officer and Executive Officer levels, bringing the total number of job sharers at that date to 478 thus creating an additional 239 jobs. Staff recruited on a job sharing basis will be offered full time appointments after a period of two to $2\frac{1}{2}$ years.

Details of the conditions of service applying to those who opt for job sharing and those recruited on a job-sharing basis are set out in the box below.

IRISH CIVIL SERVICE

Conditions of service applicable to participants in the pilot job-sharing scheme

1. *Pay*
For each grade in which job-sharing arrangements operate, the scale of pay applicable to job-sharing staff shall be a scale each point of which shall represent 50% of the corresponding point on the scale of pay appropriate to full-time staff. Increments on this scale will be granted annually if the officer's services are satisfactory. (Salary payments will issue each week to all job-sharers in weekly-paid grades, including officers following week on/week off attendance regimes).

2. *Attendance arrangements*
(i)   The principle governing attendance arrangements under the job-sharing scheme is that attendance liabilities associated with a single, full-time post will fall to be shared equally between two officers. Thus, for each individual participant in the scheme, the duration of the 'job-sharing day' will be 50% of the daily attendance liability of a full-time officer in the same grade. The conditions of service outline in the following paragraphs in relation to pay, annual leave, sick leave, superannuation and eligibility for promotion are based on this principle.

(ii) The reference at (i) above to a 50% attendance liability should not be seen as an indication that a 'half-day on/half-day off' attendance regime is the regime preferred by management. The particular regime to apply to each shared post will be determined by the employing Department, in consultation as necessary with appropriate Staff Side interests, and having regard where possible to such preferences as may be expressed by prospective job-sharers.

3. *Annual leave*
The annual leave allowances of job-sharing staff, as expressed in units, will be the same as the allowances appropriate to full-time staff. However in the case of job-sharing staff, the duration of a 'working day' for annual purposes shall be the duration of the job-sharing day as outlined in par. 2 above. (Thus, for example, a job-sharing Clerical Officer with less than 5 years service would have an annual leave allowance of 18 working days, but if such an officer was following a day on/day off or a week on/week off attendance regime and took one *full days* annual leave on a day on which he/she would otherwise be scheduled for duty, he/she would use *two* working days annual leave for this purpose).

4. *Public and privilege holidays*
In the case of job-sharing staff who are *not* conditioned to a half day on/half day off attendance regime (e.g. staff following week on/week off or day on/day off regimes) entitlements arising from public or privilege holidays will accrue to the officer who would otherwise be scheduled for duty on the day in question. In such cases, however, the normal attendance regime will, where necessary, be varied slightly by Departments with a view to allowing both job-sharing partners to benefit equally from public and privilege holidays.

5. *Sick leave*
The sick leave entitlements of job-sharing staff will, subject to the

two minor variations set out below in the uncertified sick leave arrangements, be the same as those applicable to full-time staff. However, as in the case of annual leave, job-sharing officers following a day on/day off or week on/week off attendance regime will be deemed to have used 2 days from their sick leave entitlement in respect of each full days absence from duty on sick leave.

In the case of uncertified sick leave, staff who do not follow a 'half day on/half day off' attendance regime will

(i)   have an uncertified sick leave allowance of 8 job-sharing days per annum (i.e. 4 full days) rather than the normal allowance of 7 days;

and

(ii)   will not be required to submit a medical certificate in respect of a sick absence of 2 full days (4 job-sharing days).

6.   *Superannuation*
Job-sharing staff will be eligible for superannuation benefits on the same basis as full-time staff, save that each year of service given in a job-sharing capacity will reckon as six months service for superannuation purposes. Pensionable salary will be based on full-time salary.

7.   *Probation*
The probationary arrangements for job-sharing staff will be identical in all respects to the arrangements governing full-time staff. Service in a job-sharing capacity will be reckoned as full-time so far as the duration of the probationary period is concerned.

8.   *Promotion*
Job-sharing staff will be eligible for promotion on the same basis as full-time staff, subject to the following conditions:

(i)   For the purpose of the service requirements governing promotion, each year of service in a job-sharing capacity will be reckoned as the equivalent of six months service in a full-time capacity.

(ii)   While it may be possible in some cases for officers to continue to serve in a job-sharing capacity on promotion, an offer of promotion will normally be conditional on the officer concerned undertaking to perform the duties of the higher grade on a full-time basis.

9. *Overtime*

Notwithstanding their reduced attendance liabilities, job-sharing staff will not be debarred from qualifying for overtime payments, provided that the extra attendance given by them is *outside* the span of the conditioned working day of full-time staff in the grades concerned (e.g. 9.15a.m.–5.30p.m. in the case of most general service grades) and subject to the agreed arrangements applicable to full-time staff.

10. *Outside employment*

All job-sharing staff will be required to enter into a formal written undertaking that, during the period of their service in a job-sharing capacity, they will not engage in any form of outside employment.

11. General
  (i) Job-sharing will not affect the question as to (a) whether an officer is to be employed in an established or non-established capacity or (b) whether a post is to be an established or non-established post. Thus, serving established staff who volunteer for assignment in a job-sharing capacity will in all cases retain their established status.

  (ii) Departments reserve the right to require individual job-sharing officers to resume duty on a full-time basis, for a temporary period, in exceptional circumstances e.g. for the purpose of attending an induction course of training. This right will not, however, be exercised in order to provide cover during the absence on sick or annual leave of the job-sharer's partner or as an alternative to normal overtime working by existing full-time staff. The officers concerned would be treated as full-time staff in all respects for the duration of such assignment.

  (iii) in relation to all other conditions of service, and to the regulations governing civil servants generally, no special arrangements shall apply in the case of job-sharing staff.

In the UK, the creation of new job opportunities through job sharing has been adopted by a number of local government employers. At *Sheffield City Council*, where about 160 posts are shared, its policy statement specifically declares that 'job sharing is seen as part of the general employment policy of the Authority in that the needs of staff who wish to work less than full time can help generate job opportunities at a time of continuing high unemployment'.[45] The growth of job sharing in the London Boroughs has also been particularly marked in recent years. In 1981, two boroughs were involved, now 12 have formal policies and a further nine are in the process of drawing them up. *Camden* was one of the first London boroughs to agree a policy in 1982 and currently has 75 posts shared, of which 40 per cent are amongst senior and principal officer grades (S01–P06). Two sharers are from manual grades. *Camden* has run workshops for job sharers, potential job sharers and managers and also runs a register to help employees find suitable job sharing partners. *Hackney*, the first London borough to establish job sharing policies in 1980, and *Lewisham* also maintain a system of job sharing registers. In *Brent*, 17 posts are shared, largely in the social services department, but also in housing and leisure services and in *Lambeth*, 33 posts are shared and currently further consideration is being given to extending the scheme to manual workers.[46] In central government, the *Department of Health and Social Security* has introduced a scheme, as part of an equal opportunities policy, allowing employees to opt either to job share or work part-time. About 1000 employees are involved although most have taken the part time option. The policy applies to all levels of staff and requires that management must give employees' requests serious consideration. In practice, requests are not normally turned down. Under the scheme, employees also have the option of returning again to full time hours in the future if they wish. Some of the benefits of the scheme reported by *DHSS* include improved retention of skilled and experienced staff with a consequent impact on the costs involved in training new recruits. At the *BBC*, where 12 posts are shared, a major factor in using the arrangement is to retain the services of valuable staff who, for one reason or another (child rearing, disability of dependent relatives, etc) can only work part time. Further details of the guidelines covering job sharing at the *BBC* are set out in the box below.

BRITISH BROADCASTING CORPORATION

Framework for Job Sharing Arrangements

Initiating a Job Sharing Arrangement
A job sharing arrangement is normally initiated by the staff concerned rather than the BBC. It goes without saying therefore, that those involved in job sharing should be willing participants.

Contracts of Employment
Staff participating in a job sharing arrangement should be engaged on a standard part-time continuing contract or, if currently a full-time member of staff, transferred to this form of contract and the relevant nationally agreed conditions of service, being given the option of remaining in the New Pension Scheme or becoming non-pensionable.

> *Note*: (i) Overtime cannot be required of a part-time employee.
>
> (ii) For those on part-time continuing contracts, membership of the New Pension Scheme is voluntary.

Rates of Pay and Conditions of Service
The rates of pay and conditions of service of job sharers are determined by the relevant pay and conditions of service agreements, as is their eligibility for annual leave. Although the timing of annual leave is subject to the overriding needs of the service, it would be unreasonable to insist that members of staff sharing a job should always take their leave at the same time.

Hours of Work and Extra Duty
The combined hours (excluding meals) of staff who job share are the same as those applicable to the full-time post before the arrangement was introduced. The total number of hours need not of course be divided equally if this suits the preference of all concerned. However, it should be borne in mind that staff who work less than 16 hours per week may lose certain statutory rights under current employment legislation and this should be drawn to their attention if applicable. Job sharers who do work off duty days, or who work extra hours during duty days, should be compensated in accordance with the appropriate pay and conditions of service agreement for part-time staff.

Guidelines Covering the Introduction and Operation of Job Sharing Arrangements

General

These guidelines have been agreed with the recognised trade unions. Their purpose is to set out the BBC's approach to job sharing and establish a framework for job sharing arrangements.

Job sharing should not be confused with the government's 'Job Splitting Scheme' which the BBC has assured the unions will not be implemented without prior discussion at national level. It is distinct from part-time employment, which arises from the operational needs of the BBC.

Job sharing is a working arrangement whereby two or more people share the duties of a full-time post and the various components of the work, though divided, are still regarded as constituting one job.

An essential feature of job sharing is that the arrangement is acceptable both to management and the individuals concerned. The final decision whether to introduce and then to continue job sharing rests with management. Factors to be taken into account are:

> Job sharing may enable the BBC to retain the services of valuable staff who, for one reason or another, e.g. child rearing, disability of dependent relatives, can only work part time; and

> Job sharing may be more expensive than filling a post with a single person on a full-time basis.

Union Consultation

Provided that a job sharing arrangement falls within the guidelines set out below, there is no requirement for formal consultation. However the unions do expect to be notified of all arrangements since they might impinge on local working practices.

If a job sharing arrangement falls outside the guidelines, it has been agreed that such arrangements will be subject to formal consultation and agreement.

Training and Further Development of Staff

Job sharers should be considered for all appropriate training on the same basis as their full-time colleagues. Their expectations of promotion are the same as any other member of staff and they should be given the benefit of career guidance and advice from their Personnel Officer or Appointments Department as is normal.

Advice to Staff on the Introduction of Job Sharing
Staff should be told in writing at the outset that:

— the post they are to share is full-time and there can therefore be no guarantee that the job sharing arrangements will continue indefinitely;

— if in the light of experience management conclude that the job sharing arrangement is impracticable it will be brought to an end and both partners will be given normal resettlement treatment; and

— if one partner moves on, the post will be offered to the remaining individual on a full-time basis. If the remaining partner is unable to take over the post on a full-time basis and no alternative part-time post is immediately available, his or her employment will be brought to an end.

A wide range of employment policy objectives appear in the job sharing policies of private sector organizations. For *GEC Telecommunications* at Aycliffe, County Durham, whose scheme for young people at Coventry has already been referred to, job sharing was introduced to reduce the potential impact of redundancy. Following consultations with the unions, the company re-employed 250 ex-employees who had been made redundant on a job sharing basis, together with eight current employees who opted to job share and 52 young people who were previously unemployed. Production workers operate on a week on/week off basis and clerical staff work a split week. Some of the benefits have included lower absence amongst job sharers, additional cover when a job sharing colleague is sick and a readily available pool of skilled employees most of whom are prepared to transfer to full time working during an upturn in demand.[47] A small number of office employees at *Pedigree Petfoods* work on an alternate week job sharing arrangement and also provide full time holiday cover for each other. The initiative came from the employees themselves, but it has enabled the company to retain the services of experienced people. For the last three years the company has also employed six young people on a job sharing basis linked with college training. The scheme has helped the company to assess candidates for full time vacancies and several of the job sharing trainees who have performed satisfactorily have moved to permanent full time employment with the company.

Conclusions and implications The planning and implementation of job sharing requires careful and detailed consideration, in particular how the duties and responsibilities of the
jobs concerned are to be divided. These details are beyond the
scope of this discussion, but are considered further in the IPM
publication *Employing job sharers, part-timers and temporary
staff* by Michel Syrett. A number of important lessons do,
however, emerge from our case studies and these may be summarized as follows:

- *management commitment*: senior and line managers should
  be fully briefed on the implications of job sharing before
  plans to introduce it are adopted. Within the policy
  guidelines, individual managers should retain the freedom to operate a job sharing pattern suitable to the needs
  of the department
- *union consultation*: union reaction to job sharing has been
  mixed, but unions have accepted job sharing where there
  has been full consultation over the reasons for its introduction. Where job sharing is introduced at the request of
  individual employees, trade unions would normally be
  expected to support the requests of individual members
- *promoting and supporting job sharing*: creating an aware-
  ness amongst staff has been one of the most important
  features of successful job sharing schemes. Methods used
  include the normal briefing or communications channels,
  poster campaigns and explanatory leaflets. The establishment of a job sharing register is also a feature of the more
  successful schemes
- *pension rights*: careful attention needs to be paid to the
  pension implications of job sharing for people previously
  working full time, since many pension schemes preclude
  those working less than full time hours from membership.
  In the *Irish Civil Service*, this was overcome by allowing
  job sharers to continue in membership of pension schemes,
  with each year counting as six months employment for
  superannuation purposes. Alternatively, some change in
  the rules of eligibility for pension schemes may need to be
  considered, as has happened in the case of the Local
  Government Superannuation Scheme which has included
  employees working 15 or more hours per week since April
  1986

For a small but growing number of organizations, job sharing
has proved that it can serve a range of useful purposes from the

perspective of the employer and employee, providing an alternative work pattern which can contribute to greater flexibility and productivity.

New technology homeworking and teleworking

People who work at or from home have traditionally formed a small but significant proportion of the labour force in the UK, with the occupations involved including self employed professionals, consultants, farmers, skilled tradesmen, transport workers, typists and manufacturing workers engaged in outwork, particularly in the clothing and allied industries. A recent survey covering England and Wales indicates that nearly 1.7 million people, over seven per cent of the labour force, work at or from home.[48] There is nothing essentially new about working from home, but new possibilities are being presented by developments in telecommunications technology which indicate that the nature and extent of work which may be performed from home is undergoing change. These developments, which have been referred to as new technology homeworking, 'teleworking' or 'telecommuting' are the subject of this section.

Communication with a computer from a distance has been possible for the last three decades through the use of devices known as acoustic couplers or modems which enable data expressed in digital form to be converted into modulations suitable for transfer via telephone lines. Since the 1950s, local offices have been able to communicate with head office computers in this way, but the use of this facility tended not to expand rapidly because of the relatively high cost and comparative unreliability of traditional telephone communications. Recently, a number of technological developments have made working from home using computer communications both feasible and cost effective. The cost of computer terminals is falling in real terms and their sophistication is increasing (eg in the field of microcomputers) and communications technology is undergoing swift change through the use of optical fibre cable networks and computerized telephone exchanges, making the transfer of data from remote points more cost effective and more reliable.

During the 1970s in the United States, the incidence of employees working from home, with a home based terminal linked to the 'host' computer at the employer's office, began to grow and the view has been put that remote working is becoming increasingly widely adopted for routine data processing operations.[49] In some instances, American companies have professional and managerial employees based at home also. One example is the Minnesota based *Control Data Corporation* which began its experiment amongst 60 professional and managerial staff who volunteered to work at home.[50]

A number of claims have been made about the productivity levels of home based teleworkers in relation to their work based counterparts. The South Carolina health insurance company, *Blue Cross/Blue Shield*, found higher productivity and lower error rates amongst data input operators working at home. Companies operating similar arrangements in the UK are also reported as having substantial productivity gains. *F International* (see p 248 ff) claim 30 per cent more productivity from home based employees compared to their office based counterparts in other organizations and *ICL* found that 25 hours of work in the home is equivalent to 40 hours in an office, a 60 per cent productivity increase.[55] In addition to productivity gains, there are also substantial savings to be made on the costs of office accommodation, lighting, heating and other associated overheads involved in employing people at a workplace rather than at home. One American expert has summarized the benefits to be gained from teleworking as follows:[52]

- average productivity gains of 20 per cent, reaching 100 per cent in certain cases
- greater employee satisfaction as a result of self supervision, fewer interruptions and the avoidance of the frustrations of traditional commuting
- the creation of a wider recruitment market for employers by attracting skilled employees who are homebound
- improved retention levels amongst home based staff
- greater flexibility to increase workloads without additional office space
- reduction in the office space required

Overall, teleworking is estimated to affect only a few thousand people in Western Europe and the United States, far fewer than was anticipated in the early 1970s, the principle sectors involved being data processing and electronics, banking, insurance, telecommunications and commerce.[53] In the light of the recent efforts of employers in the UK to seek more cost effective and flexible work patterns, together with the continuing pace of technological change, our contacts with employers indicate that an increasing number are giving serious attention to new technology homeworking and teleworking.

New technology homeworking and teleworking in practice   Our first example comes from *F International*, one of the country's leading software houses, established in 1962, where the working pattern adopted can best be described as new technology homeworking rather than teleworking. The company was established by a woman who wished to continue working while also being able to cope with family responsibilities and has expanded to employ around 1000 people, three-quarters of whom are self employed and working from home. Around 90 per cent of the work force is female and, although there has been no conscious decision to employ mainly women, the patterns adopted have attracted women with young families and have enabled the company to recruit scarce skills which might otherwise have been wasted. Home based employees, known by the company as 'panel members', are recruited to work as consultants, analysts, designers or programmers and are offered work on individual project assignments for which an hourly fee is paid. As freelancers, panel members are free to work for other employers if they wish, but requirements as to confidentiality and copyright are written into their contracts. Homeworkers are expected to work around 20–25 hours per week for the company, be available to make two or more client visits per week, have a telephone and their own transport or easy access to public transport.

The company emphasizes that managing a home based workforce requires special attention to the efficiency of administrative systems and to control mechanisms. Performance has to be closely monitored by means of continuous assessments of individual performance and standards have to be developed for estimating how long a job should take. The setting up of project teams requires a sophisticated skill matching system and considerable efforts need to be put into communication. Contact groups are organized at regional and local levels to reduce any sense of isolation and bring home based employees together and new recruits are visited at their homes by more experienced staff to help to deal with any problems which might arise. Because of these factors, the company has relatively high management ratios by conventional standards for programming staff of the order of 1:4 or 1:5, but it believes these are justifiable in terms of the levels of productivity achieved.[54] The company also places considerable emphasis on career development through home study methods and offers promotion prospects involving both home based and office based posts. The benefits which a home-working pattern provides the company include the following:

- flexibility to respond rapidly to fluctuations in demand since many costs are variable rather than fixed, enabling the company to expand or contract quickly and easily without costly investment in office accommodation
- overheads, such as office space and ancillary services, are reduced to a minimum
- saving on such costs as employer's national insurance and pension contributions, since panel members are self employed
- high productivity (reckoned to be 30 per cent above comparable office based employees) and low absenteeism[55]

There are few examples of teleworking in the UK, but one company which has been carrying out a limited experiment is *IBM United Kingdom Limited. IBM UK* established some experiments involving up to 60 employees at four sites for evaluation purposes. The equipment used is a company owned IBM PC, connected by telephone line to a company based, or host, mainframe computer. The company pays for the installation and costs of a second telephone line. It was felt essential to provide a telephone dedicated to the computer terminal to enable the domestic telephone to remain in normal use. The company stipulates that the home terminal is for use on company work only. The people involved in teleworking are management and professional employees (mainly programmers and analysts), all of whom are volunteers and are free to withdraw from the experiment whenever they wish. It should also be stressed that none of the employees involved work permanently from home. All the employees work a standard working week at their places of work and the role of the home terminal is to enable them to perform additional work outside normal working hours from home. Where appropriate, overtime is paid for work at home in excess of normal working hours. The company has operated a system of flexible working hours for some years and the use of a home terminal allows employees to make full use of this facility. Typically employees who might otherwise be called out in emergencies are able instead to respond by using the home terminal. The survey evaluation of the use of home terminals by employees indicates that they were used, on average, about four hours per person per week, mainly for the following purposes:

- correcting systems failures
- international communications (because of international time differences)
- assessing information

Employees involved in these experiments believe that it has enabled them to be more productive because of fewer interruptions at home and quicker access to the computer at off peak hours when the volume of data being processed is less. They also value being able to commute outside peak rush hours, the avoidance of call outs and the opportunity to spend more time with their family in the early evening when they might otherwise be at work. Employees were also asked in the company survey to express any concerns which they might have about teleworking and whilst these were not widespread, their comments included the following:

- some technical problems, particularly at installation time
- the problems of trailing cables which could be hazardous at home
- risk potential for overwork and the intrusion of work into family life

The experiments are still being evaluated by the company.

Another company with experience of teleworking is the *Digital Equipment Company (DEC)*, the American owned computer manufacturer with a head office near Reading, Berkshire. Copies of the Company's policies regarding home-based employees, the health and safety of homeworkers (including a home-office safety checklist) and a contract of employment addendum for home based employees are set out in the box below.

DIGITAL EQUIPMENT CO. LTD

Policy on remotely-based employees

PHILOSOPHY

A number of employees are not based in a Digital office on a permanent basis. These employees fall into two categories:

- Employees who are based at home.
- Employees who work from home.

In both cases, Digital will provide adequate compensation to cover any additional costs or inconvenience. The definition of these two categories is as follows:

Employees who are based at home

Are defined as those employees who have a base in a Digital office but who normally commute directly between their home and the customer.

Employees who work from home

Are defined as those employees who do not have a base in a Digital office but who are provided with the following in order to carry out their job from home:

a) Office furniture supplied by the Company (Desk, Chair, Filing Cabinet, etc).

b) Computer equipment supplied by the Company (Terminal, P.C., Printer etc).

c) A separate business telephone line with a registered DEC telephone number.

It is important that managers clearly identify and agree with employees on which basis they are employed. Before managers ask employees to be based at home or work from home, they must have the agreement of their Functional Manager.

POLICY

Employees who are based at home

Telephone Calls/Rental

Where an employee who is required to be based at home does not have a telephone, the Company will pay installation costs of one phone. The Company will also reimburse the quarterly rental charge.

All business calls will be reimbursed.

Contracts of Employment

All employees who are based at home will be issued with a Contract of Employment which specifically covers the terms and conditions attached to this requirement.

Employees who work from home

Working from Home Allowance (WHA)

Digital will compensate the employee required to work from home by paying an annual allowance. This allowance covers all additional costs incurred by an employee as a result of having to use his home as a workplace, including:

- Heating
- Lighting
- Inconvenience

The allowance is tax free and will not be taken into account when calculating pension, life insurance or any other benefit which uses base pay as the basis for calculation. The allowance will only be paid as long as the employee is required to work from home.

The allowance paid in monthly instalments will be reviewed annually on July 1st and details of the current figure can be obtained from Personnel.

Office Equipment

Digital will provide a desk, chair and filing cabinet of the same type as used in Digital offices. Where necessary other office equipmont will be supplied by the Company.

Should the employee leave the Company or transfer to an office based job, all equipment must be returned to the Company.

Telephone Calls/Rent

Where an employee is required to work from home, the Company will pay the installation costs of a separate telephone line. The Company will also reimburse the quarterly rental charge. The telephone number must be available to the Company and its customers.

All business calls will be reimbursed.

Where necessary the Company will also arrange for an answer-phone or similar equipment to be supplied. This machine will be removed should the employee leave or no longer be required to work from home.

Computer Equipment

Where an employee who is required to work from home and use computer equipment linked to an office, this will be connected to the separate business telephone line, financed by Digital. The Company will arrange delivery and installation of the equipment.

The Company will also provide a fire extinguisher as required by the Health and Safety Executive.

Should the employee leave the Company or transfer to an office based job, all equipment must be returned to the Company.

Contracts of Employment

All employees who are required to work from home will be issued with a Contract of Employment which specifically covers the terms and conditions attached to this requirement.

HOME WORKERS' HEALTH AND SAFETY

PHILOSOPHY

This policy document, including checklists, is designed to provide health and safety protection for employees who conduct office type work in their homes.

POLICY

At present there is no specific legislation covering home-office workers—after all, this is a relatively new way of operating. However, until specific provisions are made, it is the joint responsibility of DEC and its employees to ensure, so far as is reasonably practicable, adequate standards of health and safety for employees and other persons who may be affected by home-office activities.

In the absence of specific regulations, the general provisions of the Health And Safety At Work etc. Act 1974, and the specific provisions of the Offices, Shops and Railway Premises Act, 1963, will be used as references for providing and maintaining adequate standards of health and safety.

HEALTH AND SAFETY AT WORK ACT

Under this Act:

- The Company will take all reasonable and practicable steps to ensure the health, safety and welfare at work of employees, particular attention being paid to the following:

- Premises, plant, systems of work, work environment and facilities.

- The use, handling, storage and transport of articles and substances.

- Providing information, instruction, training and appropriate supervision.

- Employees are responsible for taking care of their own health and safety and that of others who could be affected by their acts or omissions at work.

- Employees are also responsible for co-operating with the Company on all matters connected with Health and Safety. This includes complying with this Policy.

One of the principal aims of this Act is to ensure that employers provide adequate health and safety facilities with regard to the premises over which they have control.

Obviously, the home-office workplace does not come within the category. Therefore, a large part of the responsibility for ensuring health and safety within employees' homes must fairly lie with employees themselves.

Nevertheless, the Company must take all reasonably practicable steps to ensure health and safety of employees is ensured and should have some control over the workplace. The following provisions are aimed at this control:

a) Employee's Manager must be allowed reasonable, pre-arranged access to employee's home-office workplace in order to inspect physically health and safety conditions. Managers must conduct initial inspection and submit a copy of the checklist to the Company's Health and Safety Manager for approval.

b) Employee/Manager Health and Safety Checklist is provided by the Company (Appendix 2).

c) Employees must submit annually, a completed checklist to their managers (managers to ensure this is done) who will consult the Health and Safety Manager as necessary.

OFFICES, SHOPS AND RAILWAY PREMISES ACT

This Act deals with Office environmental aspects, such as heating, ventilation and overcrowding, etc. Items relevant to the home-office workplace are included in the checklist appended to this Policy document.

ACCIDENT REPORTING

Employees have a legal duty to report all accidents and hazards (real or potential) relevant to their workplace.

Accidents must be reported on the Company Accident Report Form obtainable through your manager.

HAZARDS AND POTENTIAL HAZARD REPORTING

These must be reported verbally, and in writing as appropriate, to your manager who will take the appropriate steps to help remove hazards from your workplace.

GENERAL

As 'controllers' of their workplace, employees must take all reasonably practicable steps to ensure the safety of themselves, their family and others. To this end, the highest degree of communications and co-operation between employees and management is essential.

After all, it could not be considered satisfactory to find an employee sharing a heavily congested attic workplace with cans of petrol, gas cylinders, etc., especially when the only access is by way of broken stairway or ladder!

Obviously, such a situation should never exist, but it is provided to show what could very well happen if controls and commonsense are neglected.

'REMEMBER—SAFETY FIRST'

HOME-OFFICE SAFETY CHECKLIST

This checklist is to enable employees and their managers to evaluate the safety of the home-office workplace. If you can tick all the indicator boxes, the workplace should be safe and without risk to health.

In the event of 'crossed' items, you and your manager should take all reasonable practicable steps to eliminate them. Any case of failure should be referred to the Health and Safety Manager for advice.

PLEASE TICK OR CROSS AS APPROPRIATE

- Do you have safe and easy access to your workplace?
- Is your workplace a 'non-family' room, e.g. Study, Bedroom?

    If not, please state......................................

NOTE

    (Obviously, it would be hazardous to use, as workplaces, such rooms as Bathrooms, Kitchens and rooms which are generally accessible to small children).

- In the event of fire, is your workplace provided with adequate means of escape from the building?

- Are floors, passageways, corridors and staircases kept free from obstruction and in good order?
- Are all floors and floor coverings in good repair so as not to cause tripping or a falling type of accident?
- Is a general purpose, dry-powder type fire extinguisher provided and positioned at the workplace entrance?

NOTE

These can be obtained, through your manager, from Chubb Fire.

- Has all electrical equipment been competently installed?
- Is all equipment (electrical and mechanical) in good order?
- Are all repairs, etc. carried out by an authorised and competent person?
- Are all electrical wiring, sockets, plugs and leads, etc. in good condition, not overloaded and properly installed?
- Do you have enough space effectively to do your work?

ARE THE FOLLOWING WORKPLACE GENERAL HEALTH AND SAFETY ASPECTS ADEQUATE FOR YOUR NEEDS?

- Cleanliness
- Heating
- Ventilation
- Lighting
- Are you provided with adequate seating and workdesk facilities, which are safe?
- Are your storage arrangements (including Filing Cabinets) safe and secure?
- Is your workplace 'housekeeping' good?
- Is your workplace free from asbestos materials?
- Is your workplace free from highly flammable materials?
- DO YOU CONSIDER THAT YOUR WORKPLACE IS SAFE AND WITHOUT RISK TO YOURSELF, YOUR FAMILY AND OTHERS?

  If not please state ....

Contract of Employment Addendum

This addendum is made on the date hereinafter between Digital Equipment Co. Limited of Digital Park, Inperial Way, Worton Grange, Reading (Digital) and the employee whose name and address hereinafter appears (the employee). This Addendum is supplementary to the Contract of Employment in existence between Digital and the employee on the date hereof and Digital and the employee agrees for so long as Digital shall require the employee to work from home as follows:

1. That the employee will carry out the terms of the Contract of Employment from Home in consideration for which Digital will pay to the employee working from home allowance (WHA) as compensation for the additional costs and expenses of the employee including, but not limited to, heating, insurance and rates.

2. WHA will be paid by Digital to the employee in monthly instalments without deduction but will not be taken into account when calculating pensions, life assurance or any other benefits.

3. That Digital will supply the employee with all necessary equipment that may be reasonably required to enable the contract to be performed from home. All equipment shall at all times remain the property of Digital and will be returned by the employee upon termination of the Contract of Employment, upon termination of the requirement to work at home, or upon Digital's request, whichever arises the earlier.

4. That in addition to WHA, Digital will reimburse the employee for the installation costs and the quarterly rental charge in respect of one separate telephone, together with the costs of any business calls made from such telephone.

5. That Digital and the employee's joint responsibility under the Health and Safety at Work etc. Act, 1974 is to ensure that part of the employee's home which is used by the employee for the performance of the Contract of Employment (the work area) is at all times, and so far as is reasonably practicable, in a safe condition. The employee agrees to ensure that the work area complies with the requirements appearing in the health and safety checklist annexed hereto and is at all times in such a safe condition.

    That the employee will within six months of the date hereof and thereafter, upon reasonable prior notice, permit the employee's manager, or his nominated representative, into the employee's home for the purpose of inspecting the work area on behalf of Digital to ensure that it meets the required safety standards.

6. All equipment supplied by Digital for use at home will be insured by Digital.

The employee hereby agrees and acknowledges that he has read and accepts the requirements herein.

For Digital Equipment Co. Ltd.

Signature	Signature
Name	Name
Date	Date

Before leaving the subject of teleworking it is worth making reference also to the scheme known as 'networking' introduced in 1982 by *Rank Xerox International.*[56] The scheme combines a number of elements of changing work patterns described elsewhere in this book (sub-contracting, part time working and self employment) but is based essentially on the facilities provided by on-line computing to carry out work from a remote base.

'Networking' at *Rank Xerox* is a scheme which provides company executives with the opportunity of working for the company on a part time, contractual basis from home. The scheme had its origins in concerns about the cost of maintaining an expensive, administrative headquarters in central London. It was estimated that for each £1 spent on salaries, an additional £3 was needed for overheads, in particular accommodation and office equipment. The 'networking' scheme was designed to help reduce both cost and space requirements while avoiding the necessity of creating redundancies and to save the company £5 million a year. It also had a spin off effect of testing and promoting hardware and systems developed in other parts of the *Rank Xerox* organization. Senior and middle ranking executives who had reached the pinnacle of their possible career development within the company were invited to volunteer for the scheme. They were given a generous ex-gratia payment, options to buy office equipment at cost, training and a *Rank Xerox* microcomputer linked to the company's office. For the first year, each was given a contract guaranteeing two days' work per week from *Rank Xerox* at consultancy rates. After this initial year, there was no guarantee of further work from *Rank Xerox* and during this time, networkers were expected to have established their own independent consultancy businesses. Since 1982, the numbers participating in the networking scheme have risen from six to 54.

A crucial factor in the success of the scheme has been the creation by the networkers of a small business support association known as 'Xanadu'. This organization has enabled the *Rank Xerox* networkers to pool resources for marketing purposes and to share word processing, photocopying, printing and computing facilities and has acted as a focal point for contact between members of the network and between the network and *Rank Xerox*. So successful have these support centres proved to be that *Rank Xerox* are now experimenting with the concept of the 'neighbourhood office', providing local support centres and points of social contact for home based employees.[57]

6 Sub-contracting

Alastair Evans and Les Walker

Sub-contracting involves the replacement of employment contracts, and contracts of service, by commercial contracts for
services and may be seen as part of a wider trend which has
occurred over the past 20 to 30 years to pass on to others some of
the costs and risks associated with business arrangements. Some
years ago, the futurologist Alvin Toffler in his book *Future
Shock* referred to the 'rental revolution' as a characteristic of
post-industrial societies, an arrangement by which those seeking goods or services choose to rent them rather than buy them.
Thus, many consumers have opted to rent rather than buy
televisions and video cassette recorders, leaving the uncertainties and costs of maintenance and repair to the suppliers of the
goods. Companies have adopted a similar approach to their car
fleets, frequently preferring hiring or leasing arrangements to
outright purchase. Similar trends can increasingly be observed
across a wide range of business activities, including sub-contracting of manufacturing and distribution operations, franchis-
ing, licensing and so on. This follows a pattern long used in
Japan in which small businesses act as buffers to protect larger
organizations from fluctuations in the market in order to keep
costs down through competitive tendering. Similar trends can be
seen in the field of employment where independent contractors
are taking on activities formerly carried out by employees. Some
years ago, Charles Handy referred to this as the emergence of
the 'contractual organization', the growing tendency to contract
out more activities in return for fees for services rather than
wages for the time spent doing a job.[1] Handy takes the view that,
as more organizations strive for greater numerical and financial

flexibility, they also discover what activities are specific to their organization and what can be resourced externally. Such activities may be highly specialized (eg systems analysis or technical drawing) or relatively mundane activities (eg office cleaning or catering). Contractors specializing in providing such services to a range of organizations may frequently be able to do the job more cost effectively than by employing the specialists directly on a full time basis. A similar view has been put forward by John Atkinson who believes that jobs which are not firm-specific, because they are very specialized, or are relatively routine, may increasingly be seen as 'peripheral' and more likely to be resourced by sub-contractors (or temporary workers) than 'core' full time employees.[2]

Sub-contracting is not essentially new and companies have for many years sub-contracted highly peripheral activities such as catering, cleaning and security. There is growing evidence, however, that sub-contracting is now extending well beyond these traditional activities and is replacing conventional employment contracts in a much wider range of occupational groups. One study prepared for the National Economic Development Council covering 72 firms employing almost 660,000 people in the food and drink, engineering, retailing and financial sectors, found that 70 per cent of the firms surveyed had increased their use of sub-contracting arrangements since 1980.[3] Most of these firms had increased their use of sub-contracted ancillary services, but around one-third had also extended sub-contracting to non ancillary areas. Further evidence is contained in a survey of 400 organizations by Manpower Limited.[4] Between 1982 and 1985, the volume of sub-contracted business increased in 45 per cent of manufacturing firms surveyed and in 38 per cent of service sector organizations with only 15 per cent of firms in both sectors reporting that it had declined during this period. Looking to the future, around 16 per cent of respondents intended to increase their use of sub-contractors and 80 per cent expected current levels of usage to continue.

Reasons for sub-contracting

A variety of reasons are given by employers for adopting sub-contracting and many of these are interrelated, but broadly these reasons fall into one or more of the following categories:

- to concentrate resources on core business activities
- to reduce costs and increase flexibility and productivity
- to enhance job security for core employees

Each of these will be considered further, with case examples to illustrate how organizations are using sub-contractors.

Concentrating resources on core business activities It is often argued that a key element in a successful business strategy is to concentrate on what the organization knows and does best. Peters and Waterman, in their book *In Search of Excellence*, refer to this as 'sticking to the knitting' and suggest that this is one important common element in the strategies of successful organizations. The opposite is equally true in that many organizations which have lost their way commercially have often done so as a result of entering fields of commercial activity which they did not fully understand. Following a period of takeovers and diversification during the 1960s and 1970s, many businesses have recently been reviewing their portfolio of interests and have been engaged in either selling off or sub-contracting those which have not fitted successfully into the activities they know and do well.

In effect, companies are concentrating their corporate resources on core business activities and shifting the burdens or uncertainties elsewhere by buying in the expertise which they need.

Rank Xerox (see p 287 ff) is one example of a company adopting a strategy of concentrating the company's resources on core productive activities and drastically reducing peripheral activities which have high overhead costs to the company. As a result of the impact of recession and overseas competition in the world for photocopiers and duplicators in the late 1970s, the company has extensively restructured its European manufacturing and assembly operations. Before 1979, *Rank Xerox's* main plant in the UK at Mitcheldean, Gloucestershire, employed 4,800 people and produced a wide range of copiers, with a large staff also providing many support services. Following reorganization, overlapping manufacturing activity at the company's various European locations was reduced and each site was assigned more specific roles. At Mitcheldean, the company concentrated on three main core areas of production:

- high volume assembly of small copiers and the refurbishment of older, larger machines
- the manufacture of fuser rolls for worldwide distribution
- acting as an international supply centre (a function which has subsequently been considerably reduced)

Staff levels have now been reduced to around 1200. Some reductions have taken place in production areas, but the major cutbacks have come in the indirect areas by means of eliminating and amalgamating work and by sub-contracting. The company has always used some sub-contracting to cover peaks and troughs in activity, but in recent years a wide range of peripheral activities has been sub-contracted by the company, including external transport, office cleaning, maintenance engineering, civil trades (carpenters, painters, builders, etc) and internal mail. In the engineering maintenance area, a small group of highly skilled and flexible craftsmen have been retained as core employees with many years of training and experience. Some of the cost benefits and productivity improvements achieved by *Rank Xerox* as a result of these changes will be considered later in this section.

At a major oil company included in our study, the long term personnel strategy is based upon a belief that the company should concentrate its efforts on recruiting and retaining the highly skilled and experienced staff concerned with the company's core activities, but that it should contract out those skills which are not special or unique to the company. Some tasks have for some time been contracted out on an 'ad hoc' basis, including small-scale distribution, maintenance and travel services. Now, the company is examining the needs of each department to consider which of the following options apply to various categories of staff:

- permanent status
- short term contracts
- sub-contractors working within the company
- sub-contracting entirely to a separate company

Because of the number of specialized and highly skilled employees, it is expected that 80 to 90 per cent of existing employees will remain as core staff, with the remaining 10 to 20 per cent of lesser skilled jobs at the periphery being contracted out. Since the adoption of this policy, sub-contracting has been introduced in two very different areas, transport and secretarial support. In 1985, all deliveries were sub-contracted to a transport company who took on most of the company's vehicles and equipment. In 1986, the company started a process of using subcontractors (an employment agency) to provide secretarial and administrative support at its London head office, including word processor operators, administrative secretaries and their assistants. In all, 42 employees will be involved when the plan is fully in operation. At present, it is being implemented on a phased basis, with full timers being replaced by agency employees when they leave. In the light of high turnover rates amongst this group, it is thought that all employees will have been replaced by the sub-contractor's staff within two years.

Technological change was a major factor behind the subcontracting of printing services with *Cadbury Schweppes'* confectionery division. Because of the advent of on-line computing facilities and rapid changes in printing technology, it became difficult and costly for the in-house printing operation to compete effectively with the best of specialist printers. Sub-contracting widened the division's choice of suppliers and enabled it to take continuing advantage of advancing technology. It also reduced numbers on the Bournville site directly and indirectly, since direct employees are backed by a variety of supporting services.[5]

A number of other organizations in our study rationalized their use of sub-contracting in terms of concentrating on core business activities and resourcing externally those which were seen as peripheral. All these companies are American owned and it was suggested that sub-contracting such activities was probably more common in American than British organizations. *Continental Can*, for example, has always sub-contracted security, cleaning, catering, heavy goods vehicle driving and payroll in the belief that 'the company should concentrate its efforts on what it is good at'. *Kimberly-Clark*, a manufacturer of paper disposables at several UK sites, has always sub-contracted such peripheral functions as security, cleaning and catering. Haulage was contracted out three or four years ago in order to achieve greater flexibility and the company is currently moving away from having a company based charter hire fleet of vehicles towards using a variety of sub-contractors with their own vehicles on short term contracts. *Pedigree Petfoods*, part of the Mars organization, also has a philosophy of concentrating on core activities and has gradually increased its use of subcontracting in recent years. The company's approach has been pragmatic and if opportunities arise to sub-contract, they are considered on their merits. The company has always sub-contracted road haulage and laundrying was contracted out five or six years ago. More recently, cleaning has been transferred to contractors on cost grounds, with the company's former employees being employed by the sub-contractor, and a group of employees have set up their own business, at the encouragement of the company, to offer back drain cleaning and certain maintenance services.

As part of the process of concentrating on core business activities, a number of organizations have sub-contracted activities which, for one reason or another, they have been unable to manage as effectively as they would wish. In effect, they are reducing the risks or burdens to themselves and passing these on to others with specialist experience of managing such activities. In some instances these burdens have related to the industrial relations climate associated with certain functions or activities where management has been unable to negotiate the kind of flexibility and productivity it requires. At *Whitbread* the brewers, for example, the company was faced with an outdated network of depots and an industrial relations environment in which 'custom and practice' had led to inefficient working practices.[6] Industrial relations problems included sporadic disputes, out of control incentive schemes, inefficient manning and high overtime, all of which, in the company's words, 'placed a restraint on the strategic direction of the business'.[7] In its consultations with the unions, the company proposed two alternatives: either the distribution operation would continue to be run in-house on the basis of a new package of flexible working or it would be contracted out to a professional distribution firm. In the event, both these options were pursued in parallel. The company successfully negotiated an agreement involving fundamental changes in working practices, including flexible working hours, single status, the abolition of overtime pay and complete flexibility and interchangeability of labour. However, for a number of strategic reasons, the company pursued its investigation of the sub-contracting option, particularly bearing in mind the management resources which this would release and capital expenditure considerations, since substantial investment would be needed in a new depot network.[8] The decision was therefore taken to establish a separate company jointly owned by *Whitbread* and *Southern British Road Services* (part of the National Freight Consortium) known as 'BDS' (Bar Delivery Services) to handle all *Whitbread*'s distribution in the London area. All employees remaining with the company following the agreed productivity deal, some 40 per cent fewer than had previously been employed, were guaranteed a job in the new company and all the newly agreed working practices were also successfully transferred to the new set up.

A combination of industrial relations factors and the costs of an increasing legislative burden were major factors influencing the decision of *Rank Xerox* to sub-contract all its external transport operations. Up to 1983, the company operated all its own transport services, internal and external, and an examination of the costs of providing external transport revealed that they were extremely uncompetitive. Drivers' pay and allowances were far above the average for the area and periodic disputes reduced the efficiency of the service to customers. In addition, the company was also bearing the costs of an increasing legislative burden on transport operators, as well as the costs of maintaining and replacing vehicles. As a result, management considered tenders from several companies and awarded the contract for external transport to *National Carriers Ltd* on a three yearly renewable basis, reviewed annually. There was no consultation with the union prior to the announcement, but most of the employees accepted new contracts with *National Carriers* carrying out work exclusively for *Rank Xerox*. *National Carriers* also purchased the company's fleet of vehicles. Elsewhere, the company had a history of demarcation problems amongst the civil trades employees (carpenters, painters, builders, etc) which had led to considerable inefficiency. These groups of employees were declared redundant as part of the company's policy of sub-contracting, but were encouraged to become self employed and work for the company on a sub-contracted basis. Demarcation disputes have since become a thing of the past and work practices have become more flexible. The advantages of these new arrangements are considered later.

Reducing the economic risk was the major factor behind a move by a major department store retailer to reduce the volume of goods distributed by its own transport fleet and to sub-contract more of this work to outside carriers. The company points out that a large amount of capital is tied up in vehicles which are used for eight hours per day only, in addition to the problems of ensuring that vehicles carry out their full payload. The goods carried can often be bulky but not weighty, with the result that vehicles carried less than maximum tonnage. The goods being delivered to each separate store are loaded into separate roll on/roll off cages for each drop, each of which may not be loaded to capacity because of the nature of the goods required by the store. Sub-contracting the distribution operation reduced the company's involvement in these problems and their associated costs.

A final element in the process of concentrating on core business activities is the flexibility provided by sub-contracting to buy in expertise when it is needed. It was noted earlier that external resourcing may be used either to acquire highly specialized skills or relatively routine, transferable skills rather than employing people with these skills on a full time basis. One large UK company in the paper, printing and packaging business, which now employs 10 per cent of its total staff on a temporary or sub-contract basis, sees such arrangements as an important part of the pursuit of excellence in its organization. In particular, it provides scope and flexibility to buy in the best expertise and quality of people available. The company also points out that it provides flexibility to meet rapid changes in technology by buying in new skills as and when they are required, without the traditional, internal constraints and costs of change, such as negotiating new working practices, retraining, redeployment and redundancy. As well as sub-contracting parts of its transport and warehousing operations, the company's philosophy has led it to sub-contract work amongst such professional occupations as draughtsmen, design engineers, public relations, architects, surveyors, marketing and market research, personnel and training specialists.

Nabisco also has a policy of buying in specialist expertise where appropriate. At its Aintree biscuit factory, the company has an agreement with the union which states that 'external contractors will be used where specialist knowledge or equipment is deemed to be preferred; to meet surges in demand or where external resource is more competitive'. Currently sub-contracting operates in the canteen, civil trades, refrigeration engineering and fork-lift truck maintenance.

Another organization shifting towards sub-contracting in order to buy in outside expertise is the *BBC*. In addition to buying in more programme material than before, the *BBC* now buys in more equipment and services in the engineering and design areas, for example the design and construction of transmitters or broadcasting equipment, which was previously done by its own staff in house. The plan is to employ a small corporate staff overseeing standards and contract out all engineering and design work. The new philosophy is also reflected in production areas. Greater use has been made of freelancers on contract over the last few years which has offered greater salary flexibility. This has meant, for example, that the *BBC* is less likely to employ directly light entertainment producers between series when they are relatively unproductive. Around 25 per cent of production staff in television are now on contract.

Reducing costs and increasing flexibility and productivity

Apart from concentrating on core business activities, a further rationale of increased sub-contracting for many organizations is to achieve cost savings, reduce headcount and associated employment costs and achieve greater flexibility and productivity. Decisions to sub-contract (or employ temporary staff) have sometimes arisen out of 'zero base' budgeting exercises which have been carried out to establish core staffing levels. This establishes a core of essential activities which companies wish to keep fully under control and, in some cases, establishes staffing levels to meet either minimum or normal levels of expected demand. For example, the paper, printing, and packaging company which participated in our survey is moving towards the position in which its production facilities can meet normal or regular levels of demand, whilst fluctuations above this and the uncertainties associated with them are sub-contracted. This reduces the company's commitment to costly investment in plant which may be under-utilized during downturns in demand and improves control of cash flow by shifting from the fixed cost of employing permanent staff to the variable cost of employing sub-contractors. Zero basing was similarly used by the retail department store chain in the survey for establishing staffing levels (full and part time) during the period of minimum trade after the January sales. This establishes the permanent staffing complement or core which cannot be exceeded, with periods of higher demand being resourced, in this case, by short term contract staff.

One immediate benefit for companies using sub-contractors in place of permanent staff was cost. Companies which had investigated the costs of resourcing services externally were quite often surprised to find how much more cheaply they could be provided through competitive tender by sub-contractors. In addition, sub-contracting enables organizations to keep future costs under control because contract arrangements are usually renewable and the work can subsequently be transferred to another sub-contractor putting in a more competitive tender. A further advantage of sub-contracting pointed out by one company was a change in the effort/reward relationship. Employees are generally paid on the basis of time, with possibly an additional output-related incentive payment. Sub-contractors are paid for a job well done, irrespective of the time spent doing it. Thus, if sub-contractors choose to do a job in the evening or at weekends, particularly if completion is urgently required, this does not normally attract premium rates for the job, unlike those of contracts of employment.

The cost savings achieved are perhaps not so surprising when the costs of employing people are analysed. For many organizations, the real cost of employing people can add between 50 to 100 per cent or even more on the cost of the basic salary. As a guide, the box below sets out a breakdown of some of the main manpower costs of organizations, although this does not include the costs of accommodation, lighting, heating, furniture or equipment costs, nor does it take into account less readily measurable costs such as low morale or poor industrial relations.

MANPOWER COSTS CHECKLIST

1. REMUNERATION
1.1   Salary costs
1.1a   Basic pay
1.1b   Bonus payments
1.1c   Overtime
1.1d   Supplementary payments, eg shift pay, dirt pay, etc
1.1e   Merit awards
1.1f   Temporary replacements for holidays, sickness etc
1.2   Direct fringe benefits
1.2a   Car
1.2b   Pension fund contribution
1.2c   Luncheon vouchers/ subsidized meals
1.2d   Educational support for children of employees
1.2e   Subscriptions to professional bodies
1.2f   Subsidized housing including loans at preferential rates, special mortgage
1.2g   Subsidized travel via loans to buy cars etc
1.2h   Season ticket loans
1.2i   Share ownership schemes
1.2j   Location/assignment weighting
1.2k   Holiday—statutory
              —personal days
              —sabbatical
              —other discretionary paid vacation

1.3 Statutory costs (SSP etc)
1.3a National Insurance contributions
1.3b Graduated pension contributions
1.3c Occupational sick pay
1.3d Payroll administration costs
1.3e Employers' liability
1.3f Other statutory levies

2. RECRUITMENT COSTS
—applicable to avoidable and unavoidable turnover as well as to new jobs
2.1 Pre-recruitment
2.1a Preparation or review of specifications for both the job to be done and the person to be recruited
2.1b Briefing of personnel officer (and advertising staff) with line manager
2.1c Preparation of recruitment programme
2.2 Search
2.2a All indirect promotional/advertising effort directed at furthering recruitment
2.2b All direct promotional/advertising effort directed at furthering recruitment including job advertising, stationery, postage, documentation of recruitment records and related administration costs
2.2c Head hunting costs

2.3 Candidate evaluation
2.3a Interviewing including travelling, hospitality and the university/college round
2.3b Bought in selection costs
—briefing
—advertising
—preliminary selection
—complete selection
2.3c Selection tests either bought or created and including cost of subsequent administration
2.4 Induction
2.4a Inducement to move
2.4b Medical examination prior to establishment procedure
2.4c Orientation

3. TRAINING COSTS
3.1 Induction period
3.2 Remuneration of trainee and trainer
3.3 Expense of trainee and trainer including travel and subsistence
3.4 Books and materials used
3.5 Machines and buildings used in continuous training
3.6 Bought out training—school, college, government training centre fees
3.7 Development and maintenance of training programmes including cost of staff in training departments when not actually engaged in direct training

3.8 Reports, appraisal costs of those people other than the trainee and trainer, eg counselling reviews

3.9 Training for retirements

3.10 Assimilation costs—the costs incurred of employing a person after induction but before he/she is fully proficient

3.11 Higher material wastage until trainee is fully experienced

3.12 Loss of possible production from trainer whilst he/she is engaged in training

4. RE-LOCATION COSTS— temporary and permanent

4.1 Hostel charges—long term

4.2 Hotel charges—short term

4.3 Direct disturbance allowance

4.4 Cost of disturbance, eg legal fees, removal costs

4.5 Premiums paid with regard to housing price differentials or house purchase assistance

4.6 Temporary travel subsidy

4.7 Travelling expenses

4.8 *Ex gratia* re-equipment costs incurred in moving house

5. LEAVING COSTS

5.1 Loss of production between loss and recruitment

5.2 Statutory redundancy payments (less rebates)

5.3 *Ex gratia* payments

5.4 Retirement payments (other than pensions)

5.5 Liquidation of direct fringe benefits could be plus or minus costs

6. SUPPORT COSTS

6.1 House magazine

6.2 Social club

6.3 Subsidy for other social activities

6.4 Medical welfare schemes

6.5 Canteens

6.6 Safety facilities

6.7 Long service awards

6.8 Suggestion schemes

6.9 Music-while-you-work

6.10 Security service

6.11 Schemes for preferential purchase of goods including costs in purchasing department

6.12 Insurance premiums

6.13 Library and information services

6.14 Use of firm's resources for private ends (whether acknowledged or illicit)

6.15 General travel and entertaining expenses not specifically allocatable to a project

6.16 General background training not specifically allocatable to the job being done

6.17 Prestige accommodation

6.18 Car park costs

6.19 Death benefits

6.20	Rehabilitation/convalescent homes	7.1a	Personal record cards
6.21	Holiday homes	7.1b	Personal files
		7.1c	Salary administration records
7.	PERSONNEL ADMINISTRATION	7.1d	Job specification
		7.1e	Manpower planning record
7.1	Organized manpower records—these could be in more than one location in a company with decentralized company activities. These records include:	7.2	Salary review costs
		7.3	Maintenance of industrial relations including consultative committees
		7.4	Manpower research project costs

Source: BRAMHAM J. *Practical Manpower Planning*, London, Institute of Personnel Management, 1982, pp 147–149

Apart from straight cost savings, a number of other cost benefits were quoted by companies as a result of sub-contracting. These include:

- more positive attitudes on the part of sub-contractors and their staff
- higher productivity
- greater flexibility to deal with peaks, troughs and seasonal variations
- fewer disputes and stoppages
- less overtime working
- fewer restrictive practices
- saving in recruitment and training costs (especially where turnover is high)
- saving in the costs of absence (especially where absence rates are high)

A number of examples of the cost savings and other benefits achieved by organizations can be quoted. At *Rank Xerox*, whose extensive programme of sub-contracting has already been referred to, cost savings in the region of 30 per cent on a £600,000 budget for external transport operations were achieved by sub-contracting. The company also reports a number of other benefits, including:

- improvements in drivers' attitudes and efficiency
- newer and better equipment used
- no stoppages or disputes
- greater flexibility to deal with peaks and troughs
- reduction in permanent supervisory staff from four to one
- substantial savings on maintenance and replacement of vehicles
- substantial savings on such employment costs as recruitment, absence, holidays, etc

In the works engineering facilities at *Rank Xerox*, which provided maintenance across the whole range of the company's activities from cleaning to the servicing and installation of plant and equipment, sub-contracting reduced permanent staff, over a period of five or six years, from around 200 to 31 core staff, of which half are administrative, technical and supervisory staff and half are highly trained, multi skilled mechanical and electrical tradesmen. Overall, since the exercise began, costs in the department have been reduced by around 20 per cent a year, with no demarcation disputes or stoppages and greater flexibility to meet peaks and troughs. Sub-contracting amongst cleaning staff, which is now carried out by former employees who successfully tendered for the contract, reduced permanent cleaning staff by 36. It has saved an estimated 30 to 40 per cent on employment costs over the last two to three years and the service provided has been more efficient and flexible.

A number of organizations were less willing to quantify the cost savings and productivity improvements in such a precise way, many preferring to refer to them as 'substantial'. At the *BBC*, however, tenders from outside companies to provide such services as cleaning, catering and security could reduce the cost of providing the service in house considerably, sometimes by as much as 30 per cent. At *Whitbread*, whose sub-contracting of distribution operations has already been described, a package of productivity measures introduced prior to sub-contracting reduced the workforce by 40 per cent. At *Petrofina*, whose patterns of flexible weekly hours were described in Chapter 2, agreement was obtained with the unions to use drivers on sub-contracts to reduce excessive overtime working. No overtime is paid for hours in excess of the basic $37\frac{1}{2}$ per week and if extra cover is required, either because of sickness or peaks in the workload, sub-contractors or temporary staff are brought in. Under previous arrangements, management would not have used outside labour until employees' hours reached 60 per week.

As a result of the package of measures introduced, productivity has increased by 20 per cent and substantial cost savings have been achieved. At another major oil company, where the company is initiating a programme of sub-contracting amongst word processing and secretarial staff on a phased basis, it is too early to assess the cost benefits of the change. The company points out, however, that this group of employees has been characterized by high absence, high turnover and labour market shortage problems, with the result that a great deal of management time has been spent in recruitment and training. Certain cost savings are anticipated, but the main aim of sub-contracting this area is to increase efficiency.

Enhancing job security for core employees It has been suggested that one of the main reasons for sub-contracting or temporary employment at the periphery is to enhance the job security of employees at the core, with the greater risk of insecurity being born by peripheral workers.[9] With one exception, little evidence was found of companies expressly using sub-contractors in this way, although undoubtedly a number of companies have used temporary or short term contracts for this purpose, as described earlier.

One company which does use sub-contractors as part of a range of measures to enhance job security for employees at the core is *Xidex UK*, an American company employing nearly 1000 people in Brynmawr, South Wales, producing computer disks and microfilm. The policy of the company is to concentrate on the core activity of manufacturing and to sub-contract peripheral activities, such as catering, cleaning and security. One of the main objectives of personnel policy has been to maximize the job security of the core full time workforce which consists of management, administrative, clerical, engineering and technical staff and experienced production workers. Unemployment in the area is around 30 per cent and one of management's main concerns has been to provide stability of employment for its long serving employees against the background of a volatile market for the company's products. As illustrated in figure 9, the company has established a policy involving 'rings of defence' to protect the employment of its core workforce, in particular production workers who are most immediately affected by downturns in the market. On the edge of the rings of defence are 'stand by' operatives with experience of working with the com-

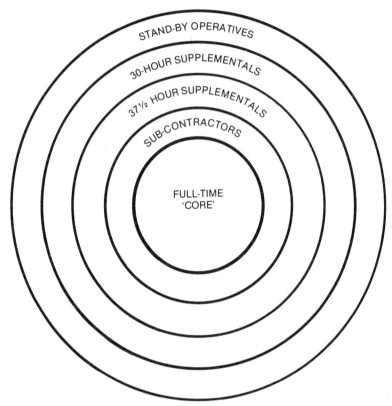

**Figure 9   Xidex UK, 'rings of defence' for the core
workforce**

pany. Management keeps a list of the names of these people and
they are called in or laid off, as and when required, on short term
contracts. Next in the rings of defence are part time and full time
supplemental employees who are employed on 10 month contracts. Sub-contractors provide the first line of defence for core
employees. They include cleaning, catering and security staff, as
well as distribution, engineering, maintenance and building
workers. If business turned down to the extent that core
workers' jobs were threatened, management would be able to use
production employees to do some of the work traditionally done
by sub-contractors (subject to contractual requirements). The
policy provides that peripheral employees should constitute no

more than 20 per cent of the workforce and currently the number stands at around 16 per cent.

Occupations involved in sub-contracting

Table 10 below provides a list of all the activities involved in sub-contracting mentioned by the organizations included in our sample. Interestingly, the most frequently mentioned was transport or road haulage, referred to by over three-quarters of the organizations using sub-contracting. Next most frequently mentioned were cleaning, catering, security and maintenance engineering, referred to by between a third and half the organizations using sub-contracting. We cannot claim that our small sample of case study organizations is representative of what is happening nationally, but the extent to which road haulage has been sub-contracted by these organizations was nevertheless unexpected.

Table 10   Activities sub-contracted by organizations in the study

Road transport	Forklift truck maintenance
Catering	Chauffeurs
Cleaning (office and industrial)	TV producers
Security	Public relations
Laundry services	Marketing
Maintenance engineering	Market research
Draughtsmen	Personnel
Design engineering	Training
Plumbing	Payroll administration
Carpentry	Gardening
Painting	Word processing
Drain cleaning	Secretarial
Internal mail	Clerical and administrative
Architects	Telephonists
Surveyors	Work study/Industrial engineering
Civil engineering	Retail management (franchising)
Development engineering	Data processing staff
Refrigeration engineering	Printing
Building maintenance	

From the comments made by organizations, it would appear that the use of sub-contracting is expanding from the traditional areas of catering, cleaning and security, which have been sub-contracted by a number of organizations for many years, into new areas such as road transport, maintenance and professional engineering and the building trades.

Potential drawbacks of sub-contractors

Reference has already been made to the range of benefits claimed by organizations as a result of sub-contracting. At the same time it is clear that sub-contracting requires careful management and a number of issues and potential problems require prior consideration. Interestingly, very few of the companies covered in our study voiced concerns about the results of sub-contracting, including companies with many years' experience of it. In principle, however, the following issues may need to be considered when contemplating the introduction of sub-contracting:

- legal status of sub-contractors
- commitment and quality control
- training and skills shortages
- industrial relations implications

Legal status and sub-contractors   The legal distinction between an employee working under a contract of service and an independent contractor working a contract for services is an issue which has occupied the courts for many years and the present position remains far from clear. Even if the parties agree to enter into a contractual arrangement which is expressly commercial rather than employment in nature, with the sub-contractor agreeing to pay his or her own tax and National Insurance contributions, this may not necessarily be conclusive evidence that there is not a contractual employment relationship between them. The courts have ruled that the intention of the parties cannot be the sole determinant of the contractual status, since it would be too easy to contract out of employment legislation by calling all employees sub-contractors.[10] The distinction between employees and independent contractors is nevertheless an important one since it fundamentally affects the legal obligations of the parties. Under contracts of employment, employees are entitled to the individual employment rights contained in the Employment Protection (Consolidation) Act 1978, including unfair dismissal and redundancy compensation. Employers are obliged to deduct tax under Schedule E, make the necessary arrangements for National Insurance contributions and insure against personal injury claims brought by employees. Employers are also vicariously liable in common law for the wrongs committed by employees. but not generally for those of independent contractors, except in certain circumstances.[11] Independent contractors, on the other hand, are liable to make their own arrangements for National Insurance contributions and tax deductions under Schedule D.

It is beyond the scope of this book to enter into a detailed analysis of the legal issues involved in distinguishing between an employee and an independent or sub-contractor. It should be noted, however, that whatever the intentions of the parties may be, in the event of a dispute, the courts will interpret the operation rather than the wording of the contract. Over the years, a number of 'tests' have been developed by the courts when interpreting the operation of the contract and these are worth bearing in mind when drawing up arrangements for sub-contracting. These tests have been usefully summarized in a publication by the Institute of Directors and include the following points:[12]

- is the sub-contractor in business on his own account, bearing the financial risks and full consequences of his actions?
- to what extent has the employer guaranteed work to the sub-contractor?
- to what extent does the employer control the way the work is done?
- to what extent is the sub-contractor integrated into the employer's business, for example through the provision of tools, equipment or vehicles?
- is payment made according to the time spent on the task or for completing a task irrespective of time spent?
- is the sub-contractor hired as an individual or is he free to supply any appropriately skilled or qualified person?
- does the sub-contractor have freedom to choose the time when the work is done?

It is not of course necessary for an employer to meet all these criteria when sub-contracting, but the courts will be looking on balance for a genuinely independent relationship between the parties in which the employer's scope to exercise control is less marked in the case of a sub-contractor than is the case in an employment relationship.

Only one organization referred to difficulties regarding the status of their sub-contractors. *Rank Xerox* wished to re-employ several electricians and fitters who had been made redundant, but wanted to return to the site as sub-contractors. Some uncertainties arose with the Inland Revenue over the status of these people and, although the Inland Revenue gave no firm ruling, the indications were that these individuals would not be regarded as self employed for tax purposes if they did more than 51 per cent of their work for one employer in the first six months. Following inconclusive discussions between the individuals and Inland Revenue, the people concerned resolved the issue by either joining together to form their own companies or by going to work for existing sub-contractors.

Commitment and quality control In a survey on *Attitudes towards employment*, carried out by the Confederation of British Industry in 1985, managers were asked their views about sub-contracting and the most commonly cited criticism related to a lack of commitment to the company.[13] We can only state that this was not the view of the managers we spoke to, who, on the contrary, pointed to greater commitment, more flexibility and productivity and better industrial relations when people were working on a sub-contractual rather than employed basis. One exception to this was *Petrofina*, which considered, but rejected the alternative of sub-contracting. The company acknowledged that it might be more economical than running the operation in house, but preferred to keep its delivery activities under company control.

It should be noted, however, that a number of organizations have introduced mechanisms to monitor and control the quality of work done by sub-contractors. At the *BBC*, for example, a small headquarters staff has been established to oversee the standards of sub-contracted work done in the engineering and design fields and at a major oil company, where secretarial and word processing work has been sub-contracted, the company imposes the following requirements on the sub-contracting agency to help ensure that it gets the quality of service required. Under these requirements, the sub-contractor must:

- test employees to ensure they have the necessary skills
- provide any necessary training and re-training
- carry out induction before employees are sent to the company (eg show them a video about the company) and ensure that they comply with standards of dress and appearance
- ensure employees do not come from an oil company, or go to an oil company when they leave
- allow the company the right to refuse to accept any employee (either before employment or during an initial two week trial period)
- try to ensure that employees stay with the company for at least six months

Training and skills shortages One consequence of the concept of core and peripheral workforces is that investment in training and development will, it is argued, be concentrated on core employees upon whom the longer term prosperity of the organization depends. This therefore raises the question of who trains workers at the periphery, given that these include semi skilled and skilled manual workers and technical and professional white collar workers, many of whose training and development have traditionally been linked to employment in medium and larger organizations. One scenario might therefore be that an increased reliance on sub-contracting might lead to a reduction in the volume of training and ultimately skills shortages in the occupational groups involved.

The growth of sub-contracting into non traditional skilled and professional employment fields is too recent a phenomenon to have yet made much impact on skills training and skills shortage. Nevertheless one organization, the *BBC*, raised this as an issue and was considering steps to overcome potential future problems. The *BBC* noted that one of the knock on effects of a greater use of freelancers and contract staff in both technical and production areas would be its implications for the corporation's traditional training role. Historically, the *BBC* has done most of the training for the television industry in Britain and, in the light of greater sub-contracting, it is now looking at ways of sharing the cost burden with the independent television companies and other independent producers in the industry to ensure that a sufficient volume of training is carried out to meet the needs of the whole industry.

Industrial relations implications   Trade unions may see the introduction of sub-contracting as a means of weakening trade union organization at the workplace, as a threat to permanent employment or as a means of cutting overtime earnings. As a result, trade unions are likely to seek to influence management's policies either informally or by formally negotiated agreement. In some companies, such as *Shell* and *Plessey*, management has undertaken to consult and keep the union informed about the extent of sub-contracting, but retains the right of management to make the decision about sub-contracting. In a few industries, for example in the building industry, some agreements lay down that sub-contract staff must be members of certain specified trade unions.[14]

A variety of approaches to the industrial relations implications of sub-contracting may be found in our case studies. At one major oil company, management's decision to sub-contract its entire transport operations and declare around 700 drivers and support staff redundant, was announced without consultation with the union (TGWU) or the employees concerned. Following union protestations, unsuccessful attempts were made to reach agreement after the announcement, but the changes were introduced nevertheless and most ex-employees were re-employed by the sub-contractor. One spin off from this has been that unions have had discussions with other oil companies to explore the possibility of inserting a clause in employees' contracts of employment to prevent sub-contracting being introduced elsewhere. A similar approach was taken amongst external drivers at *Rank Xerox*, but in the event the unions accepted the change, particularly as many redundant drivers were able to work for the sub-contractor, and concentrated their efforts on those redundant employees who did not have offers of alternative employment. At *Xidex UK*, the company's policy of sub-contracting and using 'supplemental' staff on short term contracts is a management policy and not one agreed with the union (the EETPU), although the general principles are outlined in agreements with the union.

A slightly different approach was adopted by *Whitbread* where negotiations with drivers over more flexible and leaner manning arrangements took place against the background of an announcement that the company would also be considering the option to sub-contract the whole distribution operation. In the ovont, tho compony achioved both the flexible arrangements which it wanted and the sub-contracting of the whole operation.

Elsewhere, the right of the company to engage sub-contractors has been embodied in formal agreements, quite often productivity agreements, covering a wide range of changes in working practices. At *Nabisco*, for example, a wide ranging agreement covering flexible working practices, substantial pay increases and the avoidance of compulsory redundancies also establishes management's right to use external contractors where specialist knowledge is required, to meet surges in demand or where external resources are more competitive. At *Petrofina*, a company which considered but rejected an option to sub-contract its delivery operations, agreement was reached as part of a productivity deal to eliminate paid overtime and to bring in sub-contractors or temporary workers because of sickness or peak workloads. Prior to the agreement, the union (TGWU) had strongly opposed any moves to sub-contract the delivery operation entirely and sought commitments from the company that it would not follow this course. Whilst no commitments have been given, the company has undertaken to consult the union in the event that the option to sub-contract is ever reconsidered.

At another major oil company, a productivity deal covering flexible working amongst refinery craftsmen cleared the way for the company to increase its use of sub-contractors in the less skilled maintenance areas at peak times and for special projects; the company also stresses the vital importance it attaches to consultation over the issue of sub-contracting. At the same company, under an agreement for more flexible working practices and reduced overtime working, agreement has been obtained to employ sub-contractors to meet peak periods of demand, rather than resort to overtime working amongst the permanent workforce.

7 Sabbaticals, extended leave and career breaks

Alastair Evans and Paul Massey

This chapter is concerned with innovations or changes in the traditional pattern of leave from work during the working lifetime. Various forms of special leave for domestic and personal reasons have been in existence for a long time and a new range of rights to leave for maternity, public or trade union duties became enshrined in legislation in the 1970s, but these are not the concern of this chapter.[1] Rather, we are concerned with newly emerging patterns which provide for substantial periods of leave, ranging from a few months up to five years which have been introduced by organizations for a variety of different purposes.

The schemes described in this chapter fall into four broad categories as follows:

- sabbaticals as a reward for good service
- extended career breaks and career re-entry
- arrangements for 'banking' leave
- extended leave for educational or other purposes

Sabbaticals as a reward for good service

Under this category of extended leave, employees are able to take a period of time off on full pay, on the basis of length of service. Unlike extended leave granted for social or educational purposes, employees are entitled to use the leave as they wish, which may include a long holiday, voluntary work or more time to pursue a hobby or interest. The reasons for such sabbaticals are frequently expressed in terms of opportunities to 'refresh and renew' or to 'recharge batteries', with the implicit objective that individuals will return after the break more motivated and consequently more effective in their jobs. Sabbaticals may also provide organizations with opportunities to develop employees who may take on the duties of other, possibly more senior, employees while they are away on leave.

One of the longest established sabbatical leave schemes in Britain is operated by the *John Lewis Partnership* department store and supermarket group.[2] The scheme was introduced in 1979 as a reward for long service and entitles all partners (as employees at *John Lewis* are termed), including part time partners, to a period of sabbatical leave of up to 26 weeks provided that they have completed 25 years' service with the company and have reached the age of 50 (to be reduced to 45 in stages over the next five years). The terms of the scheme recognize that "the opportunity to withdraw for a while from everyday employment without financial disadvantage and with the assurance of return to the same job is something that only the employer can give". There is, therefore, no threat to a partner's security of employment while they are on leave and they are entitled to return to their previous work, unless they request a change.

Pay during the sabbatical consists of basic contractual pay, plus a provision for any bonuses, allowances or overtime which are a regular feature of take home pay. The company believes that this benefit is highly valued by the partners and is something to strive for and look forward to. On average, 100 of the company's 28,500 employees become eligible each year and the company estimated in 1984 the annual cost of the scheme to be in the region of £300,000.[3] Two main issues have arisen out of the operation of the scheme—the problems of returning after a long break and the difficulty of senior people getting away to take their long leave entitlement. In a fast moving business such as retailing, careful thought has to be given to the process of re-entry and the company now runs a refresher programme for each employee on their return. The problem of senior people finding it difficult to get away has not been fully resolved and it has been decided that for about 100 key posts the period of leave must be delayed until immediately before retirement, but other employees are strongly encouraged to take up their entitlement.[4] Further details of the rules of the *John Lewis* sabbatical scheme are set out in the box below.

JOHN LEWIS PARTNERSHIP

LONG LEAVE

PART I General Rules

1. *Qualifications*
(a)   Partners, including part-time Partners, qualify when they have completed 25 years' membership in the Partnership and are aged 50 or over (for pre-Partnership service in acquired businesses see 1(e) below).

(b)   The upper age limit is the Partnership's normal age for retirement (65 for men and 60 for women). Membership after that date does not count towards qualification and long leave cannot commence after that date.

(c)   Partners with 25 years' membership qualify immediately on reaching the age of 50. Partners with less than 25 years' membership at the age of 50 qualify as soon as they complete 25 years.

(d)   For the purpose of long leave all broken service excluding temporary service should be added together.

(e)   The Scheme is intended for those who have been in the Partnership 25 years. For Partners in companies acquired by the Partnership, however, half the period of service in those companies prior to acquisition can be added to service in the Partnership for the purposes of both qualification and, where appropriate, entitlement.

2. *Entitlement*
(a)   One week's leave (up to a maximum of 26 weeks) for every full year of membership completed before the 50th birthday.

(b)   Service completed after the age of 50 is not added to years of service prior to this age for the purposes of entitlement; thus a Partner who joins at exactly the age of 33 becomes entitled to 17 and not 25 weeks' leave on reaching 25 years' service at the age of 58.

(c)   The purpose of the scheme is to provide long leave and under no circumstances will extra pay be given as an alternative.

(d)   No Partner is required to take long leave if he does not wish to do so.

(e)   Long Leave is the opportunity for a mid-career break without any threat to or interference with the Partner's security of employment. Partners taking long leave must know they can return to their previous work and appropriate arrangements must bo made to cnsure this is possible.

(f)   Because long leave is intended as a holiday within a long period of employment, there is no question of providing anything in lieu either by way of additional payment or artificial extension of employment for those who leave the Partnership without taking long leave even if they have previously qualified. This applies whether a Partner resigns or is dismissed and whether the reason is voluntary (eg to take up other work) or involuntary (eg ill health or redundancy).

3.   *When leave may be taken*
(a)   The idea of the scheme is to give the opportunity to take leave as soon as possible after qualifying and not to enable a Partner to give up work before his date of retirement. Individual circumstances vary, however, and every effort should be made to enable Partners to choose their own timing.

(b)   Because of the overriding commercial interests of our business, final discretion on timing must be in the hands of the Partnership's management. This generally means the Head of Branch or Principal Director concerned, but no request for long leave can be turned down or postponed for more than six months without the agreement of the Director of Personnel.

(c)   Entitlement must be taken as one period of absence and may not be split up. It can of course overlap trading years.

(d)   It may be taken either as a separate period of absence or together with any holiday entitlement (subject to the normal rules about the maximum period of regular holiday entitlement to be taken at any one time).

(e)   Notwithstanding Rules 3(a) and 3(b) above (which emphasise that the idea of the scheme is to give the opportunity to take leave as soon as possible after qualifying) Partners who qualify for long leave within five years of the Partnership's normal retirement age (or their own planned date of retirement if earlier) may be required by their Principal Directors to take long leave immediately before retirement.

4.   *How to apply*
All requests for long leave must be made in writing in advance by the Partner concerned to his Principal Director or Staff Manager. The Partnership has the right to require a minimum of six months'

notice for those below the level of Departmental Manager, and a minimum of twelve months' notice for Department Managers and above. Registrars will notify Partners and management at least one year in advance of when entitlements fall due.

5. *Pay during long leave*
(a)   Pay during long leave will consist of contractual pay plus a provision for any bonuses, allowances or overtime which are a regular feature of a Partner's take home pay. This will be made up as follows:

> (i)   contractual pay including any shift pay at the current rate.

> (ii)   a figure representing all bonuses, allowances and over-time; the weekly value of this will be calculated by taking the ranking pay for pension purposes for the last complete year, deducting contractual pay for the same period and dividing the total by 52. This arrangement recognises the special circumstances of long leave which are quite different from those affecting holidays and sickness, for which overtime and other bonuses are not paid.

> (iii)   for Partners entitled to keep tips under Regulation 150 a sum based on the most recent declaration of such earnings for tax purposes.

> (iv)   for Catering Partners, payment in respect of free meals on duty on the scale applicable to periods of holiday.

(b)   Partners may receive their pay on their usual contractual basis while on leave, ie weekly or monthly as the case may be. They may opt to collect it from their place of work or to have it sent in the form of a cheque to either their home or their bank.

(c)   Those Partners who are part-time (ie 30 hours or less calculated on a strict contractual basis) at the time they qualify for long leave shall have their pay calculated at their current hourly rate and based on the average weekly number of hours worked during the three years immediately prior to qualifying.

(d)   Partners working in units affected by any short time working arrangements will have their pay adjusted while on long leave in the manner agreed by the Director of Personnel for the unit as a whole. Any hardship this might cause to Partners already on long leave should be dealt with by referring the Partner to the Central Committee for Claims.

6. *Partnership benefits while on leave*
(a)   Partners on long leave remain full Partners in every sense of the word.

(b)   They retain their discount cards, long leave counts as continuous service, and the pay received during leave counts for the purposes of pension and Partnership Bonus. They continue to have access to the Committee for Claims, and those who are eligible retain the right to participate in Partnership Clubs and Societies.

(c)   Partners who are eligible may continue to be members of the Partnership's residential clubs and to make full use of the facilities.

(d)   While a Partner retains the right to full annual holiday entitlement in addition to long leave no adjustments will be made for public holidays which fall during a period of long leave.

(e)   Pay will be reviewed in the normal way for Partners whose long leave spans a salary review.

(f)   Annual Confidential Reports that are due within the three months following the start of long leave should be written and discussed before leave commences. Other reports should be held over until the Partner's return, and completed within three months of return.

(g)   Notice periods according to Partners' contracts continue during long leave.

(h)   Partners called for jury service during long leave will receive additional leave to compensate.

(i)   Additional leave will not be granted for periods of sickness which occur during long leave other than in exceptional circumstances.

(j)   Partners will obviously not normally expect to take on work outside the Partnership during their long leave. If they wish to do so (eg to widen their experience in some completely different operation or to supplement their income while travelling abroad) then they have that freedom of choice subject only to the normal requirement of Regulation 329.

PART II—Initial Arrangements

7.   Introduction of the Scheme

The starting date for the scheme was 18 April 1979, the 50th anniversary of the date of the signing of the First Trust Settlement.

8.   Special arrangements for those aged over 50 on 18 April 1979
The introduction of this scheme would be difficult to accomplish

without some scaling down of the entitlement of those already aged over 50 at its inception. The following provisions therefore apply:

(i)   Partners over 50 on 18 April 1979 and who have already completed 25 years' membership will have their entitlement scaled down by 2 weeks for every one complete year over the age of 50. Notwithstanding paragraph 2(a), but taking account of paragraph 1(e), of the general rules (Part I), the full number of completed years of membership before 50 (without limitation to a maximum of 26 weeks) will be taken into account before scaling down. The resulting net entitlement after scaling down, must not, however, exceed 26 weeks.

(ii)   For Partners over the age of 50 on that date but who will not complete 25 years' membership until later the same scaling-down arrangements will apply based on their age as at 18 April 1979 although they will not of course qualify until they have completed 25 years.

(iii)   Notwithstanding any scaling down resulting from (i) and (ii) above there will be a minimum entitlement for those who qualify of 10 weeks.

(iv)   Any of these Partners who on 18.4.79 were within five years of the Partnership's normal retirement age will be required to take their leave immediately before retirement.

PART III—Variation, Suspension or Termination of the Scheme

9.   Any one or more of the rules of the scheme including those affecting qualification, entitlement and pay and benefits during leave may be varied by the Director of Personnel after hearing the view of the Central Council. No Partner whose expectation for leave did not materialise would be entitled (as of right) to any compensation.

The scheme may be suspended or terminated by the Director of Personnel at any time if in the opinion of the Central Board this is necessary in the interests of the Partnership.

Any three members of the Board who were nominated for appointment to it by the Central Council may require the opinion of the Council to be ascertained on any such proposal to the Board. The terms on which any such suspension or termination would take effect would be entirely at the discretion of the Board and no Partner whose expectation for leave did not materialise would be entitled (as of right) to any compensation.

Another company providing sabbaticals as a reward for service is *McDonalds Hamburgers*. Under this scheme, which applies to salaried staff only, employees are entitled to eight weeks' paid sabbatical leave after 10 years' service which, in addition to the normal paid holiday entitlement in that year, enables a period of three months' leave to be taken. The concept was brought from the United States where paid sabbatical leave of this kind is more commonly found. Like *John Lewis*, the company does not require employees to use the sabbatical leave period for any specific purpose, but sees it as a break for employees to reflect on their careers.

A system of discretionary sabbatical leave has also operated at the *BBC* for many years where it is referred to as 'grace leave'. Originally introduced for senior staff, the scheme has in recent years been used by a variety of employees for various purposes. Applications for grace leave are considered and granted by a director in the light of individual circumstances, which might include rest, recuperation, study leave or research. No length of service is stipulated, but employees who have been granted leave have generally been with the *BBC* for at least 15 years. There is no specified length of leave laid down, but it normally lasts between two and three months. Employees receive full pay and usually a grant to help with expenses (eg for travel), the level of the grant depending on the needs of the individual and the purpose of the leave.

Extended career breaks and career re-entry

A small number of organizations have introduced a facility for extended, unpaid career breaks ranging from between three and five years, the main purpose of which is to enable employees a period of time off to bring up young children before resuming their former careers.

Two schemes of this type were introduced by the *National Westminster Bank* in 1981 to enable members of staff, male or female, to take a break in their career to care for young children and are referred to as the 're-entry' and 'reservist' schemes.

Under the *'re-entry'* scheme, the Bank guarantees an offer of re-employment to an individual at the same level of appointment or grade at which they left and provides a training programme on their return designed to update their knowledge and competence. This scheme is open to those who are seen to have the potential to reach senior management and who expect to return to work with their career commitment undiminished. Under the 'reservist' scheme, there is no commitment by the Bank to re-employ an individual, but the Bank is prepared to consider participants by placing them on a reserve list until a suitable vacancy at the level of appointment or grade at which they left the Bank becomes available. This scheme is open to those who are seen to have the potential to reach junior/middle management and who expect to return to full time employment. Both schemes operate for a period of up to five years from the date of resignation at the expiry of state maternity leave, although the offer may be extended at the discretion of the Bank.

Applicants for either scheme are normally expected to have completed five years service, on their return to have a minimum of 20 years to serve before retirement and to have received good reports during their period with the Bank. Participants in either scheme give an undertaking to provide a minimum of two weeks paid relief work per year (although many actually undertake more than this) and attend an annual one day seminar. Throughout the period of absence, contact is maintained through regular information packs and invitations to local social events. Participants are also encouraged to continue to study for the Institute of Bankers examinations, where appropriate. The Bank reserves the right to review the inclusion of individuals on either scheme where a change of residence makes the assessment of their career potential unrealistic. Selection for participation in either scheme is at the option of the Bank and those who meet the criteria described are eligible for consideration. To date there are 82 participants in total—18 re-entrants and 64 reservists.

A similar type of approach has been adopted by the *Midland Bank* with its 'retainer scheme' which was introduced in 1985. The main purposes of the scheme are:

● to encourage women, who constitute more than half the Bank's staff, to return to their careers following child rearing and also to attract career minded women to enter the Bank
● to utilize more effectively the Bank's investment in staff training and development by reducing the considerable waste of talent resulting from a lack of formal arrangements for women to return to their careers

The scheme is open to both male and female employees who have completed five years' service with the bank and wish to take a break to care for their children of pre-school age. Staff may take an unpaid service break of up to five years and the scheme is open to the following categories of employee who have a record of satisfactory performance:

- managers
- appointed officers
- management trainees or others with equivalent potential
- special grade staff

Under the terms of the scheme, employees may return to work with no loss of grade or status, which, for women, usually runs from the end of maternity leave. During the period of absence, the individual maintains involvement with the Bank by working for a minimum annual period of 10 working days. In addition there is an annual one day updating session held centrally and an annual discussion with the personnel manager. Copies of the group newspaper and any other appropriate publications are also sent to those on the scheme to assist in maintaining contact. If an individual on the scheme is willing and able to work more than the minimum, perhaps on a part time basis, the Bank endeavours to provide the relevant opportunities. In this context, the mechanism also exists for individuals to return on a part time basis at a more senior level than was possible in the past eg at senior clerical or supervisory/managerial levels. Whilst some training takes place during the period on the scheme, any further training required for updating purposes is provided on return to work.

A scheme of special leave without pay for career breaks also operates in the *Irish Civil Service* and has subsequently been extended to other parts of the public sector in Ireland. The scheme arose out of the Irish Government's Task Force on Employment and is designed to serve a number of objectives, in particular:

- to facilitate those who wish to combine a career with domestic and other responsibilities and interests
- to create new employment opportunities by filling the vacancies created by those taking a career break

Career breaks are available for both established and unestablished civil servants and cover a range of purposes (eg further education, family commitments, travel abroad, or starting a business). The break permitted is of one to three years' duration and officers returning to their careers following their breaks are assigned to appropriate vacancies as and when they arise in their former grade and department. It should be noted, however, that under the rules of the scheme, the duration of the career break does not count as reckonable service for incremental purposes, superannuation, annual leave entitlement or promotion. As of 30 April 1986, 1689 civil servants had applied for and 1666 had been granted career breaks and 3136 other public sector employees had participated in the scheme since its introduction in spring 1984. A roughly equivalent number of new, full time jobs have been created as a result. Around two-thirds of the participants have been women, mostly aged under 30. The reasons stated for applying for a career break by the 1689 civil servants were:

travel abroad	603
job abroad	220
job in Ireland	214
start a business	59
care of young family	164
other domestic reasons	294
study	135

The scheme is felt to have operated reasonably satisfactorily in relation to its twin objectives of creating additional job opportunities for young people in the civil service and the wider public sector and of providing facilities for those who wish to combine a career with domestic commitments or other interests. As with the job sharing scheme in the *Irish Civil Service*, described in an earlier chapter, a major feature of the career break scheme has been the effort put into promoting it by briefing and visiting departments, poster campaigns and promotional leaflets circulated to all staff. Whilst a number of administrative problems had to be resolved in the practical operation of the scheme in the initial stages, these difficulties have since been overcome.

Arrangements for 'banking' leave

A number of organizations operate systems whereby periods of extended leave can be earned by a range of methods, including the 'banking' and carrying forward of unused leave entitlement or additional leave on the basis of service, good attendance or other criteria.

One of the most highly developed schemes of this type has operated at *Peugeot-Citroen* in France for a number of years and provides additional periods of leave on the basis of a good attendance record.[5] The scheme was introduced against a background of pressures from employees for reduced working time and a desire on the part of the company's management to reduce absenteeism which was causing difficult organizational problems. Under the rules of the scheme, each employee accumulates a number of points for each day's attendance, with additional points being earned where shiftwork, nightwork, weekend or bank holiday working or working under special conditions is involved. More points are credited for attendance on Mondays and Fridays, when absenteeism is traditionally higher, than for Tuesdays, Wednesdays and Thursdays. Points are also credited for absences due to holidays, certified sickness or other authorized leave, but not for days lost through any unauthorized absence.

In January each year, employees are given a statement of the total attendance points credited. Where an employee has fewer than five days unauthorized absence in the year, the points accrued are increased by 50 per cent and where there has been no unauthorized absence whatsoever, the points are doubled. Employees may then convert the points credited into leave days which may be taken in the form of additional holidays each year or be banked over a number of years to provide a period of extended leave. Additionally, employees may bank their entitlement throughout their working lifetime, enabling them to retire up to one year early, with full pay and pension entitlements as if they worked the last year, or to work shorter hours or part time during a period prior to retirement. The rules of the scheme are designed to encourage the accumulation of points so that the extended leave or early retirement options are more attractive than using the accrued leave entitlement on an annual basis. Thus, employees under 35 are only permitted to use one-third of their leave entitlement immediately, one-third between 35 and 50 and the final one-third after the age of 50. In the case of employees between 35 and 50, half is available immediately and half after the age of 50. In order to encourage employees to save rather than use their accrued leave, unused entitlement at the age of 35 is doubled and doubled again at the age of 50. The scheme therefore encourages employees either to take a period of extended leave after the age of 50 or to use it for some early or phased retirement arrangement. In the event of an employee leaving for whatever reason, the accumulated entitlement is converted into a cash payment. The scheme has brought about an improvement in the absenteeism rate, has aided production planning through the taking of authorized leave rather than unauthorized absence and has provided employees with more freedom to determine the type of break which could suit them during their working lifetime.

It is not known whether any scheme of this type operates in Britain, but a number of employers do have schemes that enable employees to bank leave so that it can be taken in the form of a chunk of time off at a later date. At the *BBC*, for example, whose discretionary system of grace leave has already been referred to, management and production grades also receive an extra half-week's bankable leave as of right for each year's service after 10 years' service with the Corporation. This leave can be saved up to make a maximum of eight weeks' extra leave entitlement in that year. At *Massey Ferguson*, the reduction in the working week from 40 to 39 hours was implemented in agreement with the unions through a system of 'time banking'.[6] Under the scheme, employees continue to work 40 hours per week, against a contractual working week of 39 hours, with the additional hour each week being banked and taken in the form of additional leave. In other firms, similar banking schemes have been used to provide early retirement or lump sum payments on retirement. A number of companies, including *Lucas, Heinz, Triplex* and the *Prudential*, have also operated schemes entitling employees to save a part of their holiday entitlement each year in order to take a single period of extended leave at a later date.[7]

Extended leave for social, educational or other purposes

A growing number of organizations in recent years have adopted a system of extended leave for study or other serious pursuits and secondments of employees to participate in projects of benefit to the community or other organizations, such as small businesses. In an IPM survey published in 1980, the number of organizations providing sabbatical leave for research, study or other serious pursuit grew from 12 per cent to 19 per cent of organizations surveyed compared with 1974.[8] The 1980 survey also indicated that 14 per cent of organizations were prepared to grant social service leave and that a further nine per cent were considering making this provision available in the future.[9]

It is probable that company secondments to assist projects in the community have grown in recent years, stimulated by such organizations as the Confederation of British Industry who have been strongly supportive of such schemes in the light of growing social problems and rising unemployment, particularly youth unemployment. For businesses also, there has been a number of benefits. Involvement in the community can enhance the public image or prestige of the organization and provide new challenges to managers working in organizations where promotion opportunities have become more limited through contraction. It can also assist career blockage problems by seconding senior managers in order to open new promotion opportunities internally and can provide useful experience while secondees themselves await a further career move anticipated, for example, as a result of the retirement of a current incumbent.

A detailed description of the wide variety of schemes providing extended leave for social/educational purposes is beyond the scope of this chapter, but set out below are examples of the approaches taken by three organizations.

The sabbatical leave arrangements at *The Arts Council of Great Britain* are linked to an educational objective. The purpose of its scheme is to give members of staff the opportunity to carry out study or research which will be of benefit to both the individual and the Council. Leave for research or study is discretionary and may be granted after a minimum of seven years' service on the basis of two weeks per year of service, up to a maximum of six months. During their absence, staff receive normal basic pay. Full details of the scheme at *The Arts Council* are set out in the box below.

ARTS COUNCIL OF GREAT BRITAIN

Sabbatical leave procedure

1 *Purpose*
   The purpose of sabbatical leave is to give members of staff the opportunity to broaden their experience, acquire new ideas, skill or knowledge to the benefit of themselves and to the Council, by study or research either in this country or abroad or, where appropriate, to be refreshed by a change of environment.

2   *Eligibility*
     Sabbatical leave is not an automatic entitlement and is nor-
     mally given as a recognition of good and long service. All staff
     with a minimum of seven years service may apply, or alternati-
     vely the appropriate Director may recommend sabbatical
     leave if he/she feels it will be beneficial to a member of staff,
     or to the Council.

3   *Approval*
     Staff should, in the first instance, apply to their Director or the
     Deputy Secretary-General.

4   *Proposed Research/Study*
     When applying for sabbatical leave clear objectives for such
     leave and how these objectives will be achieved must be put
     in writing and, where appropriate, a report must be produced
     within three months of returning to work. This report must be
     given to the relevant departmental Director and a copy sent to
     the Personnel Department.

5   *Length of Absence*
     Staff will be allowed up to two weeks per year of service with
     a maximum of six months absence. Normally, only one period
     of sabbatical leave will be allowed during a term of employ-
     ment.

6   *Pay*
     Staff will receive their normal basic pay (i.e. excluding any
     long hours, overtime, premiums, night staff allowances, etc),
     during the period of absence on sabbatical leave.

7   *Sickness*
     If a member of staff falls ill during sabbatical leave and this
     lasts for eight days or more he/she must inform Personnel as
     soon as possible and obtain a medical certificate to cover the
     duration of the illness. This also applies to anyone who is
     abroad. The medical certificate should be forwarded to Per-
     sonnel. The sabbatical leave will not normally be extended
     because of illness.

8   *Training*
     Requests for in-service training, even if it is long term, should
     not be made under the sabbatical leave arrangements. The
     Council's training policy covers time off for training.

9   *External Activities*
     Staff who are on sabbatical leave are expected not to engage

> in activities which could embarrass the Council or conflict with its work. Staff must not engage in paid work when this involves use of official time or resources or involves any reference to the member of staff's official position with the Council, unless such arrangements have prior agreement by the relevant departmental Director.
>
> 10   *Cover for Absence on Sabbatical Leave*
> Normally no more than one person at a time may take sabbatical leave from any particular department. Whenever possible the work of the member of staff who is absent will be covered by other members of that department although temporary assistance may be requested through the normal procedures if necessary.

IBM has operated a secondment scheme since the early 1970s during which time 134 men and women have been seconded full time in the UK to projects of benefit to society. An employee's interest in seeking a secondment is normally first raised at their appraisal and counselling interview, either at the initiative of the individual or their manager and is considered in the light of individual and organizational career plans. At any one time in *IBM*, about 25 people are on secondment to organizations involved in work creation, education for working life, helping the disabled and to Government.

Rank Xerox introduced a provision for social service leave in the late 1970s and the company has sponsored a small number of selected staff with at least three years' service to undertake an approved social service project of their choice either in Britain or abroad for six months on full pay.[10] People wishing to be considered for such leave appear before a committee to make a case for their planned project. Activities carried out include a project helping in the rehabilitation of prisoners, voluntary service overseas and help with setting up an old people's workshop. The company also occasionally seconds senior managers to voluntary organizations such as the local enterprise agency.

8 Conclusions and considerations

Chris Curson, Stephen Palmer et al

When we set out a year ago to examine changes in working patterns since the reduction of the working week in 1979 and the onset of recession, we did so in the knowledge that whilst a great deal of work had already been carried out in different places on the mechanics of the change, there was very little empirical evidence regarding the 'macro' and 'micro' issues involved. We use these terms because flexibility in working time is perceived by many to have political, economic and social dimensions at national level, whilst, at the same time, practising personnel managers must consider what changes, if any, they should propose and which factors are most likely to give rise to the successful introduction of change at the level of the organization. This chapter looks first at issues of concern to the organization and then at national issues. Whilst the sample of about 90 organizations is not large there is no good reason to believe that what has happened in the enterprises we have surveyed is not reasonably typical of the economy as a whole.

Working time and the organization

We have explained in detail in Chapter 1 and in other chapters dealing with the specific items of change, the many reasons why particular organizations chose to adjust their traditional working time arrangements. Many of these reasons are clearly financial but sometimes introducing pay stability, eradicating low pay, and improving the industrial relations environment are also reasons for changing. In this section we consider some of the influences that seem to be present and which go a long way to ensuring the successful introduction of change, and offer a distillation of the issues that we came across in our case study interviews and in discussions with other interested parties.

Commitment   Like many aspects of management, the introduction of change requires the commitment of all managers from the board downwards. They must not only believe in the philosophy they have formulated but must be prepared to back it even if, as often happens at the beginning, there are teething troubles and an initial rise in costs. This means that managers must be prepared to back each other in implementing the strategy.

Long term strategy   We touch further on the question of a long term strategy when discussing communications below. Many organizations, especially those initiating change rather than reacting to a reduction in working hours, have developed long term plans which bring together changes in working time with flexibility and demanning exercises, all of which are an integral part of their long term business strategy.

A great influence on such strategies is the generally held belief that basic working hours are almost certain at some time to decline yet further. In many areas this will occur as a result of negotiations, but some organizations feel that such reduction in hours for manual workers will come as a result of their own harmonization policies, which are themselves the almost inevitable result of new technologies and the blurring of staff/manual demarcation lines. The added benefit of the long term approach is that it allows change to be planned on a non cost basis. The reduction in basic hours 'out of the blue' in 1979 undoubtedly caught many managements unprepared and probably accounts for why a fifth of organizations in Michael White's survey[1] had been unable to recoup any of the cost via higher productivity. "Be prepared" is therefore not a bad motto.

Expectations   Organizations which have successfully introduced change have taken notice of employee expectations,
especially those of their core staff. Regarding pay, employees
increasingly come to expect stability in exchange for flexibility,
whilst their attitude to working patterns is that time off should
be in 'usable' chunks.

Pay stability is a reason for both management and staff to
remove the disrupting effects of overtime which is easier to
achieve within the annual hours concept. Usable time off, on the
other hand, is the driving force behind the questioning of the
traditional eight hour shift unit and moves away from five day
working. Management's fears that extending the shift unit to 10
or 12 hours, to increase the periods of leisure time within a rota,
would reduce productivity levels appear, from our study, to have
been groundless. Similarly the compressed working week does
not appear to have had any adverse effects on output.

Communications and consultations . Where changes in
working patterns were envisaged a great many of our case
studies devoted a considerable amount of time both determining
their long term strategy and in getting agreement to it. Initially,
time was spent in interviewing other organizations who had
successfully adopted the chosen approach and, in some cases,
talking to consultants with an expertise in the field. Naturally,
the time spent developing the approach and consulting about it
is a function of the degree of change being made. Between 18
months and two years was cited for the full introduction of five
crew shiftworking, whereas less than six months was required to
agree a move to a $4\frac{1}{2}$ day week.

Allowing plenty of time is therefore an important factor. It
is doubly important because most successful organizations set
great store by involving their employees in the final decisions
and in getting their agreement. The time required will also be
influenced by the state of industrial relations within the organization and other factors, like its size and whether or not there
are already well established consultation and communication
procedures.

Certainly the emphasis was much more on consultation and
communication than negotiation in respect of the basic philosophy. But there is scope for a high degree of employee involvement in choosing shiftwork rotas, for example, or in moving to a
compressed working week. It also seems clear that the smaller

the workgroup the greater the scope for employee involvement in decisions of this kind.

Although adequate communication is a common feature of change, in the final analysis some organizations who introduced change did so in the teeth of trade union opposition but not without ensuring that management's case was well understood by employees generally. Very few suffered subsequent problems from this sort of unilateral management action.

Decentralization Although not an essential element in introducing change, it is worth noting that quite a few organizations, having agreed their philosophy and strategy centrally, left its actual implementation to individual units.

There are some advantages in this approach. The unit is often better placed than central personnel in deciding what approach best suits its circumstances, in communicating it and in fully involving employees. In some organizations there are even varying levels of basic working hours which depend on the amount of flexibility that has been agreed locally.

A decentralized approach will clearly work better in an organization whose constituent parts are involved in entirely different products or processes and where the make up of the workforce differs between plants. Decentralization can also be more attractive within single units, for example the introduction of a double day shift system, which may be reasonable for predominantly male, full time warehouse work, may not be acceptable to a female, part time process operation carried out in the same plant. Central head office might therefore consider an approach of agreeing the overall strategy but issuing guidelines rather than specific instructions to its unit personnel departments.

Developing new skills In those organizations where forward planning and radical thinking is taking place, management is placing great emphasis on re-learning, especially for line management. After a great deal of work in determining the shape of the flexibility granted by changes in work patterns and in finally introducing it, it is essential that employees re-learn what is required of them and that supervision is fully aware of the benefits that the changes bring them. Nowhere is this more

obvious than in the area of annual hours agreements where the
virtual abolition of overtime requires a substantial change in
attitude on the part of supervisors who have traditionally met
demand peaks in this way. Annual hours agreements, especially
if linked to elements of temporary or sub-contract working,
require that supervision can take advantage of the flexibility
allowed them under 'pay back', 'abnormal hours' or similar
clauses. This particular aspect also implies that management
carries out the often neglected duty of communicating with line
managers at all stages of the procedure as well as with its shop
floor employees.

Other factors   Although the foregoing six factors are what
appear to us the essential ingredients to successful change,
there are others that may have an influence depending on
circumstances. The monitoring of complex annual hours agreements makes essential the *computerization* of records. The level
of trust that goes with flexibility means that *recruitment procedures* should be highly rigorous and that' there should be
specific rules, for instance covering the operation of homeworkers.

In some places, management's commitment to the *harmonization* of terms and conditions of employment and/or *single
status* have been very important in achieving acceptance of
change on the shop floor. In the case of sub-contract labour
there are *financial* and *legal* implications that have to be seriously considered. And although part time working is seen as a
boon by many, some organizations have noted an increase in
expensive *turnover* and a lower level of *commitment* than for full
timers.

Our case studies contain some indication of why organizations have been successful in introducing greater flexibility
through changes in working time arrangements. Within them
there will be an approach that fits in well with the problems
faced by any organization.

A cyclical phenomenon?

It is not unduly cynical to pose the question "how permanent is
all this change likely to be?" The great issues of today are passé

tomorrow, only to come into vogue again later. Those who have welcomed, brought out and subsequently reintroduced productivity schemes—or have decentralized, centralized and decentralized again the personnel function—can recognize the simple truth that for personnel managers, as in life generally, there are few absolutes.

So, how 'permanent' are the changes outlined in this book likely to be? Certainly it is unlikely that we will see an increase in basic weekly hours. A hundred years of steady reduction does not suggest that such a change is on the cards, and it would be reasonable to assume that the changes that have resulted solely from hours reductions—the compressed working week or new shiftwork systems—are here to stay, with perhaps only those amendments that further reductions in working time may render necessary.

With the moves to part time, temporary and sub-contract working the position is less certain. The ease with which some organizations have been able to extend the use of temporary or sub-contract labour into traditionally full time occupations is partly a function of the current high levels of unemployment. At a time when it is comparatively easy to go into the market place to recruit staff in many disciplines on a short term basis, it is hardly surprising that organizations have sought to cut their costs by only employing such people as and when they want them.

Two factors, however, could reduce and ultimately reverse this trend in future. The first factor is the question of training. Much of the assumption behind the moves to temporary and part time working is that if organizations are no longer to carry out training, someone else will. The theorists argue that if the training for specific skills ceases, over a period fewer people will have those skills, demand for trained staff will rise, thus pushing up wage rates and encouraging others to undertake Government or similar courses. Unfortunately, there is no evidence to suggest that this is what happens and employers continue to report skill shortages. As the existing skilled sub-contract population ages, employers will have to train their own people in order to ensure a consistent and adequate supply of the right type of labour or find some other means of achieving the same result. Having spent that money will they really just release them back into the market for the use of competitors who may not have carried out any training themselves? Or will someone reinvent the wheel by suggesting the idea of a levy and grant system?

Secondly, if unemployment falls, organizations may find it

harder to obtain suitable employees on such a basis, and in so far as it remains possible, the going rate may increase to make it less attractive for organizations to do so. Their initial response could be to consider bringing essential employment—maintenance, transport and ultimately, administrative staff—back in house, even if for periods of the year these employees may be underemployed.

On the part time front, one organization we spoke to is already starting to express doubts about diluting its full time employees too far by using part timers. The organization has found part timers expensive to train, subject to high turnover rates and lacking employer loyalty, so much so that it is reversing the trend back towards employing full time staff. However, it must be said that none of the others that we surveyed expressed these concerns or were unhappy with their use of part time employees.

Given these influences, it would be foolish to accept without question that a trend away from 'permanent' workforce represents the future. It is certainly part of the present because at the moment it sometimes appears to be cost effective. If this ceases to be the case, for the reasons suggested above as for any others, we may see less of the 'core and periphery' approach in a few years time.

Flexible working patterns—the wider issues

We turn then from considering the implications of change as it affects individual organizations to discuss some of the more general economic and social issues raised. In doing so we are conscious of entering an area of considerable public and political concern during a period not long before a general election. It is not for a professional institute to attempt to formulate social policy at such a time, or indeed any other. Nevertheless, when both the creation of jobs and the general efficiency of the economy are matters of such widespread interest, it is surely desirable that debate on these issues should take place on as well informed a basis as possible.

The importance of this was brought home to us as long ago as November 1983 when the Institute was approached by the Department of Employment for its views on an EEC draft recommendation on the reduction and reallocation of working time. The recommendation itself covered a wide range of options forming "part of a strategy to combat unemployment". The Institute in its evidence seriously questioned the assumption that reduced working time would create jobs especially if, as one criterion upon which such change should be introduced, there should be no concomitant increase in unit costs. However, at that time, there was very little clear evidence to allow a thorough assessment of the real impact of reduced working time and changing work patterns on either costs or employment. One of the prime objectives of our particular research has therefore been to gather information in the areas of change to allow the IPM and others to draw their own conclusions. These are summarized below.

Basic hours   We have noted (Chapter 1) that the reduction in basic hours that has taken place since 1979 has been one of the major influences, along with new technology and the recession, on the working patterns that have emerged. As such, it is not always easy to disentangle its effects both from the other two influences and from changes in other areas. The reduction in the working week certainly has affected approaches to seven day continuous shiftwork, so has the new technology, but it may have had little impact on five day shift systems or overtime reductions and probably no effect at all on sub-contracting or part time working. For simplicity therefore, here we are considering the changes in hours purely in the context of the standard working week.

All the evidence suggests that the reduction in the working week has had no effect whatsoever on employment and, at worst, only a marginal negative impact on costs. The reason for this lies in the simple fact that most hours reduction agreements included a 'non cost' clause such that most of the reduction was paid for out of increased productivity. This finding concurs with the conclusions of a study by Michael White in 1982[2] which looked at hours reductions in four industries and found that only in the printing industry did some employers not achieve at least a partial recovery of their costs by offsetting agreements.

Employers adopted a number of changes to claw back the cost of the reduced working week. Compensatory improvements in productivity were sought from reducing tea breaks or other time allowances, greater flexibility, tightening up on discipline etc. The net effect was that productivity generally rose to meet the cost of the shorter working week so that the original level of output was reached with the same workforce only in a shorter time. Not much scope for increasing employment there. Indeed, according to White,[3] three per cent of all employers paid for reduced working time by *reducing* their manning requirements.

Shiftworking   The impact of shiftworking on job creation is harder to gauge. In the case of double day or three shift discontinuous shiftworking the evidence indicates that the reduction in the working week was taken on board in much the same way as outlined under basic hours above, that is, there was no increase in either employment or costs and no decrease in output. Similarly for seven day continuous shiftworking, the reduction in basic hours, in a lot of cases, did not create jobs. A great many employers have stuck with their four crew systems and met the reduction in hours out of increased overtime whilst trying to retrieve some of the on-cost out of improved productivity. The need to provide extra cover may or may not have created jobs, but our study suggests the latter because in most cases existing employees were used on relief at overtime rates.

In reality, only the moves to five crew working have created employment chances, but even these have been low because often the fifth crew is made up of the relief elements of the previous four crews. In terms of costs, employers indicated that productivity improvements had often more than compensated for any extra manning. As an aside, whilst five crew working is often introduced because of reductions in basic hours this is not the only reason. One organization introduced a five crew, seven day, shift system primarily out of a need to maximize the use of expensive capital.

This need to maximize capital equipment utilization could well be the most important influence on shiftworking and, through that, on jobs in the future. In countries like Britain, where the capital base is comparatively small and declining, and where technical change and, therefore, obsolescence are rapid, the most important influence on unit costs in the future could be to maximize the utilization of that capital that exists. In its most recent survey, the CBI[4] shows that 57 per cent of British manufacturing companies are under-utilizing their capital stock. The problem is that the opportunities presented to increase employment via shiftworking are largely restricted to the primary and manufacturing industries which now only employ a quarter of Britain's workforce. In the rapidly growing service sector the use of shiftworking is necessarily circumscribed by the fact that a particular service must be provided at the times that its customers require it and outside those times, there is little if any, demand for staff in most instances.

Overtime It has long been argued by trade unions, and others, that a ban on overtime would create jobs. At the last count[5] the total number of hours of overtime worked in the UK was nearly 12 million which, assuming an average basic working week of 37½ hours, amounts to 320,000 jobs.

That such an analysis is too simplistic is obvious, as was shown in an article published by two IPM members in 1981.[6] It fails to take account of where the overtime is worked, who works it and why. For example, it is doubtful whether abolishing overtime working for railway workmen in the south east of England will do much for unemployed fishermen in Hull, quite apart from the fact that it would be unlikely to do much for south eastern train services either. The other problem is that a great deal of overtime arises on a short term, last minute or emergency basis, or is of limited seasonal duration. In fact, not only would eliminating it be impossible to bring about but it would hardly create any jobs at all, except possibly in some shift systems. Even abolishing 'custom and practice' overtime may have little effect, as much of this type of overtime is probably unnecessary in the first place.

Certainly the concept of annual hours has reduced overtime working in those organizations that have adopted it, primarily by introducing greater flexibility in manning, thus ensuring that the availability of employees closely matches the peaks and troughs of production needs. Often this flexibility has been purchased by including all or most of previous overtime earnings into basic pay. But whilst costs are unchanged, few, if any, jobs have been created except in some cases of five crew shiftwork.

Part time, temporary and sub-contract working We have put these three items together because their impact on jobs and costs are very similar. They all form differing parts of the periphery in the 'core and periphery' model and their attraction lies in their comparative cost effectiveness when compared to full time employees. Part time, temporary and sub-contract working are all used to meet specific, comparatively short term needs. This in itself is cheaper than employing full timers who would be surplus to requirements at times, but there are further substantial cost savings from (probably) a reduction in manning needs and from the fact that such employees, certainly temporary and sub-contract workers, are unlikely to receive benefits like holidays, sick pay and pensions to the same extent as full time permanent staff.

Whilst there are undoubted cost savings from moving some way towards the peripheral workforce, even these may be questioned in the long run. However, some would say they do have a role in creating jobs. In the sense that more people are now employed than in the past and that the major growth areas have been part time and temporary working this is true. But the whole argument hinges upon the definition of 'job'. Some would argue that 'real jobs' are only those performed by a person who works 'full time' weekly hours. Others would argue that if what was previously one job were divided amongst two part timers there would be two jobs for statistical purposes.

Extended leave arrangements We enquired about extended leave arrangements as a possible means of creating jobs because it had been suggested that they might assist in achieving that result. However very few organizations offer extended leave and, where they do, it is so often restricted to certain groups or grades that no conclusions about either costs or job creation can be drawn. The evidence is that the scale of extended leave is so small that its effects in both areas are minimal and this is unlikely to change in the near future.

Conclusions

The evidence we have gathered leads us to the conclusion that most of the changes in working patterns that have so far taken place have not, and probably will not, create new employment. The changes have little to do with creating employment *per se* and a great deal to do with the business needs of the organization and the aspirations of the existing workforce. This is not to deny their undoubted influence on improving productivity which, it may be argued, has added to the security of the 'core' workers.

From our study there emerge some areas of concern at the national level. There have been few successful examples of reduced overtime working and, where they do exist, few, if any, employment opportunities have been created; reductions in working time have not created work and have been paid for in part or in total out of increased productivity. Of the areas we have studied, only the extension of shiftworking seems to offer any long term hope for increasing *employment*, and the scope of this is limited. Part time working, on the other hand, has increased *jobs*. This is because, making increasing use of part time, temporary and sub-contract workers has primarily the effect of spreading the available work around in a different pattern without significantly increasing the overall amount of employment. The extent to which this is helpful in combatting unemployment depends on what the aspirations of workers really are. There may be a significant number who would be willing to work on such a basis but further research would be necessary to determine the extent of this, and, in any case, the very features that may make part time and temporary working attractive to employers—freedom to lay off staff, lower levels of fringe benefits, and so on—must by definition render it a less desirable pattern from most workers' point of view. The evidence suggests that the actions of employers and, where relevant, the results of collective bargaining, will not change this and one is led to conclude that legislative and perhaps also fiscal change (ie through taxation) would be necessary to make part time employment more secure and attractive to individuals and hence provide a real contribution to reducing unemployment. And this is perhaps the point at which the wider political debate needs to commence.

References

Chapter 1
Emerging themes in flexible work patterns

1 See, for example, ATKINSON J. Manpower strategies for flexible organizations. *Personnel Management*. August 1984. pp 28–31; ATKINSON J. Flexibility: planning for an uncertain future. *Manpower Policy and Practice*. Vol I, 1985. pp 26–29; INSTITUTE OF MANPOWER STUDIES. *Flexibility, uncertainty and manpower management*. Brighton, Institute of Manpower Studies, 1984; INSTITUTE OF MANPOWER STUDIES. *Flexible manning; the way ahead*. Brighton, Institute of Manpower Studies and Manpower Ltd, 1984
2 NATIONAL ECONOMIC DEVELOPMENT COUNCIL. *Changing work patterns: how companies achieve flexibility to meet new needs*. London, NEDO, 1986
3 MANPOWER LIMITED. *Flexible manning in business*. Slough, Manpower Limited, 1985
4 HANDY C. The organization revolution and how to harness it. *Personnel Management*. July 1984. pp 20–23
5 MANGUM G, MAYALL D and NELSON K. The temporary help industry: a response to the dual internal labour market. *Industrial and Labour Relations Review*. vol 38, No 4, July 1985. p 559
6 TRADES UNION CONGRESS. *Labour market flexibility*. Circular No 91. London, TUC, 3 December 1985
7 RATHKEY P. *Trade union involvement in changing job structures*. Unpublished paper presented at a Royal Institute of Public Administration Conference, 11 March 1986; and RATHKEY P. Trade unions, collective bargaining and reduced working time: a critical assessment. *Employee Relations*, Vol 8, No 1, 1986. pp 4–9

Chapter 2
New patterns of flexible dayworking

1   BREWSTER C and CONNOCK S. *Industrial relations: cost-effective strategies.* London, Hutchinson, 1985. p 70
2   See also INCOMES DATA SERVICES LTD. *Productivity and working time.* London, IDS, April 1984. (Study 312) pp 29–30
3   DOBSON G. *Working patterns in the north of England.* London, British Institute of Management, 1986. pp 31–32
4   *Ibid.* pp 32–34
5   FERNER A. Political constraints and management strategies: the case of working practices in British Rail. *British Journal of Industrial Relations.* March 1985. pp 47–70
6   Flexible rostering at British Rail. *Industrial Relations Review and Report.* No 267, March 1982. pp 11–13
7   *Ibid.* p 13
8   FERNER A. *op cit,* p 56
9   *Ibid.* pp 58–59
10 DE LANGE W. Control of working time: attuning working time to organizational or individual needs. *Labour and Society,* Vol 11, No 1, January 1986. p 98
11 ROTHWELL S and STEEL A. *Report on flexible working patterns in Great Britain.* Centre for Employment Policy Studies, Henley—the Management College. July 1983. p 42
12 Quoted in EVANS A and PALMER S. *Negotiating shorter working hours.* Basingstoke, Macmillan, 1985. p 65
13 *Ibid.* p 65
14 DE LANGE W. *op cit.* p 98
15 ROTHWELL S and STEEL A. *op cit.* p 42
16 WHITE M. *Shorter working time through national industry agreements,* Research paper no 38. London, Department of Employment, 1982
17 EVANS A and PALMER S. *op cit.* pp 131–132 and INCOMES DATA SERVICES LTD. What engineering companies are doing about the 39-hour week. *IDS Report,* no 357. p 3
18 EVANS A and PALMER S. *op cit.* pp 132–133
19 EVANS A and PALMER S. *op cit.* pp 133–134 and INCOMES DATA SERVICES LTD. *Hours of work.* London, IDS, February 1980. (Study 211) pp 16–17
20 35-hour, 4-day week agreed at Winn and Coales. *Industrial Relations Review and Report.* Pay and Benefits Bulletin. 5 November 1985. p 6
21 Inland Revenue in experimental four-day working week scheme. *Financial Times.* 14 June 1985
22 DICKENSON F. When the shorter week is a fortnight. *Personnel Management.* April 1982. p 3
23 EVANS A and PALMER S. *op cit.* pp 134–135

24 EVANS A and PALMER S. *op cit.* p 6

25 DOBSON G. *op cit.* p 34

26 TERIET B. Flexiyear schedules—only a matter of time?. *Monthly Labor Review.* December 1977. pp 62–65

27 EVANS A and PALMER S. *op cit.* pp 24–25

28 LYNCH P. Annual hours: an idea whose time has come. *Personnel Management.* November 1985. pp 46–50

29 *Ibid.* p 47

30 *Ibid.* p 48

31 *Ibid.* p 48

Chapter 3
Overtime and its alternatives

1 EVANS A and PALMER S. *Negotiating shorter working hours.* Basingstoke, Macmillan, 1985. p 16

2 *Ibid.* p 67

3 *Ibid.* p 84

4 FLANDERS A. *The Fawley productivity agreements.* London, Faber, 1964

5 See, for example, Shift work 2: reducing working hours. *Industrial Relations Review and Report.* No 302, November 1983. pp 2–4 and INCOMES DATA SERVICES LTD. *Productivity and working time.* London, IDS, April 1984. (Study 312) pp 13–16

6 Why Petrofina is abolishing overtime. *Financial Times.* 24 August 1984

7 LYNCH P. The abuse of overtime. *Industrial Society.* December 1985. pp 22–25, 44

8 NATIONAL ECONOMIC DEVELOPMENT COUNCIL. *Changing working patterns: how companies achieve flexibility to meet new needs.* London, NEDO, 1986

9 For further details, see EVANS A and PALMER S. *op cit.* pp 88–91

10 Overtime—restricting its level. *Industrial Relations Review and Report.* No 270, April 1982. pp 2–8

11 EVANS A and PALMER S. *op cit.* pp 107–108

12 Methods to contain overtime. *Industrial Relations Review and Report.* No 330, October 1984. pp 2–6

13 LYNCH P. *op cit.* p 25

Chapter 4
New forms of shiftworking

1 NATIONAL BOARD FOR PRICES AND INCOMES. *Hours of work, overtime and shiftworking.* Cmnd 4554, London, HMSO, 1970. (Report 161)
2 EVANS A and PALMER S. *Negotiating shorter working hours.* Basingstoke, Macmillan, 1985
3 INDUSTRIAL SOCIETY. *Survey of shift working practices 1979.* London, Industrial Society, 1979. (Information survey and report series no 198)
4 INCOMES DATA SERVICES LTD. *Shift patterns.* London, IDS, 1985. (Study 335)
5 INCOMES DATA SERVICES LTD. *Productivity and working time.* London, IDS, 1984. (Study 312)
6 INCOMES DATA SERVICES LTD. *op cit.* (Study 335)
7 RUSKIN COLLEGE. Trade Union Research Unit. *Five team working and eight hour, seven day, continuous shiftworking.* Oxford, Turu, 1981 (Technical Note no 74)
8 INCOMES DATA SERVICES LTD. *op cit.* (Study 335)
9 CHEMICAL INDUSTRIES ASSOCIATION LTD. *Introduction of the shorter working week.* London, CIA, 1982

Chapter 5
Alternatives to full time permanent staff

1 MEAGER N. *Temporary work in Britain: its growth and changing rationales.* Brighton, Institute of Manpower Studies, 1985. p 29
2 MANPOWER LIMITED. *Flexible manning in business.* Slough, Manpower Ltd, 1985. p 9
3 MEAGER N. *op cit.* pp 11–13, 13–19
4 Top executives tempted by temporary work. *Industrial Relations Review and Report.* No 363, March 1986. pp 15–16
5 MEAGER N. *op cit.* p 26
6 *Ibid.* pp 35–38
7 Quoted in MEAGER N. *op cit*
8 SYRETT M. *Employing jobsharers, part-time and temporary staff.* London, Institute of Personnel Management, 1983. pp 78–80
9 Quoted in MEAGER N. *op cit.* pp 37–38
10 *Ibid.* pp 38–40

11 Using temporary and sub-contract labour. *Industrial Relations Review and Report.* No 365, April 1986. pp 4–5
12 *Ibid.* p 5
13 INCOMES DATA SERVICES. *Temporary workers.* London, IDS, August 1983. (Study 295)
14 SYRETT M. Temps: a blind spot for personnel? *Personnel Executive.* September 1983. pp 31–34
15 ROTHWELL S. Comparative labour costs: getting the right mix. *Manpower Policy and Practice.* Spring 1986. pp 15–18
16 Part-time work in 15 countries. *European Industrial Relations Review.* No 137, June 1985. p 21
17 INCOMES DATA SERVICES LTD. *Part-time workers.* London, IDS, June 1982. (Study 267) pp 1–2 and EVANS A and PALMER S. *Negotiating shorter working hours.* Basingstoke, Macmillan, 1985. pp 49–50
18 EVANS A and PALMER S. *op cit.* p 50
19 Quoted in SYRETT M. *Employing jobsharers, part-time and temporary staff.* London, Institute of Personnel Management, 1983. pp 10–11
20 INCOMES DATA SERVICES LTD. *Part-time workers.* London, IDS, June 1982. (Study 267) p 20
21 *Ibid.* p 28
22 *Ibid.* p 24
23 *Ibid.* p 29
24 Part-time work—a survey. *Industrial Relations Review and Report.* No 320, 22 May 1984. p 3
25 *Part-time workers. op cit.* p 23
26 SYRETT M. *Employing jobsharers, part-time and temporary staff.* London, Institute of Personnel Management, 1983. p 13
27 *Ibid.* p 13
28 Part-time work—a survey. *op cit.* pp 2 and 5
29 Shift to part-time work—a case study. *Employment Bulletin and IR Digest,* May 1985. p 2
30 Maintaining a flexible workforce—Lyons Tetley. *Industrial Relations Review and Report.* 18 December 1984. pp 7–10
31 Part-time work—a survey. *op cit.* pp 3–4
32 SYRETT M. *Employing jobsharers, part-time and temporary staff.* London, Institute of Personnel Management, 1983. p 45
33 *Ibid.* p 41
34 *Ibid.* p 41
35 WALTON P. Job sharing. In CLUTTERBUCK D, *ed. New patterns of work.* Aldershot, Gower, 1985. pp 110–126
36 EVANS A and PALMER S. *op cit.* p 59
37 EQUAL OPPORTUNITIES COMMISSION. *Jobsharing.* Manchester, EOC, 1981. p 5
38 WALTON P. *op cit.* p 117
39 EVANS A and PALMER S. *op cit.* pp 59–61
40 *Ibid.* pp 61–62

41 SYRETT M. *Employing jobsharers, part-time and temporary staff.* London, Institute of Personnel Management, 1983. pp 48–49
42 *Ibid.* pp 52–53
43 HEELEY L. Tackling the problem that will not go away. *Local Government Chronicle.* 11 January 1985. p 40 and Job sharing in practice: the Staffordshire experience. *Local Government Chronicle.* 16 March 1985. pp 203–204
44 SYRETT M. *Employing jobsharers, part-time and temporary staff.* London, Institute of Personnel Management, 1983. pp 106–108
45 *Ibid.* p 53
46 *Job sharing in the London boroughs.* London, New Ways to Work, 1986
47 SYRETT M. *Employing jobsharers, part-time and temporary staff.* London, Institute of Personnel Management, 1983. p 49
48 HAKIM C. Homework and outwork: national estimates from two surveys. *Employment Gazette.* January 1984, pp 7–12
49 HUWS U. New technology homeworkers. *Employment Gazette.* January 1984. pp 13–17
50 *Ibid.* p 15
51 Homeworking. *Labour Research.* July 1984. p 172
52 KELLY M M. The next workplace revolution: telecommuting. *Supervisory Management (USA).* October 1985. pp 2–7
53 *Telework: impact on living and working conditions.* Dublin, European Foundation for the Improvement in Living and Working Conditions, 1984, quoted in *European Industrial Relations Review.* April 1985. pp 21–23
54 HUWS U. *The new homeworkers.* London, Low Pay Unit, 1984. p 58
55 *Ibid.* p 58
56 See also JUDKINS P, WEST D and DREW J. *Networking in organizations: the Rank Xerox experiment.* Aldershot, Gower, 1985. pp 56–58 and HUWS U. *The new homeworkers. op cit.* pp 55–56
57 SYRETT M. *Goodbye nine to five.* London, New Opportunities Press, 1985. pp 57–58

Chapter 6
Sub-contracting

1 HANDY C. The organization revolution and how to harness it. *Personnel Management.* July 1984. pp 20–23
2 ATKINSON J. Manpower strategies for flexible organizations. *Personnel Management.* August 1984. pp 28–31

3   NATIONAL ECONOMIC DEVELOPMENT COUNCIL. *Changing working patterns: how companies achieve flexibility to meet new needs.* London, NEDO, 1986
4   MANPOWER LIMITED. *Flexible manning in business.* Slough, Manpower Limited, 1985
5   CADBURY, SIR ADRIAN. *The 1980s: a watershed in British industrial relations.* Brighton, Institute of Manpower Studies, 1985. p 9
6   BDS: new employment package, new company. *Industrial Relations Review and Report.* No 342, April 1985. pp 7–12
7   *Ibid.* p 8
8   *Ibid.* p 11
9   ATKINSON J. *op cit*
10 LEWIS D. *Essentials of employment law.* London, Institute of Personnel Management, 1983. p 35
11 *Ibid.* p 35
12 INSTITUTE OF DIRECTORS. *Labour market changes and opportunities: new patterns of work.* London, the Institute, 1985. pp 24–27
13 CONFEDERATION OF BRITISH INDUSTRY. *Managing change.* London, CBI, 1985. p 20
14 Using temporary and sub-contract labour. *Industrial Relations Review and Report.* No 365, April 1986. pp 2–7

Chapter 7
Sabbaticals, extended leave and career breaks

1   For a further discussion of the full range of leave arrangements operated by organizations, see JAGO A. *Special leave.* London, Institute of Personnel Management, 1980
2   See also MAY S. Sabbaticals: the John Lewis experience. In CLUTTERBUCK D, *ed. New patterns of work.* Aldershot, Gower, 1985. pp 104–109
3   MAY S. *op cit.* p 108
4   DEVINE M. Time off for a step back. *Manpower Policy and Practice.* Vol 1, No 2, Winter 1985. pp 10–11
5   See also TAVERNIER G. Car workers shift to flexible leisure time. *International Management.* October 1978. pp 39–40; More holidays for less absence. *European Industrial Relations Review.* No 62, March 1979. pp 15–16; Benefits for the French motor car industry: holiday scheme for good attendance. *Department of Employment Gazette.* January 1978. pp 31–33
6   INCOMES DATA SERVICES LTD. Massey Ferguson agrees 18 month pay and conditions package. *IDS Report.* No 453, July 1985. p 3

7 Sabbaticals—a review of current practice. *Industrial Relations Review and Report*. No 238, December 1980. pp 7–9

8 JAGO A. *op cit*. p 29

9 *Ibid*. p 33

10 See also *Industrial Relations Review and Report*. No 238. *op cit*

Chapter 8
Conclusions and considerations

1 WHITE M. *Shorter working time through national industry agreements*. London, Department of Employment, 1982. (Research paper 38)

2 *Ibid*

3 *Ibid*

4 CONFEDERATION OF BRITISH INDUSTRY. *Industrial trends survey*. London, CBI, April 1986

5 DEPARTMENT OF EMPLOYMENT. Overtime and short-time operatives in manufacturing industries. *Employment Gazette*. March/April 1986. Table 1.11, p 518

6 KINCHIN SMITH M and PALMER S. Getting to the bottom of overtime. *Personnel Management*. February 1981. pp 27–31

Select bibliography

BREWSTER C and CONNOCK S. *Industrial relations: cost effective strategies.* London, Hutchinson, 1985

CLUTTERBUCK D, ed. *New patterns of work.* Aldershot, Gower, 1985

CONFEDERATION OF BRITISH INDUSTRY. *Managing change.* London, CBI, 1985

EVANS A and PALMER S. *Negotiating shorter working hours.* Basingstoke, Macmillan, 1985

INCOMES DATA SERVICES. *Productivity and working time.* London, IDS, 1984. (Study 312)

INCOMES DATA SERVICES. *Shift patterns.* London, IDS, 1985. (Study 335)

INCOMES DATA SERVICES, *Temporary workers.* London, IDS, 1983. (Study 295)

NATIONAL ECONOMIC DEVELOPMENT COUNCIL. *Changing working patterns: how companies achieve flexibility to meet new needs.* London, NEDO, 1986

MEAGER N. *Temporary work in Britain: its growth and changing rationales.* Brighton, Institute of Manpower Studies, 1985

SYRETT M. *Employing job sharers, part-time and temporary staff.* London, Institute of Personnel Management, 1983

Case studies

1 Annual hours and seven crew shiftworking at Blue Circle Industries plc

Blue Circle manufactures cement and sanitary ware as separate businesses at several sites throughout the country. There are 10,941 employees in the UK.

In 1985 major changes in working patterns were agreed for two of the company's cement plants, at Cauldon and Dunbar (see box below). The agreement was with GMBATU, AUEW and EETPU. It covers all manual employees at the two sites except lorry drivers (28 on one site, 65 at the other). Changes were also made at the same time to the pay and conditions of staff employees.

The strategy

In recent years, profits in the British cement industry have been squeezed. Production has been static over the past four or five years and manning levels have been reduced drastically over the same period. Because of the threat of imports, there had until recently been no price increase for $3\frac{1}{2}$ years. Because of its general knowledge of Europe and other major countries, management at Blue Circle was aware of developments on the Continent of which it wanted to have first hand experience. The company wanted to develop up to date plants in the UK in order to be as competitive as possible. The decision was taken to embark on a major investment programme at Cauldon and Dunbar and between £30 and £40 million was invested at each site. These two plants were selected because of the availability of the right type of raw material and because they were seen to have a long term future.

The company used the opportunity of the introduction of new technology to introduce integrated working and establish new working patterns at the two sites. The aim was to get away from the old manual conditions of work such as payment for hours attended and minimize manning levels, while at the same time reducing hours of work and improving conditions for employees. Previously hourly paid employees were working an average of 50 hours, although the basic week is 39 hours. It was clear to management that normal attendance-related pay systems provided an opportunity for employees to extend work in order to enhance their earnings. There were also demarcation problems within the craft unions and between process and craft employees. There were 11 process grades and three craft grades.

A great deal of work went into research and the formulation of the new proposals before they were put to the unions. The whole process took about two years to complete. Other companies were visited, mainly continuous process industries and many in greenfield sites. Management decided to approach the exercise as if it were starting from scratch, while recognizing the obvious constraints of having to modernize its existing sites and deal with its existing employees.

The company's aim was to minimize unit labour costs and raise labour productivity, ie maximize the use of employees' time. Management wanted to move away from attendance-related pay and to offer employees reduced hours of work. The new structure had to be designed with scope for incorporating possible future developments, eg harmonization or further cuts in the working week, while recognizing traditional trade union claims.

The agreement

Negotiations on terms and conditions for process and craft employees in the cement industry are conducted at national level. It was decided to develop the new agreement, within the framework of the national agreement, to apply only at the two plants. The company presented it to the unions without previous joint consultation. The unions made a positive contribution to the proposals while at the same time seeking to get the best terms for their members,

The final outcome was an agreement called 'The Stable Income Plan for Integrated Working'. The main elements of the agreement are:

- *flexible working* ie skills were enhanced and restrictions reduced so that employees are able to work more effectively throughout attendance time
- *annual hours* contract introduced on the back of more socially acceptable working patterns
- *new continuous shift patterns* introduced
- *new stable income plan* established with standard cashless payments at extended periods

Each plant started with a workforce of around 450 which has now been reduced to just over 300.

A selection procedure was agreed with the unions whereby all employees were initially assessed on a 20 point matrix which takes into account skills, health, absence and disciplinary records, with length of service only as a final deciding factor. All employees were interviewed to ascertain whether they wished to work under the new system and all were individually counselled on how the changes would apply to them. Employees were also given a chance to discuss any problems. Volunteers were sought for redundancy or early retirement, but some compulsory redundancies were unavoidable. Management reports that the exercise went very smoothly and the company now employs an adaptable skilled workforce which has undertaken the extensive extra training necessary. It was not felt this could all have been achieved through traditional last in first out selection.

Flexible working

The aim of the integrated or flexible working provisions is to make the most effective use of employees' time. Detailed job specifications have been abolished and employees are now categorized only by skill and work pattern. There are three grades of process operator and one engineering craftsman (cross traded) grade. Demarcation has been reduced and all employees are within their competency required to:

- carry out any duty with due regard to relevant safety regulations, policies and safe working practices
- work without direct supervision
- assist other personnel as necessary in any part of the works

In order to increase flexibility all employees are required to train to acquire extra skills, if possible to a recognized level (eg Engineering Industry Training Board module). Electrical and mechanical craftsmen have to acquire a skill in the other function. When employees have qualified in four skills they receive a 15 per cent skills payment. There is commitment by the unions for training to be an ongoing programme for all employees, with craftsmen becoming fully multi skilled and cross traded.

Manning levels have been reduced so that the plant is now manned for the normal operating situation. Peak workloads are covered by contracting.

Annual hours

The aim of the annual hours contract was to ensure that employees work approximately equal hours so that pay relativities are based on skill and working patterns, not attendance.

The company wanted the distribution of working hours to be as fair as possible, but recognized that there would still be peaks and troughs in the demand for work. An annual hours contract was agreed which includes a 'flexible hours' provision that allows the company to call upon employees to work limited extra hours above the basic hours when necessary. Flexible hours replace overtime and constitute up to an additional $12\frac{1}{2}$ per cent of basic hours. Experience in other companies had indicated that there had been problems with annual hours contracts if time off in lieu was offered when overtime was worked at peak load times, as it was not always possible to release people to take their time off. Under this system the extra hours are already counted in the annual hours and paid for. The unions had no basic objection to the introduction of annual hours but they were concerned that all the flexible hours could be saved up till the end of the year and then employees might be exploited. So the company agreed to mandatory flexible hours limits in periods of 2, 10, 20 and 65 days, and the maximum number of outstanding flexible hours available to the employer are gradually diminished on a sliding scale throughout the year. The agreement includes a statement of obligations and requirements. The company said it would endeavour to share out flexible hours, call out and bank holiday working fairly between employees. The hours worked are monitored by a computer linked to an electronic time clock. Printouts are available to the employees. Without computer technology, it would not have been possible to operate the system on a long term basis. Management accepts the fact that people sometimes have prior commitments and will be unable to work flexible hours when requested. However, employees must accept that they have over a period of time to do their fair share of flexible working. Flexible hours working is a contractual requirement, and all things being equal, employees do not have an option to refuse a company request to work these hours.

A joint planning and review meeting takes place at local level at three-monthly intervals to appraise hours, call out etc. Management will, if possible, advise the unions of the future use of flexible hours if it can be foreseen.

The annual hours agreed are:

45.8 working weeks and 4 days at 39 hours per week	1786
23 days annual holiday plus 8 public holidays at 39 hours a week	242
ie minimum hours	2028
Built in flexible time at 12½% of 1786 hours	223
Contract hours (maximum)	2251

Shifts

Traditionally continuous shiftworkers had a four crew shift pattern. In 1981 when hours were reduced from 40 to 39, these employees took one extra shift off every eight weeks and the duties were either left uncovered or covered by inclusion in another work pattern. This was recognized as an unsatisfactory long term solution which would not be able to continue if hours were further reduced. In addition employees automatically covered for each other's absence, so any increase in holidays or reductions in the basic week would have led to increased overtime.

Management considered a variety of different shift systems before coming to the conclusion that a seven crew system was most appropriate. Although it was costly there were advantages for the company and its employees. As well as employees working the three traditional shifts, two 'spare' shifts are written into the rota. Employees on 'spare' shift are used first to cover absence and then work on other integrated duties. Some spare shifts are reduced to seven hours in order to accommodate the 39 hour week. For the employees, working hours have become more acceptable. They get two weekends off every seven week cycle, and one of these is a five day break. Only $2\frac{1}{4}$ weeks are worked in unsocial hours although they receive shift allowance all the time.

This system can cope with increased holidays and a shorter working week (as far as the mechanics are concerned) if they become part of the UK industrial scene. In order to establish the new system, several dayworkers had to be recruited to shift-work. The yard gang employed on day shift was abolished and shiftworkers are expected to do cleaning and simple maintenance work previously done by that gang. This new system means that the traditional antipathy between dayworkers and shift-workers should be diminished, and shiftworkers are given an additional sense of responsibility for their working environment. Now everyone shares because everyone is on the same hours ie $39 + 12\frac{1}{2}\%$ if necessary.

Pay

Pay rates are based on the existing national agreement. Management recognized that it was essential to get improved productivity to justify the new pay structure. In return for what amounted to an average increase of around five per cent in gross pay (ie including former average overtime earnings) employees had to undertake to work more flexibly.

The new 'Stable Income Plan' provides a guaranteed, regular and equalized level of earnings based on the annual hours contract of 2251 hours. On top of the basic rate for the 39 hour week there are: a 15 per cent integrated working allowance, the 15 per cent skills classification allowance (when four skills are acquired), the flexible hours payment, shift allowance and payments where a defined work pattern requires weekend working. The integrated working allowance incorporates a whole range of special payments and allowances paid previously. The only additional payments now come from a company wide productivity scheme and special payments to charge-hands and first aiders. Most previous earnings protection payments are superceded. Because the new levels include an average of former overtime earnings, most employees have increased their take home pay, although some had it reduced depending on the amount of overtime worked previously, but all employees will now work fewer hours than before. Hourly paid employees moved from weekly payment, mainly by cash, to payment by credit transfer every four weeks.

Holiday and sick pay provisions have been improved since under the Stable Income Plan, pay is maintained at the same level as when the employee is at work, whereas under the industry agreements previously applying, pay for holidays and sickness absence were at different levels.

Staff

The agreement for staff was negotiated separately with the British Cement Staffs Association which deals with all staff negotiations with the Company. Management originally took the view that since all hourly paid employees were on 39 hours the staff should be too. Previously staff hours varied from 42 to 37 per week plus overtime in many cases. At the end of the day it did not seem logical to increase working hours against the trend of reduced working weeks. So it was agreed that where applicable staff hours should be reduced to 39, but staff already working less than 39 hours a week should stay on their existing hours. All staff jobs were reappraised through the existing job evaluation system and new job descriptions issued; the redesignation yielded on average a one grade increase.

Staff at the two plants who were eligible for overtime

payments were extracted from the Blue Circle agreement on overtime and compensated by a five per cent exemption payment, a provision for which already existed for certain occupations. A further three per cent payment was made to all staff working at the two sites. If staff are transferred to other locations these payments cease and they return to the normal company arrangements. The changes have enabled the company to ensure that supervisors now work the same hours as their subordinates. There will be times when staff are required to work extra hours and management recognizes its responsibility to ensure these are distributed fairly.

Conclusions

The agreement was implemented at Cauldon in September 1985 and at Dunbar in January 1986. Although it is too early as yet to come to any conclusions about the impact on productivity, the indications are that there has been as much as a 50 per cent reduction in the time traditionally taken on tasks. At Cauldon, work which used to take five or six days to complete is now being done in three days, leaving extra time available for maintenance.

INTEGRATED WORKING

THE STABLE INCOME PLAN FOR INTEGRATED WORKING AT SINGLE STRAND PRE-CALCINER WORKS (SSPC)

CAULDON AND DUNBAR

Introduction
Integrated working will provide much greater scope for the employees to use their skills and abilities, and the Company wishes to broaden the opportunities for them to do so.

The new arrangements enable each retained employee to learn additional skills so that he is able to undertake as part of his normal duties, a wider range of tasks. Thus he becomes less restricted to a single operation and is able to make a positive contribution to all parts of the works operations through his added skills, versatility and co-operation.

The pay system described below brings all pay rates to a common basis. It will provide regular, equalised payments in exchange for a contracted number of hours and coupled with safeguards in case of sickness will result in better, stable incomes.

General Description

1. This Income Plan applies to retained employees paid under the terms and conditions of the NJIC or Craft Committee agreements and such terms and conditions shall continue with application and supplementation as set out in the following paragraphs and appendices.

2. Persons who have qualified for full holiday entitlement and who are employed under this income plan will be paid for 2251 hours* in 12 calendar months commencing 6 am on April 1st each year. Of this figure, 1786 hours forms the basic defined work pattern component with 2009 hours being the maximum working time should operational requirements so demand, the balance being the annual and public holiday components.

* 45 working weeks and 4 days at 39 hours per week	1786
23 days annual holiday plus 8 public holidays at 39 hours per week	242
Minimum hours	2028
Built in flexible time at $12\frac{1}{2}$% of 1786 hours	223
Contract hours (maximum)	2251

N.B. In a leap year; and where the number of public holidays in a scheme year varies because Easter is a moveable feast; and depending on how the 7×3 shift cycle relates to the start and finish of the scheme year, the components of the 2251 hours will be adjusted accordingly, but the maximum contract hours and built-in flexible hours will not exceed 2251 and 223 hours respectively.

When a person joins the Company during a scheme year, and/ or he has not earned the full holiday entitlement, the contract hours will be pro-rated in proportion to the defined work pattern days available (i.e. after taking account of public and annual holiday entitlement). When absence occurs due to holidays, certified sickness, bereavement leave, training courses, recognised Trade Union duties and approved public duties, the annual contract hours available to be worked will be reduced by the defined work pattern hours for those days concerned.

To avoid excessive accumulation of contract hours, management will programme employee attendance so that normally a person will work not less than his defined work pattern of 39 hours each working week (average 39 hours for 7×3 shift-workers). The extra flexible time element of 223 hours in the contract will be used as operations require, but will be scheduled within limits which provide employee safeguards without restricting the operating of the works.

There will continue to be a time recording system.

3. Stable Income Payments will incorporate all existing payments both for defined pattern working and those which are earned as extra items over and above defined pattern earnings. The payments will incorporate:

   a. a skills classification allowance which recognises the range of extra skills to be learnt both within and additional to the employees main discipline, and which will not be paid until the requisite standards have been attained.

   b. a composite SSPC integrated working allowance to accommodate the various extra payments listed in paragraph 6 below which will no longer be paid as extras and to recognise the variety of activities that the employee will undertake using his acquired skills, and the improved co-operation and attitude.

4. Payments will all be related to nationally negotiated rates as shown in the attachment. Stable Income payments will apply in all normal employment circumstances, whether the employee is working, on holiday, sick or absent with permission for other reasons, for the period of eligibility specified in the national agreements for each circumstance.

   Payments will therefore be constant except in the following circumstances:

   a. When entitlement to sickness payment is exhausted under the rules of the sickness scheme.

   b. If the employee takes unpaid absence.

    c. In circumstances defined under rule 18, clauses (b) and (c) of the NJIC and Craft Committee agreements.

    d. When undertaking a temporary change of duties as defined in Appendix VII, rule 8.

    e. When requisite skill standards have not been attained.

5. Payments will be made under credit transfer arrangements direct to a bank or other account at 4-weekly intervals (initially payments at Cauldon and Dunbar will be made at 2-weekly intervals).

6. The following national and company payments and allowances have been incorporated into the composite SSPC integrated working allowance:

Working on Customary Holidays
Recalls to Duty
Crane Allowances
Lieu Day Payments
Craft Grade 1 and 2 Personal Protection Payments
Abnormal Condition Payments
Kiln Repair and other incentive bonus payments
Unsocial Hours Payments
Christmas Day Working

Therefore with the exception of those items in paragraph 7 below, no payments or allowances will be made in addition to the Stable Income Payments.

7. Supervisory and first-aid allowances will be paid independently to those qualifying for such payments. Earnings protection payments are treated separately in the attachment. Continuity Bonus and Productivity payments will be made in accordance with the respective agreements.

8. All Process/Plant trainees will be paid as Plant Attendants but excluding the skills classification allowance until they are qualified and allocated to a particular employment category.

Craftsmen who are not cross-traded will not receive the skills classification allowance until they have attained the necessary qualification standards (See attachment to Appendix IV.)

9. The supply and cleaning of overalls will be in accordance with the appropriate clauses in the NJIC and Craft Committee agreements.

10. The wearing of safety helmets and safety footwear in the manufacturing environment and the equipment designated for use in specific areas will be a condition of employment,

reflecting the varied duties and departments in which each employee may work. The safety footwear subsidy will continue to be paid each year to each employee at the national rate, and additionally each year there will be an issue of one pair of safety boots for emergency purposes. This is apart from statutory and other requirements to provide suitable protective equipment.

11. List of appendices:
    Work Patterns
    Job Classification
    Annual Hours and Attendance Scheduling

INTEGRATED WORKING

SINGLE STRAND PRE-CALCINER OPERATIONS—WORK PATTERNS

The Works will continue to utilise daywork and 2-shift work patterns, and its continuous operations will be serviced by a new 7×3 shift pattern of which an example is set out below.

Week/crew	M	T	W	T	F	S	S	Hours
1	M	M	M	M	M	—	—	40/40
2	—	A	A	A	A	A	A	48/60
3	A	—	—	N	N	N	N	40/52
4	N	N	N	—	—	S	S	40/52
5	S+	S+	S+	S	S	—	—	37/37
6	—	—	—	S+	S+	S	S	30/42
7	S	S+	S+	—	H	M	M	38/50
								39/47.57

1. S= Spare day used to cover shift absence or to undertake other integrated working duties. Days marked+to be 7 hours to yield average 39 hour week over 7 week cycle.

2. On any day for each position, there will be one man on morning shift, one on afternoon shift, one on night shift, two men resting and two men on spare man duties.

3. Shift payments made for each working day, whether on shift or spare day duties; 8 hour shifts except where marked+.

4. Shift activities grouped apart from spare days. 5 weeks out of 7 are worked under daytimo conditions in normal circumstances. Two weekends off in 7 weeks, one of which forms part of 5 consecutive days off, rest periods in all other weeks.

INTEGRATED WORKING

SINGLE STRAND PRE-CALCINER OPERATIONS: JOB CLASSIFICATION

General: Within their competency, all personnel, whatever their classification will be required to:

    (i) carry out any duty with due regard to relevant safety regulations, policies and safe working practices,

    (ii) work without direct supervision,

and (iii) assist other personnel as necessary in any part of the Works.

A. PROCESS OPERATIONS

1. Senior Process Operator

Essential Education, Training and Experience

Technical education or training to a recognised standard. Extensive knowledge and comprehension of the entire works process. General maintenance knowledge, skills and experience. Supervisory and training skills or experience. General driving skills.

Main duties

To control and operate a wide range of process plant and equipment. To apply maintenance knowledge and skills. To drive a range of mobile plant and equipment as required. To direct continuity of plant operation or maintenance work as necessary. Undertake semi-skilled and unskilled work wherever required.

2. **Process/Plant Operator**

Essential Education Training and Skills

A good general education. A thorough knowledge of the works process. General driving skills or a thorough knowledge and understanding of works mobile and fixed plant and a high degree of driving skills. First line maintenance skills and experience.

Main duties

To operate all plant and equipment within any section of the process and drive a range of mobile plant; or to drive all mobile and fixed plant within a section of the works or process, and drive any other mobile plant and equipment as necessary. To carry out first line maintenance on plant and equipment. To undertake semi-skilled and unskilled work wherever required.

3. **Plant Attendant**

Essential Education, Training and Experience

A general education. A general knowledge of the plant and process.

Main duties

To attend to and assist with the operation of all works fixed and mobile plant and equipment. To undertake any unskilled work wherever required.

B. **MAINTENANCE AND REPAIR OPERATIONS**

Engineering Craftsmen (Cross-traded)

Essential Education, Training and Experience

Recognised technical training with relevant qualifications. Cross-trading training or experience in other specified skills and disciplines. A thorough (main discipline) knowledge of all works plant and machinery. A knowledge of process operations and skills. General driving skills. General supervisory and training skills.

Main duties

To maintain and repair works plant and equipment using main discipline skills and cross-traded skills. To supervise repair and maintenance work as required and train others in maintenance skills. To drive a range of mobile plant and equipment. To apply process skills and knowledge in undertaking semi-skilled work and to carry out unskilled work if circumstances require.

INTEGRATED WORKING

ENGINEERING CRAFTSMEN

1. Introduction

There has been, over the years, a blurring of the edges where one craft stopped and another started, and this is further highlighted by apprentice training which teaches a whole range of basic skills before specialisation occurs.

The Company needs to make use of craftsmen who are more versatile than before and whose time and skills can be used to the fullest extent without undue delays.

2. Objectives

In order to achieve maximum utilisation of craft resources, a fundamental requirement is that craftsmen must be competent to practice their basic trade together with added skills in any part of the Works. Therefore all craftsmen who are selected must already possess, or have the potential to possess, a number of added skills to a defined standard.

It is recognised that the achievement of the agreed objective of full versatility will need to be progressed beyond commissioning and that its implementation will help to minimise the need for flexible hours.

The first step to the objective, however, is to ensure that each person employed in a main category will, in addition to his basic skill, have acquired at least four added skills, one of which will be in another main category. In the case of Engineering Craftsmen (Mechanical) the added skill in another main category as part of the first step, will be isolation. These attainments will qualify for the 15% skills classification allowance, subject to continuing to train to achieve full versatility and satisfy the terms of the definition.

3. **Main Categories and Specified Skills**

   Main Categories

   Engineering Craftsman (Mechanical)
   Engineering Craftsman (Electrical)
   Engineering Craftsman (Process Control)
   Engineering Craftsman (Vehicle Repair)

   Basic or Added Skills to specified trade or module
   standard, i.e. not every skill necessarily to trade standard.

   Mechanical Maintenance and Repair
   Electrical Maintenance and Repair
   Process Control Maintenance and Repair
   Vehicle Maintenance and Repair
   Fitting
   Turning
   General Machining
   Slinging and Rigging
   Isolation
   Pipe Fitting and Plumbing
   Fabrication
   Hydraulics
   Pneumatics
   Mobile Plant Operation
   Process Plant Operation
   Erecting
   Scaffolding
   Gas Cutting
   Gas Welding
   Arc Welding
   Mobile Plant Maintenance and Repair
   Auto-Electrics
   PLC Fault Finding
   Electronics

   Existing occupational classification and job titles will no
   longer be separately identified.

4. **Applying the Skills**

   It is anticipated that, in normal circumstances, an engineering
   craftsman will practice his basic trade for around 75–85% of his
   time with the remainder being spent upon added skills. In the
   great majority of cases these will be used in association with
   work requiring use of the basic skill. Those tools necessary to
   undertake added skills, other than those which a craftsman is
   expected to own so as to practice his basic trade, will be
   provided by the Company on a loan basis.

INTEGRATED WORKING

FIRST LINE MAINTENANCE

First line maintenance duties covering both preventative and repair activities will be undertaken by both craftsmen and process personnel, giving due regard to safety requirements, policies and safe working practice as set out in the General Statement at the commencement of Appendix IV. Such activities can best be illustrated by examples, all of which fall within an overall description which involves the use of simple hand tools such as:

Screwdrivers
Spanners
Pipe Wrenches
Hammers
Grease Guns
Single Phase Electric Tools
Saws
Chisels
Belt Repair Equipment
General Cleaning and Painting Equipment
Small Jacks and Chain Hoists
Gas Cutters/Torches

Thus, a selection of jobs that would be categorised under the first-line maintenance activities would include:

Belt tracking, splicing and emergency repairs
Lubrication to defined standards
Changing sensing devices and probes
Changing cooler plates
Routine painting
Packing glands on pumps
Changing fuses on electric plugs and rewiring (110v)
Changing PLC cards from indicated fault location
Replacing refractory brick lining
Isolation
Changing Mill Liner Plates
Routine Mobile Plant Maintenance
Dust Plant Repairs/Servicing
Lifting/Rigging
Scaffolding
Lubricating

The tools necessary to undertake first-line maintenance will be provided by the Company on a loan basis, except where a craftsman undertakes work with tools which he would be expected to own so as to practice his basic trade.

INTEGRATED WORKING

ANNUAL HOURS, FLEXIBLE HOURS AND
ATTENDANCE SCHEDULING

Annual Hours

An individual will accumulate 'attendance' towards his annual contract on the following basis:

1. When at work—according to the defined start and finish times of the work pattern. When flexible time is worked, the additional hours must be authorised by the supervisor. When lateness occurs (i.e. less than one shift) no deduction will be made and the lost hours will be required to be made up unless otherwise instructed by management. Disciplinary procedure may be applied.

2. When absent due to holidays, certified sickness, bereavement leave, agreed training courses, recognised Trade Unions duties and approved public duties, 'attendance' will accumulate at the rate of the defined work pattern hours for those days concerned.

3. Unauthorised absence will result in the loss of pay for each day involved, but the defined work pattern hours for each day will be credited.

Four Tiers of Protection

The Company recognises that there must be a proper structure and reasonable safeguards for employees in regard to the use of flexible time which is built into the annual hours component of the Stable Income Plan. The employees will realise that any structure must cope with the varying situations that are likely to occur at any cement works.

To this end, the Company will apply four tiers of protection:

1. Joint planning and periodic review meetings supported by individual monitoring and employee advice.

2. Mandatory limits which restrict the amount of time any employee might be asked to attend in specified periods.

3. Provisions for a reduction in the amount of flexible time available for the remainder of a scheme year in certain circumstances.

4. A statement of Company intent regarding the standards it will aim to uphold, and the standards it expects of the employees.

1. **Joint Planning and Periodic Meetings;
    Individual Monitoring and Employee Advice**

    Prior to the commencement of each scheme year (1st April);
    Works Management and employee representatives will hold
    an overall preview meeting to discuss and plan what events
    and demands on attendance may be required in the forthcom-
    ing year (e.g. major kiln repairs, Christmas working).

    During the year, at quarterly intervals, further joint meetings
    will review the scheduling of flexible time in the previous
    period, recommend where improvements in the methods of
    scheduling employees individually could be made, and update
    the original overall preview.

    Records will be available to each employee to show how many
    annual hours he has accumulated as the scheme year pro-
    gresses, clearly identifying the flexible hours, so that the use of
    this time is as closely balanced between individuals as pos-
    sible to provide the fairest situation in practice. The accumu-
    lation of hours will be notified to each employee at regular
    intervals.

    Further records will be kept to show the number of occasions
    when individuals work on rest days, are 'called out' or work on
    a public holiday, again with the aim of ensuring fairness.

2. **Flexible Hours Attendance with Mandatory Limits**

    Mandatory limits will save any employee from working ex-
    cessive amounts of flexible time in particular periods, except
    when a force majeure situation prevails (see below). This does
    not mean that employees will be required to work up to these
    limits each time—merely that when they are asked to work
    flexible time, they will not be asked or permitted to work
    beyond these times.

    The mandatory limits will mean that no one will be permitted
    to work more than:

    a. 16 flexible hours in any 2 day period

    b. 66 flexible hours in any 12 day period

    c. 76 flexible hours in any 28 day period

    d. 120 flexible hours in any 13 weeks

    e. 223 flexible hours in a full scheme year

    If a 7 hour break cannot be taken between the finish of the last
    period of work on any day and the start time of the next
    defined pattern work day, then authorised absence will be

granted for the defined work pattern of the following day. Where the following day is a rest day, a 7 hour break must have been taken before any work is undertaken on that rest day.

(British Summer Time—The 1 hour change to and from this period will be disregarded for flexible hour mandatory limit purposes.)

In addition to the above, three further mandatory limits will be applied.

f. No one would be asked to attend more than 20 rest days in any scheme year, and no more than two consecutive rest day periods as defined in the work pattern, either in whole or part.

g. Any person who works for more than 14 consecutive days will not be asked to attend on any of the next four rest days as defined within the work pattern.

h. Defined work pattern hours cannot offset flexible hours or vice versa, (except when a leap year occurs and subject to where the start of a scheme year relates to the 7×3 shift cycle).

Force Majeure—In the face of a major emergency—flood, landslide, explosion etc.—the flexible time scheduling system would be suspended. As soon as possible, the parties would meet do discuss the resetting of the scheduling system and to deal with any exhaustion of the contract hours.

3. **Flexible Time Reductions**

The system described below will be applied to gradually reduce the employees contractual commitments over the year when little or no flexible time has been used in the early part of a scheme year, without limiting the works operations and repair requirements.

The system has been designed to keep sufficient hours in reserve in the earlier part of the year so as to meet possible demands in the later part of the year, whilst at the same time ensuring that an employee cannot be asked to provide all the flexible hours for a full scheme year in the final months of that year.

The table shows the maximum number of flexible hours that can be contracted at any point in time for the remaining months of the year, assuming that little or no flexible time has been used up to that date, by reducing the contract requirements. The scheme, however, falls within two main rules:

a. No one can work more than 223 flexible hours in a scheme year.

b. When applicable the mandatory limits described in section 2 will also apply.

	Limit on use of outstanding flexible hours in a scheme year
Start of year	223
End of: April	223
May	221
June	218
July	213
August	205
September	194
October	179
November	160
December	137
January	109
February	76
March	0

4. Statement of Company Intent and Employee Obligations

Employees will be obliged to meet their contractual requirements up to 223 flexible hours, subject to the above protection arrangements. In addition, management will endeavour:

a. to minimise the use of flexible time. It would be considered against the spirit of the agreement to seek attendance unreasonably and without proper explanation of the requirement.

b. to share 'call-outs' and working rest days and public holidays as equally as possible;

c. to share all flexible time requirements as fairly as possible;

d. whenever possible, to give a minimum of 24 hours notice to attend.

Management acknowledges that exceptionally, an employee's prior commitments may restrict his availability to work flexible time on that occasion, without absolving him from the responsibility of working his fair share.

2 Five principles—the vehicle for change and overtime elimination at British Caledonian Airways Limited

The company was formed in November 1970 as the result of a merger between Caledonian Airways and British United Airways and became British Caledonian Airways in November 1971. In May 1985, the company employed 7262 people. The company is part of the Caledonian Aviation Group plc with interests in airline operations and the travel and hotel business.

Background to the changes

Against a background of greater competitiveness in the airline industry, in part brought about by increasing deregulation, the Board of Directors initiated an extensive policy review of its operations in 1983. As a result, the board committed the company to the objectives of creating an airline with a highly paid workforce, but with the lowest unit labour costs, in order to be a fully effective competitor in the airline industry.

The three key aims of the policy review were:

- to become the best airline in the world
- to provide service to the point of obsession
- to make a giant stride in people relations

The achievement of change in the existing climate of industrial relations was seen as fundamental to the achievement of these aims.

Industrial relations background

The workforce is subdivided into seven bargaining units, as follows:

- engineering and maintenance staff
- surface transport and goods handling
- supervisory engineers and technical
- air cabin crew
- clerical; staff/supervisory
- flight engineers
- pilots

The achievement of the company's longer term industrial relations objectives would require separate negotiations with each of these groups since the issues to be resolved varied between them. It was coincidental that in order to keep the task within manageable proportions, changes to existing arrangements would first be negotiated with the engineering and maintenance staff (E&M). Having established a set of basic principles with all negotiation groups these could then be generally applied in negotiations.

The E&M staff group consists of unskilled, semi skilled and craft employees below supervisory level and the following unions are recognized within the bargaining unit: AUEW, EETPU, TASS, FTAT, GMBATU, UCATT and TGWU. The issues to be resolved within this group included the following:

- industrial relations characterized by traditional confrontation between management and union representatives
- informal, spoken agreements between managers and shop stewards, supplemented by numerous formal, written agreements
- demarcation lines between different groups of employees
- a complex wage structure with over 100 pay elements, supplements and allowances
- relatively high levels of overtime working
- unstable and fluctuating earnings levels
- a commitment already given to reduce the basic working week from 39 to $37\frac{1}{2}$ hours

Establishing industrial relations objectives

In order to achieve the changes sought, a team was established consisting of the director responsible for industrial relations, an industrial relations manager supplemented by appropriate line managers. Five principles were developed as a vehicle to meet the desired objectives:

- security
- mutual trust
- involvement
- people matter
- co-operation

Stemming from these principles, a number of negotiating objectives were established in order to give effect to them. These included:

- the rationalization of the wage structure to provide stable salaries in place of the traditional fluctuating wage levels previously based on hourly rates, supplements and overtime
- the abolition of overtime as such, but with a provision for extended time to meet 'emergencies', and the commitment to cover the task in an average of $37\frac{1}{2}$ hours as had previously been achieved in 39 hours plus overtime, ie substantial increases in productivity
- greater flexibility in working arrangements, with removal of demarcation always within the limits of safety and training and a greater willingness to take on a wider range of tasks, as the need arose
- further moves towards the harmonization of terms and conditions of employment
- development of a different management style enabling the greater involvement of individuals and representatives in making inputs to decision making machinery in order to achieve better decisions and enhance the climate of trust and co-operation

Introducing the changes

With the full support of the board for the objectives outlined, the process of preparing the ground prior to negotiation commenced during 1983. The set of proposals were entitled 'The Way Ahead' and initially seminars and workshops were held with line managers to examine in detail their implications. Changes in attitudes are rarely instantaneous and the proposals were initially met with some scepticism. Considerable efforts were put into this discussion process, not least because they placed greater onus upon managers to plan and organize work more effectively without relying upon additional overtime to get tasks done. Following this, extensive briefing sessions and workshops were held with the shop stewards and trade union officials and eventually, commitment was given to the five principles underlying the approach. All the employees concerned were then briefed in small groups reinforced by video, prior to the formal negotiations and a leaflet describing the broad philosophy was published and distributed.

Joint sessions of managers and shop stewards were then held prior to the commencement of formal negotiations to discuss the proposals in more detail. Negotiations started in November 1984 and the agreement was eventually agreed and implemented in July 1985. After concluding the negotiations, joint workshops were held with all the employees involved in order to brief them in detail on what had been agreed before a ballot was conducted.

The achievements of the agreement

Some of the key achievements may be summarized as follows:

- the elimination of overtime: it was agreed that extended time would be worked in an emergency, but that it would be compensated only by time off in lieu to maintain an average of $37\frac{1}{2}$ hours
- the consolidation of nearly all pay elements into annual salaries, paid on a weekly basis; it was hoped to get agreement to monthly payment by credit transfer, but this was not given high priority and in the event was not

agreed. It was agreed that a small number of additional allowances would be retained: shift pay, call out pay, standby pay, an allowance for working away from base and first aid money

- a rationalization of the number of grades, with jobs being more broadly defined so as to achieve greater flexibility
- the removal of demarcation always within the limitations of safety and training
- the reduction of the basic working week from 39 to $37\frac{1}{2}$ hours, with no increase in workforce size and no increase in unit labour costs
- further moves towards harmonization in such areas as holiday and sick pay entitlements
- employees and shop stewards making their contribution through involvement prior to discussions being made, examples of which included:

    joint departmental discussion and problem solving groups to promote efficiency, safety improvements

    joint investigations by managers and shop stewards where there were failures to achieve required standards

    the establishment of a joint Disciplinary and Grievance Appeals Panel, consisting of line manager, industrial relations manager and shop steward

    greater reliance on trust and co-operation, working without (constant) supervision, with more responsibility devolved to employees to organize their own work and the work of the people needed to assist them

Key factors in achieving a successful outcome

- full commitment from the board
- the establishment of carefully planned objectives
- extensive briefing, consultation and negotiation with all those involved
- attractive reward package involving higher, stable salaries, harmonization of benefits and shorter working hours
- changes in management style which encourage mutual trust and the greater involvement of employees and representatives in future decision making

Conclusions and future developments

The company points out that the agreement is a radical departure from traditional industrial agreements and negotiating the agreement is only the beginning. The agreement provides a system in which involvement, co-operation and trust can flourish to ensure the challenges of the future can be met. The response has been encouraging with major changes in attitude, co-operation and flexibility. The company stresses that the amount of time involved in making such a change is substantial and should not be under-estimated. The company's next task is to extend 'The Way Ahead' agreement to the other bargaining groups mentioned previously.

3 Annual hours and five crew shiftworking at Continental Can Limited

Continental Can is an American owned company which manufactures two-piece cans for the beer and soft drinks market. It started production at its Wrexham site in 1980. There are now 255 employees, all employed on the same terms and conditions and all members of the TGWU, except for eight senior managers. This is a continuous process industry, and 165 of the employees at Wrexham work shifts.

From the start there has been a single union agreement and common terms and conditions throughout the plant. Since the original agreement there have been two major innovations. In 1983, integrated job evaluation was introduced, and in 1985, the plant moved to five shift working.

Background

At the time of opening, there were talks with several unions, but the TGWU was eventually chosen because it had a good reputation locally, and a full time official based in the area. The agreement with TGWU was radical when it was introduced, although it is less so now. Management recognizes that it was easier to negotiate such an agreement for a greenfield site than at an established plant, but the employees still had traditional attitudes towards work which the company has tried to change.

One of the ways in which the company is trying to change

233

attitudes is in its relationship with the union. Representatives
are called 'employee reps' rather than union reps. Meetings with
the union are kept to a minimum—normally they are held
quarterly. The full time official was originally entitled to attend
quarterly meetings as of right, but following a request from the
employee reps, he now only comes by invitation. For example, he
was brought in by the employees for negotiations on job evaluation and five crew working as his experience was much broader
than the representatives and he also had some knowledge of job
evaluation in local companies.

The management philosophy is to 'keep moving', in the
belief that if working practices are not constantly reviewed,
'traditional' practices will become established and overmanning
and demarcation could reappear. As a consequence, there is a
very strong management commitment to training, partly to
prevent 'custom and practice' developing, but in the main to
ensure that the job is being done in accordance with requirements.

All employees at the plant receive an annual salary, paid
monthly by credit transfer. There are no additional payments
except for overtime. There is no clocking on for any employees.

There was a five year plan for the plant which included job
evaluation, a reduction in working time and the eventual elimination of overtime. The first two have been achieved. Overtime
has been reduced, but not yet eliminated.

Five crew working

Five crew working was introduced as part of a two year agreement which included an annual hours contract, a reduction in
weekly hours to 39 with no loss of earnings and a 10 per cent
salary increase.

Since 1982 management had come under increasing pressure
to reduce working hours. Dayworkers were on a 40 hour week
and those on shift worked 42 hours including two hours contractual overtime. Management said it was not prepared to make a
'cosmetic' reduction in working hours ie to give one shift off
every six weeks (which would require cover) or to increase
overtime. There was, however, concern that if management did
not face up to the issue, reduced working hours might be forced
upon the company by union pressure and the company would not

necessarily get the best from it. Management therefore started to investigate alternative shift systems in continuous process industries.

Management was aware that there was already a gap between the working hours required and the hours a person was available. Already, holiday and absence cover plus the two hours contractual overtime were costing around 15 per cent overtime. If hours were reduced, there would have to be a radical change if further increases in overtime were to be avoided.

A change to five crew working would have reduced weekly hours to 33.6 per week, so management decided to include holidays in the roster to bring weekly hours up to 36. In addition, crews would be rostered for extra maintenance shifts every month or two to bring their hours up to an average of 39 per week. These shifts, which last 12 hours, are used for several purposes. Every month each of the four production lines has to be shut down for routine maintenance. The whole shift is bought in and while some employees work on maintenance, others take the opportunity to do tasks which cannot be fitted in during normal working hours.

The company used the services of consultants to design several alternative shift systems. Formerly employees had been working 12 hour shifts, but the workforce was divided, with some in favour of 12 hour shifts and others preferring to revert to eight hours. The new five crew system, jointly chosen by employee representatives and management, has a combination of eight and 12 hour shifts, which it was thought would please everybody. To everyone's surprise, when it was put to ballot, it was rejected overwhelmingly.

Management was not prepared to give up at this stage, so it spent a further two months explaining the system to employees and trying to convince them to support it. A 30 page document was produced for employees. Management gave an undertaking that, once five crew shiftworking was established, a joint working party would meet with a view to producing a revised version of the rota. In a second ballot, the change was approved by a small majority. With hindsight, management believes that it should have done more early on to 'sell' the new system to employees, rather than leaving this to the employee reps who were not always able to answer detailed questions from employees.

During the first year, two new shift systems were jointly designed by employee representatives and management and put to employees with necessary explanations. After a ballot, there was a majority of employees in favour of eight hour shifts.

One of the reasons why employees who had previously requested 12 hour shifts changed their views was that the move to five crew working was achieved with almost no increase in staff. In total, five extra employees were recruited, including a new shift supervisor. The fifth crew was created by substantially reducing crew numbers on the four existing crews. One of the results of the reduction in manning was that work became more onerous and employees found it more difficult to cope on a 12 hour shift system.

Another reason for the rejection of 12 hour shift patterns was that they had provided employees with four-day breaks, but this was lost with a combined eight and 12 hour rota. With five crew working, employees could have four-day breaks when they worked eight hour shifts. The new rota is based on six, eight hour shifts, followed by four days off. The four days are reduced to three when employees work a 12 hour 'maintenance' shift.

The current roster has all the holidays built into the system, except for 48 hours (six shifts) known as 'floating' hours which can be taken off at any time during the year with management's agreement. Eighteen shifts are taken off in the summer and the plant closes for Christmas and New Year. Management thought that denying employees the opportunity to choose when to take their holidays might have been unpopular, but this has not been so. The next year's rota is issued well in advance so that people know when their holidays are and can book their holiday travel.

Shiftwork employees (some 75 per cent of total) work a shift rota which requires the crew to provide cover for 1825.58 hours per year, out of which each person has to attend work for 1777.58 hours per year, ie each person can take 40 hours off with pay. The person's annual hours contract is therefore to follow the shift rota on 1825.58 hours per year and to attend work as follows:

Basic hours	1777.58 hours (paid)
+ paid for	48.00 hours (time off)
+ paid for	64.00 hours (public holidays)
+ paid for	144.00 hours (fixed holidays)
	2033.58 hours paid/per annum

$2033.58 \div 52.143$ weeks/year = average 39 hour week.

Day staff are also on an annual hours contract, but are free to choose when to take their holidays in consultation with management. They work 9.00am to 5.00pm Mondays to Thursdays and 9.00am to 4.30pm on Fridays. They used to have more flexible hours, but start and finish times have now been standardized.

Results

One result of the introduction of five crew working was a drop in overtime from 16 to eight per cent. It is now possible to cover for most absence and odd days of holiday without overtime by working short crewed. Only one to two per cent of overtime goes on absence cover, the rest is used for project work and training.

Because of the reduction in overtime, there was a saving on payroll costs. This paid for the 10 per cent salary increase and the increase in overtime rates brought about by the reduction in working hours with maintenance of earnings. Therefore the package was mostly self financing.

The biggest advantage of the new system as far as management is concerned is that working patterns are established which should last for the next 10 years. The new shift system would allow weekly hours to be reduced to 33 if necessary, but at this level all the holidays and maintenance days could not be built into the rota.

Administration has been considerably simplified by the introduction of rostered holidays. One of the consequences of rostered holidays and annual hours is that new employees qualify immediately for holidays on their roster, but employees who leave do not qualify for holidays if they leave before the dates of their crew's holiday period.

The future

On the principle of 'keeping moving', management is considering several changes for the future. One possibility is that the job evaluation scheme might be changed to allow for more individual recognition, for example by allowing employees to qualify for extra payment by acquiring new skills.

The elimination of overtime pay is a high priority and the company would be prepared to eliminate overtime payment, but it is thought that overtime levels will have to be further reduced to less than five per cent before this is worth discussing formally with the representatives.

Linked with the reduction of overtime, management believes that it can also attain a simpler salary structure. Although sickness absence has been consistently low at around

$2\frac{1}{2}$ per cent since the plant opened, management would like to do away with the belief that people are 'entitled' to be ill. If a guaranteed salary were paid and overtime pay were abolished, it would also make sense to consider the need for having separate provisions for sick pay. It would also make the administration of the payroll considerably easier. Employees would have security of earnings and there would be a greater discipline on management to deal with persistent absenteeism. The removal of a sick pay scheme in favour of a guaranteed annual salary is more difficult to come to terms with, partly because of State sick pay arrangements and partly because it is such a major step forward that it needs to be considered very carefully. The company believes it must strive to gain total commitment from every employee and that all that it has done so far merely provides the mechanisms and removes the barriers: the real task is to establish the relationship between its supervisors and its employees which will bring about the commitment.

4 Annual hours and five crew shiftworking at Don & Low plc

Don & Low plc is part of the Don Brothers, Buist Group and manufactures industrial textiles. The original family business was founded in 1794. Its main business was jute manufacture until 1960 when the company branched out into the manufacture of polypropylene, an oil based product which is now established as the standard backing material for carpets.

The move from jute to polypropylene has involved very high levels of capital investment by the company in recent years, and has meant a move away from a labour intensive to a capital intensive structure. The company has ceased to be a traditional textile manufacturer and now runs a modern continuous process industry. The high capital cost of the equipment has meant that it is imperative to keep the machinery in operation for as many hours as possible.

The company has 1300 employees based at several sites in Tayside. There are 1100 weekly paid employees of whom between 600 and 700 are shiftworkers. Three hundred are monthly paid employees. The workforce is roughly 40 per cent female, 60 per cent male. The TGWU is the main union, although there are just over 100 AEU members and a further 70/80 in a specialist technician union.

Background

Until January 1986 the company worked a four shift continental system with employees working 42 hours a week (including two hours rostered overtime). Basic pay was for the 42 hour week plus a flat rate shift disturbance allowance. Additional overtime was around five per cent,

The company was operating for 46.4 weeks a year with traditional shutdowns for Christmas, summer, spring and autumn holidays. Shiftworkers received a total of 30 days holiday, non shiftworkers 29 days.

In January 1986 a new five shift system was introduced following an 18 month period of research, development and then negotiation within the company.

In 1984 management found itself under increasing pressure to reduce working hours. Most companies in the local area had already reduced the working week, so management agreed in principle to a reduction to 39 hours the following year.

Management felt it had two options if the working week were to be effectively reduced. Either it could keep the existing four shift system and build in extra days off which would entail employing more staff to cover, or it could try to find a system which would increase production time to as near 52 weeks a year as possible while still giving employees an increase in leisure time.

The union was looking for an increase in leisure time without any loss of income and a roster which would give more leisure time at the weekend.

The unions were invited to join a working party to examine the possibilities, but they declined saying they preferred to receive proposals from management and negotiate at that stage.

A senior management team was set up to examine the options available. An intensive period of research followed with members studying the available literature, attending seminars at the Industrial Society and visiting several other companies for detailed discussions. Shift systems at five companies were examined in detail.

Management decided that it wanted to go for a five shift system and to increase operating time by having only one shutdown period at Christmas. At this stage a specialist shift-working analyst was brought in to give advice. He was given all the company's requirements as regards holiday periods etc and created two alternative shift systems for management to examine. After some changes to give equal numbers of morning, afternoon and night shifts over the year to all employees, management chose the system which has now been implemented. The rejected system gave shorter breaks. The analyst has now computed the rosters for the next five years. Shifts are given a different roster each year so that popular holiday times are fairly distributed.

Consultation and negotiation

Management was in the process of carrying out a training exercise for supervisors, so it was decided to present the new proposals to the supervisors, in confidence, as part of their training in order to get some initial reactions.

Management made a presentation to the supervisors outlining its preferred choice and offering as an alternative the system used at one of the companies visited in the petrochemical industry which gives much more intensive periods of work and longer periods off. It was thought that this system would be less attractive because it was more suited to the all male workforce in the petrochemical industry. The supervisors came back with their comments a week later and nearly all were in favour of management's choice. They did, however, offer several constructive observations and comments.

Their main concern was that 213 shifts were rostered, whereas a 39 hour week required 226 shifts to be worked. At that stage management was expecting all 13 shifts to be 'paid back'. This, it was thought, would have a significant effect in reducing overtime. The supervisors said it would be impossible to fit in 13 payback shifts in the year.

Given the reaction of the supervisors, management decided to present only their preferred option to the workforce. Meetings were set up with the trade unions and the company's joint consultative committee at which management gave a presentation and distributed written handouts on the new system. Then the proposals were taken to plant level, where line managers explained them to each shift. Management said that the proposals had to be accepted as a package, but it was prepared to negotiate on wages and payback shifts.

Surprisingly, there was little hostility to the loss of traditional holidays, but there was employee concern about the level of wages and the payback shifts. Employees also asked to be able to consider an alternative system.

It was decided that in order to strengthen the newly formed joint consultative committee, it would be given the chance to consider the options and would be asked to report back to management. When the employee representatives returned, they reported that four out of five plants favoured the five shift system preferred by management.

Negotiations then began with the unions. Management proposed that current earnings should be maintained, with the overtime factor consolidated to give a higher shift disturbance allowance. In return, management proposed that manning should not be increased pro-rata when the fifth shift was introduced. Management wanted to increase the workforce by 15 to 20 per cent (instead of 25 per cent) by the use of more flexible manning. The unions accepted the offer on wages and it was established that manning would be increased by 18 per cent for shift operations. For day operations there would be no increase in manpower although they were also to reduce their working hours to 39 per week. They were told they would have to work out a roster for holidays which provided adequate day service cover.

On payback shifts, the unions agreed that the extra 13 shifts should in theory be worked, but argued that it was not practical to do so. They also accepted that a reduction in overtime should be sought. Management said it was prepared to concede on payback shifts to the level of a 38 hour week. It was agreed that five payback shifts should be worked at short notice to cover for absence and emergencies. Two further payback shifts would be pre-planned and used for training which would be of benefit both to the employee and the company. Payback shifts would be monitored by local management weekly and a printout would be available monthly. Employees would not be asked to work more than two payback shifts a month, but a responsible attitude was necessary and more than one refusal to work a payback shift was not expected from individual employees. Management insisted that despite its concessions on payback shifts, the 39 hour week was still the point from which negotiations would start in the future. Employees were being paid for a 39 hour week, and day staff work 39 hours.

Conclusions

The new system was introduced in January 1986 and, so far, is reported to be working smoothly. As a result, 120 new jobs were created. Forty were filled internally because of the closure of one unit, and there were 1000 applicants for the remaining 80 new jobs. So far, the overtime bill has been reduced by half.

The company estimates that there will be an increase in production of between nine and 10 per cent because of the longer working time. All things being equal, management estimates that there will be a net surplus on the exercise despite the fact that manning has been increased by 18 per cent and the working week cut by three hours. It is hoped that the net surplus may be doubled if other possible cost savings are achieved. These might come from reduced absence and more labour stability because of greater leisure time. There should also be a reduction in maintenance problems because a more sophisticated preventative maintenance system has been introduced since there are fewer shutdown times available for repairs. The move to only one closure a year will also save the heavy costs of shutting down and starting up the plants.

The new structure is expected to last for at least 10 years. The 'payback' system means that reductions in the working week to 35 hours can be accommodated in the present system. Management believes that the change to five shift working will give the company an edge over its competitors as it is the first company within the industry to make such a fundamental change to working time.

DON & LOW PLC

REDUCED WORKING HOURS

CONTINUOUS SHIFT EMPLOYEES

At a meeting held on Friday, 16th August, 1985 between management representatives of Don & Low plc and T. & G.W.U. employee representatives, the following principles were agreed as the way in which working hours would be reduced for Continuous Shift employees:

1. Five-shift working will be introduced with effect from 3rd January, 1986.

2. Contracted hours of work will be reduced to an average of 39 per week.

3. There will be no reduction in gross wages which are currently being paid for the present Four-Shift, average 42-hour week, although the make-up of those wages will require to be altered.

4. A new, annualised working pattern will be introduced, the detail of which has yet to be finalised, but with the following provisions:

   (a) each working shift will be of 8 hours' duration;
   (b) there will be only one complete shutdown each year—between Christmas and New Year;
   (c) 213 shifts per annum will be rostered for each employee.

5. In order to fulfil their obligation to work an average 39-hour week, employees would be required to work 226 shifts per annum and it was agreed that this forms the basis of each employee's Contract of Employment.

   It was also agreed, however, that the Company will call back only a further 7 shifts per annum from each employee. Five of these shifts will be for 'production' purposes and will be valued at time-and-half; 2 shifts will be for 'training' purposes and will be valued at straight time. Whilst 7 shifts will be worked, therefore, $9\frac{1}{2}$ shifts will be 'paid back'.

   It was agreed that these shifts will be called back on the following basis:

   (a) not more than 2 per calendar month:
   (b) part shifts can be worked;
   (c) not during a long break period, during weekends off, or following nightshift working unless mutually agreed.

6. It may be that not all employees are asked to 'pay back' a total of $9\frac{1}{2}$ shifts in each year, the organisation of which will be the responsibility of local management. It was agreed that those who are required to 'pay back' $9\frac{1}{2}$ shifts will not be considered to have been treated unfairly when compared with those who are required to 'pay back' less than $9\frac{1}{2}$ shifts.

7. Consultation with employees will be concluded within a 2-week period in order to identify the annualised working pattern which will be introduced, from 2 alternatives offered by the Company.

5 SHIFT PROPOSAL WORK PATTERN

	Work rota		Notes
	On	Off	
START	5	5*	213 days on, 152 days off
	7	4	
	7	5*	21 weekends off
	7	5*	
	7	4	13 weekends outside holidays
	7	5*	
	7	5*	8 weekends during holidays
	7	4	
	7	10**	All weekends but one have more than Friday, Saturday, Sunday
	7	2	
	7	2	32 periods off]
	7	5*	32 periods on]
	7	5*	
	7	4	9 periods of 2 days off
	7	3*	1 period of 3 days off
	7	2	6 periods of 4 days off
	5	2	12 periods of 5 days off
	7	2	3 periods of 10 days off
	7	17***	1 period of 17 days off
	9	2	
	7	5*	
	7	5*	27 periods of 7 days on
	7	2	2 periods of 5 days on
	7	2	1 period of 4 days on
	7	10**	1 period of 1 day on
	7	4	1 period of 9 days on
	7	5*	
	7	5*	
	7	4	
	7	5*	
	4	2	
FINISH	1	10*	
	213	152	

* Denotes weekend off

1986
Shorter Working Year

	M	T	W	T	F	S	S	M	T	W	T	F	S	S	M	T	W	T	F	S	S	M	T	W	T	F	S	S	M	T	W	T	F	S	S
			JAN 1	2	3	4	5	6	7	8	9	10	11	12	13	14	15	16	17	18	19	20	21	22	23	24	25	26	27	28	29	30	31	FEB 1	2
1	—	—	—	—	N	N	N	—	—	—	—	M	M	M	A	A	N	N	—	—	—	—	—	M	M	A	A	A	N	N	—	—	—	—	—
2	—	—	—	—	A	A	A	N	N	—	—	—	—	—	M	M	A	A	N	N	N	—	—	—	—	M	M	M	A	A	N	N	—	—	—
3	—	—	—	—	M	M	M	A	A	N	N	—	—	—	—	—	M	M	A	A	A	N	N	—	—	—	—	—	M	M	A	A	N	N	N
4	—	—	—	—	—	—	—	M	M	A	A	N	N	N	—	—	—	—	M	M	M	A	A	N	N	—	—	—	—	—	M	M	A	A	A
5	—	—	—	—	—	—	—	—	—	M	M	A	A	A	N	N	—	—	—	—	—	M	M	A	A	N	N	N	—	—	—	—	M	M	M

	3	4	5	6	7	8	9	10	11	12	13	14	15	16	17	18	19	20	21	22	23	24	25	26	27	28	MARCH 1	2	3	4	5	6	7	8	9
1	M	M	A	A	N	N	N	—	—	—	—	M	M	M	A	A	N	N	—	—	—	—	—	M	M	A	A	A	N	N	—	—	—	—	—
2	—	—	M	M	A	A	A	N	N	—	—	—	—	—	M	M	A	A	N	N	N	—	—	—	—	M	M	M	A	A	N	N	—	—	—
3	—	—	—	—	M	M	M	A	A	N	N	—	—	—	—	—	M	M	A	A	A	N	N	—	—	—	—	—	M	M	A	A	N	N	N
4	N	N	—	—	—	—	—	M	M	A	A	N	N	N	—	—	—	—	M	M	M	A	A	N	N	—	—	—	—	—	M	M	A	A	A
5	A	A	N	N	—	—	—	—	—	M	M	A	A	A	N	N	—	—	—	—	—	M	M	A	A	N	N	N	—	—	—	—	M	M	M

	10	11	12	13	14	15	16	17	18	19	20	21	22	23	24	25	26	27	28	29	30	31	APRIL 1	2	3	4	5	6	7	8	9	10	11	12	13
1	M	M	A	A	N	N	N	—	—	—	—	M	M	M	A	A	N	N	—	—	—	—	—	M	M	A	A	A	N	N	—	—	M	M	M
2	—	—	M	M	A	A	A	N	N	—	—	—	—	—	M	M	A	A	N	N	N	—	—	—	—	N	M	M	A	A	N	N	—	—	—
3	—	—	—	—	M	M	M	A	A	N	N	—	—	—	—	—	M	M	A	A	A	N	N	—	—	—	—	—	M	M	A	A	N	N	N
4	N	N	—	—	—	—	—	M	M	A	A	N	N	N	—	—	—	—	M	M	M	A	A	N	N	—	—	—	—	—	—	—	—	—	—
5	A	A	N	N	—	—	—	—	—	M	M	A	A	A	N	N	—	—	—	—	—	M	M	A	A	N	N	N	—	—	M	M	A	A	A

	14	15	16	17	18	19	20	21	22	23	24	25	26	27	28	29	30	MAY 1	2	3	4	5	6	7	8	9	10	11	12	13	14	15	16	17	18
1	A	A	N	N	—	—	—	—	—	—	—	—	—	—	M	M	A	A	N	N	N	—	—	M	M	A	A	A	N	N	—	—	—	—	—
2	—	—	—	—	—	—	—	M	M	A	A	N	N	N	—	—	M	M	A	A	A	N	N	—	—	M	M	M	A	A	N	N	—	—	—
3	—	—	M	M	A	A	A	N	N	—	—	M	M	M	A	A	N	N	—	—	—	—	—	—	—	—	—	—	M	M	A	A	N	N	N
4	M	M	A	A	N	N	N	—	—	M	M	A	A	A	N	N	—	—	M	M	M	A	A	N	N	—	—	—	—	—	M	M	A	A	A
5	N	N	—	—	M	M	M	A	A	N	N	—	—	—	—	—	—	—	—	—	—	M	M	A	A	N	N	N	—	—	—	—	M	M	M

	M T W T F S S	M T W T F S S	M T W T F S S	M T W T F S S	M T W T F S S
		JUNE			
	19 20 21 22 23 24 25	26 27 28 29 30 31 1	2 3 4 5 6 7 8	9 10 11 12 13 14 15	16 17 18 19 20 21 22
1	M M A A N N N	— — — — M M M	A A N N — — —	— — M M A A A	N N — — M M M
2	— — M M A A A	N N — — — — —	M M A A N N N	— — — — M M M	A A N N — — —
3	— — — — M M M	A A N N — — —	— — M M A A A	N N — — — — —	M M M M A A A
4	N N — — — — —	M M A A N N N	— — — — M M M	A A N N — — —	— — — — — — —
5	A A N N — — —	— — M M A A A	N N — — — — —	M M A A N N N	— — A A N N N
		JULY			
	23 24 25 26 27 28 29	30 1 2 3 4 5 6	7 8 9 10 11 12 13	14 15 16 17 18 19 20	21 22 23 24 25 26 27
1	A A N N — — —	— — — — — — —	— — — — — — —	M M M M A A A	N N — — M M M
2	M M A A N N N	— — A A N N N	— — M M A A A	N N — — M M M	A A N N — — —
3	N N — — M M M	A A N N — — —	M M A A N N N	— — A A N N N	— — M M A A A
4	— — — — — — —	M M M M A A A	N N — — N N M	A A N N — — —	M M A A N N N
5	— — M M A A A	N N — — M M M	A A N N — — —	— — — — — — —	— — — — — — —
	AUG				
	28 29 30 31 1 2 3	4 5 6 7 8 9 10	11 12 13 14 15 16 17	18 19 20 21 22 23 24	25 26 27 28 29 30 31
1	A A N N — — —	M M A A N N N	— — A A N N N	— — M M A A A	N N — — — — —
2	— — — — — — —	— — — — — — —	M M M M A A A	N N — — M M M	A A N N — — —
3	N N — — M M M	A A N N — — —	— — — — — — —	— — — — — — —	M M A A N N N
4	— — A A N N N	— — M M A A A	N N — — M M M	A A N N — — —	— — M M A A A
5	M M M M A A A	N N — — M M M	A A N N — — —	M M A A N N N	— — — — M M M
	SEPT				OCT
	1 2 3 4 5 6 7	8 9 10 11 12 13 14	15 16 17 18 19 20 21	22 23 24 25 26 27 28	29 30 1 2 3 4 5
1	M M A A N N N	— — — — M M M	A A N N — — —	— — — — — — —	M M A A N N N
2	— — M M A A A	N N — — — — —	M M A A N N N	— — M M A A A	N N — — M M M
3	— — — — M M M	A A N N — — —	— — M M A A A	N N — — M M M	A A N N — — —
4	N N — — — — —	M M A A N N N	— — — — M M M	A A N N — — —	— — — — — — —
5	A A N N — — —	— — M M A A A	N N — — — — —	M M A A N N N	— — M M A A A

The following is a shift rota chart (rotated on the page). Day numbers run along the top of each band, and the five rows correspond to the five shift teams. The month labels NOV and DEC mark the start of each new month.

Band 1

Team	6	7	8	9	10	11	12	13	14	15	16	17	18	19	20	21	22	23	24	25	26	27	28	29	30	31	**NOV** 1	2	3	4	5	6	7	8	9
1	–	M	M	A	A	–	–	N	–	–	M	M	M	–	A	M	–	N	–	–	N	A	A	–	–	–	A	A	A	N	N	N	–	–	–
2	A	N	A	–	A	–	–	M	M	M	–	–	N	A	M	–	–	N	N	N	A	A	A	N	N	N	M	M	M	A	A	A	N	N	N
3	–	–	A	–	–	N	M	M	–	–	N	A	A	M	–	–	N	A	A	A	M	N	N	A	A	A	–	–	–	A	A	A	N	A	A
4	M	M	N	A	–	–	M	A	A	N	A	–	M	M	M	N	A	–	M	M	–	–	N	M	M	M	–	–	N	M	M	M	A	A	A
5	N	N	–	M	N	–	–	–	N	A	A	M	–	–	–	N	A	–	–	N	–	–	N	M	–	–	N	N	A	M	M	–	M	M	M

Band 2 (NOV → DEC)

Team	10	11	12	13	14	15	16	17	18	19	20	21	22	23	24	25	26	27	28	29	30	**DEC** 1	2	3	4	5	6	7	8	9	10	11	12	13	14
1	M	M	N	–	–	–	M	–	–	–	M	M	M	–	A	A	N	–	–	N	A	–	–	M	M	M	A	A	A	N	N	N	–	–	–
2	M	M	A	N	–	–	–	N	–	M	N	A	A	–	M	M	N	–	–	N	A	M	M	–	–	N	A	A	A	N	A	A	N	N	N
3	–	–	A	A	N	–	–	N	A	N	A	A	M	–	–	N	A	–	–	N	A	N	N	–	–	N	A	A	A	–	–	–	N	A	A
4	N	–	–	N	A	M	–	–	N	A	A	M	M	N	–	–	M	A	A	–	M	A	A	N	N	N	–	–	–	A	A	A	N	A	A
5	A	N	–	–	A	A	M	–	–	M	M	–	–	A	N	–	–	N	A	A	M	M	M	A	A	A	N	N	N	M	M	M	A	A	M

Band 3 (DEC)

Team	15	16	17	18	19	20	21	22	23	24	25	26	27	28	29	30	31
1	M	M	A	A	N	–	–	M	A	–	–	–	–	–	–	–	–
2	–	–	M	M	A	N	–	–	M	–	–	–	–	–	–	–	–
3	–	–	–	–	M	A	N	–	–	–	–	–	–	–	–	–	–
4	N	–	–	M	M	A	–	N	–	–	–	–	–	–	–	–	–
5	A	A	N	N	–	–	M	A	N	–	–	–	–	–	–	–	–

M = Morning
6am to 2pm

A = Afternoon
2pm to 10pm

N = Night
10pm to 6am

5 New technology homeworking at F International Limited

F International was founded in 1962 and is now one of the country's leading computer software houses. The majority of the company's workforce has always worked flexibly and from a home base, with only a small office based management, administrative and sales staff, and it is possibly the leading example in this country of a business which has been successfully built on new working patterns.

The company was founded by a woman who wanted to continue working while also being able to cope with family responsibilities. She realized that a break from work in the rapidly changing computer industry would damage her career, so she established herself as a freelance programmer working from home. The company grew during the 1960s, flattened out for a while after that, but has been expanding rapidly since the late 1970s. In the last year, business has increased by 30 per cent. The company now offers a full range of information systems and software services and has regional offices throughout the UK, as well as subsidiaries overseas.

The company now has a workforce of around 1000. Three-quarters of the workforce is self employed and working from home. Of the 250 salaried staff, only 27 per cent are office based, and these are mainly management and administration staff. The remaining salaried staff, including many senior managers, are home based. Some 90 per cent of the workforce is female. There is no union involvement.

The company has throughout its history had a very clear philosophy that it exists to offer employment opportunities to people who are unable to work in a conventional environment. The principle has been to employ a majority of home based people who work flexible hours. In an industry with severe skill shortages, the company makes use of skills which would otherwise be wasted because the individuals are unable to work regular hours in an office. This approach inevitably attracts women with young families, but it also provides employment for men and women who want to combine working with other activities such as academic study or writing a book. The large number of women employed by the company is seen as an outcome of its working patterns rather than as a conscious decision to employ only women.

Self employment

The majority recruited to work in the 'technical' area (consultants, analysts, designers, programmers) are self employed and freelance. On selection they are given a detailed account of the terms for the supplying of their services. This describes their relationship with the company and their responsibility for such matters as income tax and National Insurance. They are not employed on fixed term contracts, but are offered work on individual project assignments. As freelancers, they are free to work for other employers if they wish, but requirements as to confidentiality and copyright are written into their terms.

Individuals inform the company of the amount of time they want to work and work is offered to them as it becomes available. They are free to accept or reject the offer. This gives people the opportunity to vary their working time to suit their own arrangements, for example by taking time off for extended holidays or to cope with family needs.

When they accept an assignment they sign a project assignment sheet which outlines the nature of the work and the standards expected; it provides an estimate of the time the work is expected to take and describes the fees to be paid. Payment is by the hour for working and travelling time.

Although these individuals are working from home, not all of their work is done at home. They are expected to be available to visit clients at least twice a week.

The use of flexible working patterns by freelancers for the majority of the company's work means that management and administration has to be highly efficient. Performance has to be closely monitored and standards have to be developed for estimating how long a job should take. The setting up of project teams requires a sophisticated system to match up the skills and work requirements of the workforce with business needs.

Although management does not have to deal with many of the problems which arise with office based staff, considerable effort goes into maintaining communication with home based employees. Each of the nine regional offices is responsible for communication within its region. Local events and contact groups are often organized on a voluntary basis to help reduce any sense of isolation which might arise from working at home. New recruits are given induction and visited by more experienced staff who can help deal with any problems which might arise.

The self employed status of the majority of the workforce has legal and financial implications for personnel management which have to be taken into account. In particular, the company must take care not to endanger the self employed status of the workforce according to Inland Revenue definitions. Management reports that each problem which arises has to be worked through from scratch because so few precedents are available.

Recruitment

Because it is trying to attract people who might not necessarily be actively looking for a job, a different approach to recruitment is needed.

The company does very little direct advertising for recruits, but instead relies on maintaining a high public relations profile. It only employs computer specialists who already have considerable experience in the industry, so many recruits approach the company when their personal circumstances make working from home an attractive alternative.

Close links are maintained with other companies in the field, so that employees who leave, for example to have children, can be pointed in the direction of F International. If recruits are needed in a particular area, a public relations campaign is mounted using local radio, newspapers, open days etc.

The selection procedure has to be rigorous because the lack of close supervision means that much has to be based on trust.

Individuals have to be responsible and self disciplined in order to work successfully from home.

Training

Although the company employs experienced staff only, and therefore undertakes no basic training, considerable emphasis is placed on appraisal and career development. There is a mix of traditional and modern training methods.

Some training can be done at home by self study methods, and the company provides learning packages for this purpose. Some training courses are necessary, and these are often held at evenings and weekends to fit in with the workforce's other commitments. The company has found that its flexible approach has sometimes caused problems with other organizations in this respect. For example, there has been much discussion with the MSC to obtain grants towards training because the company was not providing conventional daytime courses.

There are considerable opportunities for career development within the company as most managers are recruited from among the self employed. Currently all regional managers have been promoted from within the company.

Salaried staff

Because the majority of the workforce is self employed it has been necessary for the company to define clearly which roles must be retained for salaried staff. A quarter of the workforce is salaried, and this includes management, administrators and the sales force. Salaried status does not necessarily mean that staff have to be office based. Less than 30 per cent of salaried staff work from the company's head and regional offices, the rest are home based. Many senior managers, for example, work from home and have home based secretaries who live nearby. Others work partly from home. The company reports no major problems with having managers based at home. They perhaps spend more time on the telephone than they would if they were office based, and there is not the same informal communication as there

would be if they were working in the same building as other
managers. But there are advantages to working at home, such as
lack of interruption which can often lead to higher productivity.

Conclusions

F International is one of the very few examples in this country of
a company whose success has been based on flexible working
patterns. The flexibility which is built into the system works
both to the advantage of the company and its workforce. For the
company, the nature of the workforce helps it to make a rapid
response to fluctuations in demand. The attraction for the self
employed workforce is that they can organize their working
lives to fit in with other commitments. For many of the staff, it
provides an opportunity to work which would not otherwise be
available. A recent attitude survey carried out by the company
among freelance staff showed very positive results. Most like the
flexibility that working for the company allows. However,
management reports that there are occasional problems with
people who cannot cope with working from home or find they
want to work in an office for social reasons.

For the company there are other advantages. Fixed overheads are reduced to a minimum, although the communication
costs inevitably increase. The company does not have to provide
office space nor any of the ancillary services normally necessary
for an office based workforce. It is not responsible for National
Insurance, pensions etc for most of its staff.

In an area where recruitment is difficult and skilled recruits
are in great demand, the company can tap the skills of employees
whose talents would otherwise be wasted. Management reports
that productivity levels are extremely high, as is the level of
commitment to the company. Although absence is difficult to
measure, it is thought to be lower than normal because of the
flexible nature of working patterns.

As far as customers are concerned, management reports
that there is often some initial concern from new customers
about the unusual nature of the organization. But once they are
convinced that the company can provide a good service, this
concern disappears and much of the company's business comes
from repeat sales. The company now has such a well established
reputation that this is far less of a problem than it used to be.

Although the company is involved with new technology, by the nature of its business, the use of computers is, perhaps surprisingly, not regarded as significant in the development of the company's working patterns. Certainly when the company began, and still to a large extent, most of the home based work is done with paper and pencil. Staff are not required to have their own computers, nor are they provided by the company except occasionally when they are lent out for a specific project.

However, technological innovations will undoubtedly improve the organization's efficiency. For example, the company has recently installed an electronic mail system linking all managers and sales staff and is now looking towards the introduction of a communication network that could enhance all the freelance panel. This is targeted for 1987, the company's jubilee year and will make communication much easier with home based staff.

6 Three crew, 12 hour continuous shiftworking at Imperial Brewing & Leisure Limited

Imperial Brewing and Leisure Limited is a wholly owned subsidiary of the Imperial Group plc and is involved in brewing (Courage Limited) wines and spirits, retailing, hotels and restaurants. In total, around 30,000 people are employed by the company.

Its London headquarters staff numbers 230, of which 120 are based at the data processing centre in West London. The only employees to work shifts at head office are about 21 computer operators who work at the data processing centre. These employees are crucial to the company's business as they operate the computers which monitor sales and distribution as well as running the company payroll. In March 1986 a new shift system and a new shift allowance payment was introduced in this department. No union agreement operates for this group of employees.

Previous system

Previously, employees at the data processing centre worked three shifts: 11.30pm to 8.00am, 8.00am to 4.00pm and 4.00pm to 11.30pm. The working week started on a Sunday night and ran through until Friday afternoon. Some weekend work is necessary for maintenance and trying out new programs and this is paid for at overtime rates. Employees worked straight shifts ie one week each of days, evenings and nights. A flat rate shift allowance of £1000 was paid to all shiftworkers, irrespective of attendance or grade.

Management became concerned at the high levels of absence among these employees, especially on Mondays, Thursdays and Fridays. Absence had become a constant problem and management had been forced to resort to disciplinary warnings and docking pay in an attempt to stop it. It was also felt that there was a demoralized attitude among the employees on shift.

Management came to the conclusion that a change in the shift system was needed. A departmental meeting was called to discuss the issue and the employees were asked for their suggestions for improvements.

12 hour shifts

The employees considered the matter and returned with two concrete suggestions: they proposed a new shift system, still based on three shift working, but with 12 hour shifts worked on a 3,4,3 basis over a three week cycle. Shifts would run from 8.00am to 8.00pm and 8.00pm to 8.00am (see box below). The employees also proposed that the shift allowance should be raised, but that in order to discourage absence it should become a shift attendance allowance ie it would only be paid for those shifts when employees attended work. Management suggested that while the implications of these changes were being examined, employees should work the proposed new shifts on a trial basis for three months with no changes to shift pay. This was agreed and it very soon became clear that the new system had several advantages for management.

Productivity and morale both improved markedly. Management reports that invoicing, for example, is completed three or four hours earlier than before. Two shift changeovers a day, instead of three, made administration and communication easier. The new system also did away with problems which had caused bad feeling in the past; in particular the evening shift had tended to leave all the heavy jobs for the night shift. Now it was felt that all shifts were pulling their weight. The new shift pattern also enabled greater continuity of workflow because of

SHIFT PATTERN

	SUNDAY	MONDAY	TUESDAY	WEDNESDAY	THURSDAY	FRIDAY	SATURDAY
WEEK 1	Red (N)	Red (N) White (D)	Red (N) White (D)	White (N) Blue (D)	White (N) Blue (D)	Blue (D)	
WEEK 2	Blue (N)	Blue (N) Red (D)	Blue (N) Red (D)	Red (N) White (D)	Red (N) White (D)	White (D)	
WEEK 3	White (N)	Blue (D) White (N)	Blue (D) White (N)	Blue (N) Red (D)	Blue (N) Red (D)	Red (D)	

Notes:
1. Meal Breaks : 90 minutes per shift.
2. Tea Breaks : 3×15 minutes per shift.
3. Holidays : Each 12 hour shift not attended through holidays will count as $1\frac{1}{2}$ days holiday against your annual entitlement.

only one shift change in a 24 hour period, resulting in far fewer misunderstandings or problems.

In the meantime management put considerable effort into researching the implications of the proposed change. Levels of absenteeism were monitored during the trial period. There was a decrease, but this was not as great as management had hoped for. While certified sickness dropped markedly (from 35 days to $8\frac{1}{2}$), uncertified sickness hardly dropped at all. However the shift attendance payment had not yet been introduced and a good proportion of the absence was due to one individual. There was also some fatigue during peak processing times amongst operators working three days at a time, but it is felt that the additional time off built into the system more than compensates for this.

The implications of the new hours for such matters as breaks, holiday entitlement and 'beer allowance' also had to be considered. Because of the nature of the work several breaks are needed. Previously in an eight hour shift there was one mealbreak and two teabreaks. For the 12 hour shift there is one 60 minute mealbreak, one 30 minute break and three 15 minute breaks.

Management also did a survey of shift allowances for similar employees in other companies. Companies in the brewing industry, and some other local companies, were approached. Thirteen responded, and from their responses it became clear that while levels of basic pay were fairly average, the company's shift allowances were below average for the industry and area. It was decided that the shift allowance should be increased. Both managers and employees argued strongly against a graded increase ie having shift allowance as a percentage of salary, as they thought this would be inequitable.

A recommendation was therefore made to the board that the new shift system should be introduced and that the shift allowance should be increased by £500 to £1500, but that it should become an attendance payment. The allowance would be paid for attendance per shift, with part shifts being paid pro-rata. The shift allowance would be paid for holidays, but not for any other absence.

When the board had given its approval, a letter was prepared for the employees involved and a joint meeting of all three shifts called. Employees were given the option of going back to the old system or accepting the new proposals as a package. Only two employees were not in favour of the new system and one of these has since been transferred out of the unit.

The new system was introduced at the beginning of March. As the shift allowance will now be paid in arrears a flat £100 allowance was paid to tide employees over the first month. This will be repaid at a later date.

Conclusions

The company is still concerned about absenteeism and this will be monitored for the next three months to see if the new payment system makes a difference. There have, however, already been several advantages for the company including: 'immensely' increased productivity, smoother changeovers, higher morale, more time available for the development of projects. It is hoped that the increased productivity will also lead to a reduction in overtime.

The new hours work well for the company. Much information about sales and deliveries comes in' during the late evening and can be dealt with by the night shift when it takes over: for example, salesmen send in daily reports and the computer invoices customers and compiles the next day's schedules. Similarly the computer sends out delivery schedules to depots all over the country every night.

For the employees there is more concentrated and 'usable' leisure time. Travelling is reduced and at more convenient times. Morale is better and improved productivity means they can spend time on more interesting project work.

The company is hoping at least to break even on the costs of the change and it is thought possible that savings could be made. The increase in the shift allowance could cost the company around £10,000 a year, but it is hoped that there will be considerable savings now that the allowance has become conditional on attendance. Any reduction in absenteeism will also save on the costs of bringing in expensive contractors to provide cover. If overtime is also reduced, there will be further cost savings. There has also been a saving because the company used to provide a hot meal for the night shift. Now that the shift starts at 8.00pm, employees eat before they come to work, so only cold food is provided and a cook does not have to be employed.

7 Annual hours and four crew shiftworking at Kimberly-Clark Limited

Kimberly-Clark is an American owned company that manufactures disposables at several sites in the UK. Altogether there are around 3000 employees. Terms and conditions are negotiated separately for each location.

In 1981 the company opened the first of two greenfield sites in North Wales. The first site, Sealand, was followed by a mill on a much larger site at Flint in 1982.

The industrial relations arrangements were established first at Sealand with the intention of carrying them through to Flint when it opened. There are presently 200 employees at the two mills, of which 170 are hourly paid.

Amongst its various industrial relations objectives at the new site, management particularly wanted the greatest possible flexibility from the workforce and considered having a single union agreement. It also wanted to improve on the industrial relations practices introduced at the last new site to open which was in Northumberland in 1969/70. The approach in Northumberland was very radical at the time, but the company found it had to backtrack on some of its aims.

In North Wales therefore it was decided to take a moderate approach, eg to try and achieve maximum flexibility, but not do away completely with overtime. This 'broad brush' approach was based on the concept of annual hours. There were also several minor matters which the company hoped would create the right sort of working environment eg all staff have the same entrance, shared car parks, free coffee, a landscaped site, and a working environment kept clean and attractive. Management believes that it would have been difficult to achieve thc flexibility and commitment required from the workforce if employees had been asked to work in the traditional British working environment.

Discussions were held with several unions, but it was finally decided to go for a single union agreement with TGWU because they had a predominant local presence.

The advantages of a single union agreement for the company are that it does away with demarcation disputes and makes negotiating easier. The main disadvantage is that craft employees may dislike being represented by a general workers' union.

Heads of agreement were signed with the TGWU before any employees were recruited. Agreements based on annual hours contracts were concluded at both sites when they opened.

Annual hours

Although the North Wales mills are not part of the British Paper and Board Industry Federation, some of the company's other mills are and therefore the company was aware of the annual hours contracts being introduced in paper mills. There had to be some 'education' of the union on the concept of annual hours and management had discussions with other companies such as Continental Can.

The annual hours concept requires a new attitude on the part of those involved. It is sometimes difficult for employees to understand that a fundamental change has taken place in their working arrangements. Employees are paid for working the annual hours stipulated in their contract, all the rest of the time is their own. Their annual salary is based on their contract and all that is required is that employees work the hours rostered. If they are sick when they are off the rota, the company does not need to know about it. If time off is to be increased, negotiations do not focus on extra holidays, but rather on a decrease in annual hours.

The annual hours agreement necessarily applies a 'current year' approach to holidays for all employees. It is recognized that it could be very expensive to introduce such a system on an existing site where holiday is accrued in arrears for hourly paid workers.

Employees take some holidays during shutdowns and the rest are by arrangement with the shift leader when it is possible to work short crewed. The rota incorporates 13 more shifts than employees should work to complete their annual hours, and it is up to them to arrange to take these shifts off in consultation with colleagues and supervisors.

Shifts

The technology introduced at the new sites was very advanced and largely untried. The Flint plant was only the second of its type in the world, so for the first 18 months or so management and employees were involved in a lengthy learning process.

At Sealand, shift workers were employed on a discontinuous three shift rota. At Flint, where maximum flexibility had to be retained during the learning period, staff were employed either as dayworkers or as continuous shiftworkers. Over the 18 month period, shiftworkers had a variety of different shift patterns. They moved from continuous work for short periods with two crews working 12 hour shifts (ie run seven days, shut five), through a three crew system to a conventional four crew system with eight hour shifts and four-day shutdowns. As demand increased, some days off were taken during the roster and shifts worked short crewed.

Working patterns were adapted to fit in with the learning process and to cope with increasing demand. These frequent changes to shift systems were only possible because all employees were employed on annual hours contracts.

Eventually the shift system settled down to the current 12 hour system. The 12 hour shifts were introduced at the request of the employees, several of whom had worked 12 hour shifts while they were in training at the mill's sister plant in the United States. They felt that 12 hour shifts gave them more usable leisure time. Most employees are fairly young and place a great value on leisure time.

Twelve hour shifts were first introduced for an experimental period. Most employees found they liked them. Only two employees opposed them and they eventually left of their own accord. Management saw advantages and disadvantages to 12 hour working. There was concern about physical fatigue, but in the event this has not proved a major problem, partly because the most physically demanding product failed.

Management was also concerned about providing absence cover on a 12 hour system. It would not be possible to cover by the traditional method (ie with half shift overtime working by employees on the previous and subsequent shift) because employees could not be expected to work continuously for 18 hours. This has not proved a major problem, however, because shifts can either work short crewed or because there are sufficient people on days off who can be called in to work an extra shift, but in any case absence at short notice is extremely rare.

Sickness absence among shiftworkers is remarkably low at 1½ per cent. Absence among shiftworkers is less than among salaried staff. It is thought that part of the reason for this is that the number of attendances is less, so the chances of employees being ill when they are due on shift is correspondingly less.

An overtime experiment to provide the option of time off in lieu has had little response from employees and only three employees have taken advantage of the opportunity to have time off in lieu instead of overtime pay. However management has decided that the facility will continue as it may reduce overtime costs and allow for some additional flexibility.

Flexibility

Most of the employees taken on at the two mills had previous experience of shiftwork. The company was very careful in its selection procedure to find employees who would be flexible in their approach. There are few problems with the flexibility demanded by the company and most employees say they prefer the new system.

At Sealand all the machine operators are craftsmen. At Flint no craftsmen are employed on shift, but the process crews all contain people with experience in either the mechanical or electrical crafts and they are expected to use their knowledge to deal with any immediate problems during their shift. All craftsmen at Flint are on day work. The company uses them fairly traditionally, but all are expected to be flexible.

Pay

The TGWU stressed that there should be a commitment by the company to pay good wage rates in return for flexible working. Under the terms of the agreement, the company is committed to pay wage rates competitive with those of the major companies in the area. Wage rates are monitored by a variety of local surveys and management reports that the company is regarded as the highest paying in the immediate location.

All employees are paid monthly by credit transfer. The company has agreed to cash cheques for employees who cannot get to a bank and up to 60 per cent of dayworkers take advantage of this facility. One of the reasons for this is that all employees (day and shift) are paid for meal breaks and are required to be available at all times during working hours. Employees are therefore not allowed to leave the site during working hours and a good canteen is provided. The rule is accepted by employees and is thought to avoid problems of lunchtime drinking. The only protests have come from contract and assigned staff working temporarily on site.

The future

The company is hoping to introduce five crew working at several other plants in the near future. Management would prefer to stay with an eight hour shift pattern but will not resist if employees insist on moving to 12 hour shifts.

Management has come to the conclusion that in continuous process industries with weekly hours below 42 a change to five shift working is inevitable in the long run.

It is relatively easy to demonstrate that the move to five crews is cost effective, eg four crews with seven members each need either two spares each or have to work 15 per cent overtime in order to provide cover (often in practice there is a combination of both). So there must either be a total of eight spares employed (more than an extra crew) or overtime paid at $22\frac{1}{2}$ per cent (15 per cent at time and a half). The cost of a fifth crew is 25 per cent, ie cheaper than carrying two spares on each shift or $2\frac{1}{2}$ per cent more expensive than 15 per cent overtime working.

8 Flexible manning and temporary working at The Nabisco Group Limited

Nabisco is an American owned, multinational company traditionally best known in Britain for its Shredded Wheat cereal product and employs 12,000 people in the UK. In 1983, it considerably extended its UK presence through the acquisition of Associated Biscuits Limited, an association of three family owned businesses—Jacobs, Huntley and Palmer and Peak Freans. The associated companies were run relatively independently and, against a background of an industry increasingly dominated by United Biscuits, had begun to go into economic decline. This decline was all the more significant since Huntley and Palmer had once been the largest biscuit manufacturer in the world. The companies had become characterized by a number of serious problems, including overcapacity, underinvestment, low productivity, low pay and generally poor morale.

Since 1983, the fortunes of the biscuit business have improved substantially and can be related fundamentally to Nabisco's style and approach of doing business. Nabisco is a financially strong, entrepreneurial, performance-orientated organization, whilst Associated Biscuits was traditional, paternalistic and underinvested. Central to the changes introduced, was the way in which people were managed and organized in order to support and help drive the dramatic commercial and financial turnaround.

Strategies for change

On the people side of the business, the priority issues requiring attention were agreed to be:

- revitalizing managerial performance
- revitalizing the personnel function
- improving the personnel administration
- improving industrial relations
- tackling the low pay, low productivity problem
- improving employee communications
- obtaining greater industrial relations stability
- creating a corporate identity without destroying local loyalty and commitment
- introducing equity and consistency into personnel policies and practices

In order to improve *managerial* performance and rationalize the structure of the organization, a number of measures were introduced, including the following:

- the clarification and rationalization of the management grading structure
- the sharpening of objective setting and performance measurement through the introduction of performance appraisal for managers, as well as supervisory, administrative and clerical staff
- the introduction of salary progression on the basis of merit only, signalling to managers the new emphasis on rewarding performance and the achievement of results. (The salary progression system for all non management staff was also changed to a merit/performance link basis.)
- an improvement in the pay and benefits package from lower to upper quartile, signalling a break with the previous low pay, low efficiency culture
- the creation of stronger links in the rewards for performance paid to senior management and directors through the introduction of a bonus programme linked to financial and personal targets
- the introduction of an annual management audit linked to succession plans, the identification of high potential and the gaps requiring to be filled through external recruitment

A range of reforms have also been undertaken amongst unionized *manual workers* to tackle the problems of low pay and low productivity. Such reforms include:

● a progressive reduction of the number of bargaining units in order to streamline the existing complex structure of bargaining
● an improvement in the quality of the physical working conditions to match the desired image of becoming a high quality producer of premium food products
● moves towards greater harmonization of conditions of employment
● a clear commitment to the development of employee communications (including the introduction of briefing groups), participation and involvement
● the introduction of two or three year agreements to provide a stable framework within which to implement productivity and manpower plans, including extensive changes in working practices. This measure, together with the reduction in bargaining units, has also served to reduce the number of potential sources of conflict over pay by more than half
● the provision of substantial pay increases in real terms in exchange for real productivity gains in order to raise the previously low level of manual workers' pay

The remainder of this case study describes how this strategy has been implemented in practice at the company's Aintree biscuit factory.

Changes in working patterns and practices at the Aintree biscuit factory

In order to achieve a number of the productivity and industrial relations objectives described above, three year enabling agreements were signed with the four trade unions (GMBATU, AUEW, EETPU and UCATT) providing substantial pay increases and 'no compulsory redundancy' in return for flexible working patterns and practices and reduced manning levels. These agreements became effective in December 1984. In all, approximately 2100 employees at Aintree in unskilled, semi skilled and skilled occupations were covered by the agreements.

In exchange for guarantees on job security the agreements provide for the introduction of revised working practices, manning levels and procedures which are designed to improve the efficiency and contribution of employees. Specifically, the craft agreement includes movement towards staff status for craftsmen, changes in working practices and the removal of restrictive practices, plus the acceptance of training to extend skills and flexibility. For process workers the agreement includes an investigation of manning levels, the acceptance of the use of temporary labour and the acceptance of adjustments to grading differentials. A new seven grade structure will be introduced in January 1987. It also includes a statement on the elimination of boundaries between production and engineering departments.

Both agreements include a 'no enforced redundancy' clause and also that no industrial action be taken before a full and secret ballot.

Fundamental to the agreements is the concept of 'enabling' change to occur. The agreements do not itemize a list of working practices which are being bought out. Instead, trade unions have undertaken to operate any change in work practice proposed by management for a trial period of one month. At the end of the trial period, the effects of the changes introduced are reviewed by a joint management–union monitoring committee. No grievances can be raised during the one month trial period and the final right to implement any change lies with management after due consultation. Initiatives are then passed to a departmental joint consultative committee for implementation. In the nine months since July 1985, 85 initiatives have been tried out (mostly related to demanning), 82 have been implemented and a further 23 (at March 1986) were undergoing trial periods. Any reductions in manning are handled initially by redeployment or by voluntary redundancy during the period of the three year agreement.

Temporary working   One part of the agreement involves an undertaking to move towards the employment of temporary workers (both full and part time) in place of permanent employees in routine jobs requiring little training, in order to meet temporary and seasonal demands. The agreement includes a clause enabling management to employ up to 25 per cent of total number on temporary contracts before trade union representatives are notified, up to an absolute maximum of 30 per cent. A list of people prepared to do temporary work is kept and the people concerned are called in, as required, according to season or to meet demand during special promotions. They are normally employed in packing jobs, working three daily shifts per week of about five hours each.

Sub-contracting   The agreements state that 'external contractors will be used where specialist knowledge or equipment is deemed to be preferred; to meet surges in demand and where external resource is more competitive'. Currently sub-contracting has been applied in the following areas:

- canteen
- civil trades
- refrigeration engineering
- forklift truck maintenance

Effects of the agreements   Gross pay rates over the three year period of the agreement will have increased by between $27\frac{1}{2}$ and 30 per cent. Significant productivity gains are also anticipated and numbers employed are being reduced though voluntary redundancy and natural wastage by 110 and further reductions are likely to continue.

9 Annual hours, four and five crew shiftworking at Pedigree Petfoods

Pedigree Petfoods, part of the American owned Mars organization, enjoys a major share of the UK petfood market. It has 1800 employees, of whom 1200 are based at Melton Mowbray, and the rest at two smaller sites at Peterborough and Waltham on the Wolds. The company is not unionized.

Annual hours

The company has implemented common conditions in many respects for several years. For example, all employees clock on, including managers. In 1977 hourly pay rates for manual workers were abolished, and all employees went on to weekly pay. In 1980 employees worked a variety of hours:

- two-shift workers on double days with scheduled overtime
- three-shift workers on $37\frac{1}{2}$ hours
- four-shift workers on an average of $39\frac{1}{4}$ hours
- office dayworkers $37\frac{1}{2}$ hours
- other dayworkers on 39 hours

In an attempt to rationalize working hours between all these different groups, the management decided to convert to an annual hours system. Using office workers as the base, the annual hours calculation was:

52 × 37.5	1950
LESS annual holidays	150
	1800
LESS statutory holidays	60
	1740
LESS 4 year effect	1
Annual hours	1739

A working party, which included first line managers, was set up to consider how annual hours should be applied to shiftworkers and it took four months to produce their report.

The annual hours system was introduced for all employees in 1981, but there were some initial problems explaining the new system and persuading employees (and senior managers) of its advantages. It took six months to explain and implement the changes, and management now recognizes that probably further preparation was needed before the introduction of annual hours.

One of the difficulties was that four-shift workers, who were said to have been on a $39\frac{1}{2}$ hour week, were actually only working an average of $38\frac{1}{4}$ hours when the effect of bank holidays and shutdowns were taken into account in the annual hours calculation. Thus the reduction in nominal weekly hours was only three-quarters of an hour rather than two hours as first thought. Another problem which had to be dealt with was that office staff working days did not really benefit from the change.

Management reports that, with hindsight, the most important factors in introducing a successful annual hours scheme are:

- careful and detailed preparation
- tight control
- an efficient time keeping system
- to revise shift systems as little as possible
- to integrate pay systems in advance

However, there continue to be advantages to annual hours, some of which the company is only now beginning to realize. For employees there is the benefit of a regular weekly income. All employees receive basic weekly pay based on their grade rate and annual hours divided by 52, plus any overtime pay. For the company, one advantage was that holiday arrangements were tidied up, as every hour now has to be accounted for.

Management sees annual hours as an 'enabling' concept

which 'uncouples' the use of assets and equipment from the weekly hours worked by individuals, and allows for easier implementation of more flexible working patterns. One example is the possibility of introducing variable hours, for example in the accounts department where work peaks at certain times in the month.

The cost of the reduction in hours for manual workers was considerably offset by savings from more flexible working practices.

Since 1981 two days extra holiday have been granted and annual hours as a result have been reduced to 1724.

Shift systems

Over 800 employees (including managers) work a four crew shift system. The rotas are produced for four years at a time to equalize the number and type of shifts worked by each crew. There is one major summer shutdown, but because certain parts of the plant have to be kept open this year, some employees will take alternative summer holidays. There are also seven 'flexible' days holiday which employees can choose to take at any time with management permission. There is an unusual arrangement on Saturdays whereby the morning shift works $5\frac{1}{2}$ hours, and the afternoon shift 10 hours, so that more employees can attend more Saturday afternoon activities.

A variation on the four crew rota has been introduced at the company's Peterborough site where employees now work 12 hour shifts at weekends. This gives two weekends off in four rather than only one in four and has proved very popular with employees. There have been no disadvantages for the company.

A five crew system was introduced for security staff three years ago. No extra people were employed as the fifth crew was created from existing employees by the reorganization of work. The introduction of the five crew system provided a valuable opportunity to examine the benefits from both an employee and company viewpoint. With the introduction of the security fifth crew, overtime was reduced from around 28 per cent to virtually nil. Under the annual hours system these employees 'owe' the company 60 hours a year. These hours are used for training and to cover for sickness. Training hours are written into the rota. The company's experience is that employees dislike the uncertainty of owing hours to the company.

The introduction of five crew working in a small area has provided some valuable insights which management is hoping to use in its consideration of alternative systems for the majority of shiftworkers. For example, the current five crew rota gives employees several 10 day breaks as well as a longer break in the summer. It has been found that long breaks in winter are unpopular with employees and these times are better used for training.

There have been several other changes to shift systems since the introduction of annual hours. The double day shift has been abolished. Another recent innovation is to permit the interchangeability of shifts. This works particularly well with a five crew system, and as far as management is concerned it makes no difference who is doing the shift as long as it is covered by a qualified employee.

10 Flexible rostering and the abolition of overtime at Petrofina (UK) Limited

Petrofina (UK) Limited is a Belgian owned oil company with 17 operating centres in the UK. The company and its subsidiaries have 2200 employees in Britain.

In September 1984 new working arrangements were introduced for 300 drivers, depot workers and blending plant operators. These employees are all members of the TGWU. The agreement known as the 'New Approach' reduced working hours, abolished overtime, and introduced a new pay structure and more flexible working practices.

Background

Petrofina is a company which operates very flexibly in order to react quickly to changing market conditions. This means that there is a 'stop-go' policy on sales. If the price is high and it is profitable to sell then the company needs to move very quickly; when prices drop, sales are restricted. The effect of these fluctuations in activity had a direct impact on the take home pay of manual workers, who were working an average of nearly 10 hours overtime a week. Some were working as much as 58 or 59 hours a week.

Management was concerned that the pay of manual workers was very unstable, while other employees were unaffected by fluctuations in activity. Because a large proportion of manual employees are in the older age range, there was also concern about the effect of the pay structure on pensions. Typically drivers were earning £130 basic a week and £60 overtime. But only their basic earnings were pensionable, so employees faced a very substantial drop in income on retirement even if they had long service with the company.

The company made an unsuccessful attempt to eliminate overtime in the 1960s when the first productivity deals were agreed. Since then overtime had grown, especially in the winter with its high demand for heating oils, and employees often worked at weekends. Management believed that the reliance on overtime earnings encouraged employees to work inefficiently and led to restrictive practices.

It was therefore decided to initiate a new productivity deal which would give employees a more stable income linked to retirement pensions, and to take the opportunity to introduce more flexible working practices. The company also planned to introduce larger vehicles into its fleet at the same time.

The alternative of sub-contracting was considered but rejected. Management believes that, while it is economical, it is better to keep delivery staff under company control. There was also opposition from the union which had tried to obtain a commitment from the company not to sub-contract deliveries. The company has not given this commitment, but it has promised to consult the union on any major changes.

The company also came under pressure from the union for a reduction in working hours and management believed that there would soon be a demand for pensions to be related to average earnings. The 'New Approach' was an attempt to meet several of the union's aspirations, while at the same time increasing productivity for the company.

A working party consisting of three managers and four lay delegates spent nine months discussing the package in detail. Full time union officials were not involved. No major changes were made to the management proposals, but the union played a significant role in simplifying the package and making suggestions for improvements. Compromises were reached, for example on the guaranteed day. The company would have preferred no guaranteed day or a shorter one than was finally agreed.

The aim was to make the package as 'watertight' as possible, to avoid ambiguities and to place constraints on managers as well as employees to ensure increased flexibility and prevent the reintroduction of overtime.

When the changes were agreed they were explained to shop

stewards, and a booklet was distributed to all the employees who would be affected. The workforce was asked to vote on the proposals as a package. The union recommended acceptance and the lay delegates from the working party visited the depots to explain the new arrangements. In the ballot, 85 per cent of employees voted in favour, a much higher percentage than management had anticipated. All the depots voted in favour, even those where employees would lose money through the abolition of overtime earnings.

The New Approach

The package was the first of its kind in the industry. The three parts of the package were: a reduction in working hours linking with the abolition of overtime, a new pay structure and new flexibility requirements.

Working hours were reduced from 40 to $37\frac{1}{2}$, to be worked between Monday and Friday. There is a guaranteed six hour day, except when this means a total of more than $27\frac{1}{2}$ hours worked in the week. Employees are required to work up to 11 hours on any one day, if required. If hours exceed $37\frac{1}{2}$ in any one week, they are deducted from the following week's hours.

There is no paid overtime. If extra cover is required, either because of sickness or peaks in the workload, temporary workers or sub-contractors are employed. If peak workloads continue, extra permanent staff will be recruited. Previously management would not have used outside labour until employees' hours reached 60 a week.

Rostered Saturday working has been abolished. If employees are required to work at weekends or on public holidays, a minimum of $7\frac{1}{2}$ hours is guaranteed at enhanced rates. Time off in lieu is also given. Originally time off had to be taken in the following week, but after an approach from employees, a 'banking' system for hours has been introduced. The high premium on weekend/holiday working is designed to discourage its use. Weekend working has to be specifically authorized by one of two managers.

The new *pay structure* increased basic earnings by up to 45 per cent. These earnings became pensionable so that for an employee with $37\frac{1}{2}$ years' service the annual pension would increase from £5000 to £7000 a year. The basic annual salary for a driver increased from £7584 to £11,001 in September 1984. By 1986 it was £12,216. An annual unsocial hours payment is added for shiftworkers and is also pensionable.

Shift sharing has been introduced and has proved popular with employees. With management agreement, employees can choose, for example, to work two weeks on shift and two weeks on days and receive half the monthly unsocial hours allowance. As far as the company is concerned, as long as the shifts are covered it makes no difference whether the unsocial hours payment goes to one person or is divided between two.

All employees moved to monthly pay by credit transfer and the company gave interest free loans to help them over the change. Formerly there were three payrolls with employees on monthly, fortnightly and weekly pay.

'Total' *flexibility* was required from employees and all previous 'local agreements' were abolished. New operating standards were introduced and employees were required to work without supervision. Complete flexibility meant that all employees were expected to undertake any work for which they were competent. For example, some depot staff were also required to drive when necessary and drivers were obliged to deliver to any location (previously local agreements restricted the area). There was to be no restriction on vehicle capacity up to the legal maximum.

A major innovation was the abolition of restrictions on loading from any point, either company or non company. Restrictions on the use of sub-contractors and temporary workers were also abolished, subject to agreed guidelines which include the stipulation that contractors' drivers must receive the same rates as company drivers when they work for Petrofina.

Results

The company estimated that the changes would result in an increase of 12.8 per cent in the paybill and 12 extra drivers were employed when the package was introduced. It was expected that 70 per cent of the extra costs would be recouped in the short term through increased efficiency.

Initially costs were far higher than expected. Indeed, management admits that the new system did not work well for the first six months, mainly because managers and supervisors were not ready to make the best of it. They did not make use of the new operational flexibility available to them and they found it difficult to think in terms of the hours available, rather than in terms of volume as they had done before.

At the start, it was difficult for everyone to adjust to the New Approach. Managers often found that by Thursday all the employees had used up their $37\frac{1}{2}$ hours and contractors had to be brought in to cover for Friday and weekend work. As a consequence, costs increased substantially and for the first six months it was feared that the increase would be some 20 per cent above the original estimates.

But productivity also increased immediately by around 20 per cent, and has continued at a high level. Slowly, as staff came to terms with the new arrangements, the changes started to show real benefits. Management now believes that it was necessary to allow time for the new system to settle. It was also fortunate that the managing director was committed to the scheme and gave it strong backing through the difficult early months.

Now costs have been reduced below the original estimates and the scheme is self financing. The workforce has also been reduced to the original 300 by natural wastage.

As well as the gradual change in attitude which was necessary for the New Approach to be successful, there were three factors which management believes contributed to the scheme's eventual success:

- *the planned introduction of larger vehicles* led to a drop in the number of contractors employed
- *the use of 'back loading'*: previously local agreements had restricted loading points and the company had not been able to make use of other companies' facilities, or their own facilities, by another depot's drivers. Now the aim is to have tankers loaded at all times by making use of all available facilities. This takes considerable organization but it has led to substantial increases in productivity
- *the centralization of vehicle scheduling*: this has been an important influence on the success of the new working arrangements, although it was not planned to coincide with their introduction. Indeed, some managers had serious reservations about the effects of centralization before it was introduced. Previously routing was done by clerks at the individual depots, now it is all done centrally by computer. Now that the overall picture can be seen, there

is total flexibility between depots. If peaks arise at one depot, work can be diverted to others, sometimes creating a 'domino' effect as work moves up or down the country. Many of those who now work at head office were formerly local supervisors, so they can call on local knowledge to use the system to best advantage

Another significant change is that the computer provides a total job time. Previously there were separate estimates for loading/unloading etc. Jobs are timed to the minute and employees are expected to make up for lost time whenever possible. All delays have to be substantiated by tachograph discs.

Management reports that the New Approach is now popular with the workforce. Basic earnings levels are said to be the highest in the industry, although in other companies, employees may earn more because of overtime. Petrofina employees are also said to have come to value their increased leisure time. Although around 30 per cent of the employees affected lost money because of the abolition of overtime pay, the pensions provisions made the new pay structure attractive to a workforce which included many employees with long service. Income stability resulted in an upsurge in mortgage requests when the package was introduced. The package also abolished most of the differences between staff and manual employees.

Although there were some problems early on with employees trying to avoid work, these have now been dealt with and management reports a significant change in attitude on the part of employees. Management has agreed to use 'its best endeavours' to let employees know the hours to be worked on the previous day. The aim is for employees to work an average of $7\frac{1}{2}$ hours a day, although they can be scheduled for between six and 11 hours. Weekly hours only go over $37\frac{1}{2}$ on Fridays if unseen emergencies arise. Weekend working has been cut to a minimum, unsocial hours working has been reduced and the shift system rationalized.

Since the package was introduced, overtime pay has been abolished for supervisory and clerical staff, who now receive time off in lieu for working extra hours.

11 Flexible manning with four, five and six set shiftworking at Pilkington Glass Limited, Greengate works

Pilkington opened its Greengate plant in 1981. There are now 404 employees all, except 16 managers, employed on the same terms and conditions. GMBATU represents the process workers, tradesmen are represented by the AUEW and EETPU and ASTMS represent office staff and foremen. All the employees recruited to work at Greengate when it opened were transferred from other Pilkington sites. They were used to traditional working practices, but there was careful selection to recruit staff who would be adaptable to the new working practices introduced at the plant. Several employees decided not to move to Greengate when they heard that overtime pay was to be abolished.

Background

Pilkington was very successful during the 1960s and early 1970s, but by the mid 1970s inflation in the UK and the strength of sterling started to have a serious effect on the business. There was overcapacity in the worldwide glass market and foreign competition became intense. The company's share of the UK market dropped from 85 per cent to around 50 per cent. The heavy cost of investing in the new Greengate plant made it imperative that maximum productivity was achieved.

A management team, initially 10 strong, was set up two years before the plant opened to plan for the future and recruit and train staff. Management's aim was to break away from the traditional working practices which had grown up at Pilkington over the years. The new plant also gave the company an opportunity to break with the company's well established centralized negotiating structure. Greengate negotiated its own multi union agreement separately from the company-wide agreements which applied to the rest of the Pilkington employees. The management team at Greengate tried to create a new attitude among the workforce which would lead to increased flexibility and efficiency and make the plant competitive in the world markets. The issues they wanted to deal with were:

● overmanning
● demarcation
● unhelpful attitudes
● high sickness absence
● a complex pay structure which was abused and manipulated (eg the bonus scheme did not operate as an incentive since nearly all employees were on the top rate)
● divisions between union memberships

Management wanted efficient manning, maximum flexibility and multiskilled craftsmen. The aim was for an open management style and to do away with 'indefensible status differences' between different groups of employees. All employees would have the same terms and conditions and it was hoped to encourage a high level of commitment to the plant from the workforce.

The management team were influenced in their approach by the experience of one of the company's Swedish plants. The Greengate agreement has since been regarded as a 'flagship' for the rest of Pilkington's sites in the UK. In 1984, centralized bargaining was abolished and all plants are moving towards the Greengate model in their local negotiations.

The agreement

All employees (except managers) have the same terms and

conditions. All work a 39 hour week and all, including managers, have to use the computerized clocking system. Most staff employees in the rest of Pilkington work 37½ hours and have flexitime. There is no flexitime at Greengate.

All Greengate employees have 25 days holiday and receive sickness benefit from day one. Facilities such as the canteen and car parks are shared by all employees. Periods of notice, grievance procedures etc are the same for all.

The only difference between employees is union membership and membership of separate pension schemes. However, the benefits and contributions of the two pension schemes are now virtually identical.

There is a single integrated pay structure. When the plant opened, management carried out job evaluation using the HAY/ MSL Guide Chart Profile method. This was followed by a joint union-management review. There are 10 grades covering 51 jobs. All employees receive an annual salary paid monthly by credit transfer. The only additions to the basic salary are shift commitment payments, on-call allowances and public holiday *premia*; only the public holiday payments are related to the number of occasions worked—the others are paid in equal amounts. A site bonus scheme was introduced in 1984. Because the plant had been so successful, there were union requests for a profit centre. However, it proved impossible to introduce profit sharing, but the bonus scheme operates in a similar way. It is site output bonus, based on the efficiency of the process and output through the gate. The bonus is accumulated weekly, but paid every six months. Management reports that the scheme is seen as a way to give everyone 'a share of the cream'. Because it is a flat-rate bonus based on the output of the whole site, it has developed an interest among employees in the performance of the plant as a whole and it is not seen as having a direct motivational effect.

There is no payment for overtime at Greengate. All employees receive time off in lieu for working over the 39 hour week. The extra hours—called 'alternative' hours—attract time off on a one for one basis, even for weekend working. Alternative hours are kept to a minimum by realistic manning levels to provide cover for absence. Employees accrue alternative hours and take them off at a time convenient to themselves and the company. Management reports that alternative hours working is highest among engineering personnel who sometimes have to work long extra hours to deal with emergencies. Management has a relaxed approach to credit hours, so that employees may allow them to accumulate and take several days off at a time. It is not permitted to accrue odd minutes, however, as nothing less than half an hour is regarded as alternative working.

In 1982, in the run up to the annual pay negotiations, there was an overtime ban at Greengate. Employees were concerned that there might be abuse of the alternative hours system and wanted reassurances about how, when and why they might have to work overtime.

The dispute was resolved by an increase in shift payments and management assurances about 'typical' alternative hours working expected. This provided some reassurance to those who feared abuse of the system. Management also agreed to joint monitoring of the alternative hours worked and banked. Recent results show that most employees on site are in the lowest category of credit hours, ie nil to 10 hours.

Holidays are not rostered but agreed with management within shift groups.

Shift systems

Greengate has a range of different shift systems designed to meet the varying operating requirements in different areas of the plant. The objectives which management wishes to achieve in operating these various shift patterns are as follows:

- to provide the right type of people, in the right numbers, at the right time, to meet departmental workloads
- to provide effective cover for both planned and unplanned absences
- to give both individuals and teams responsibility for smooth, efficient operations in their sections
- to allow day to day operation with minimal involvement from supervision
- to inconvenience employees if there is excessive absence (especially for short notice/short term absences)
- to limit 'alternative hours' working to a mutually acceptable level (given that the site has no paid overtime)
- to provide working arrangements that are generally acceptable to employees

Out of a total workforce of 404, the number involved in the various working patterns in operation breakdown as follows:

Type of work	Numbers
Days	114
2 sets non-continuous	50
4 sets continuous—Warehouse	136
—Others	30
5 sets continuous	50
6 sets continuous—Engineering	24
	404

Under these arrangements, typical manning levels at any one time are up to 194 in the daytime, 61 to 80 in early mornings and evenings and 42 to 55 at night and at weekends.

Four set shiftworking   The four set shift pattern is worked in the warehouse and stockroom areas and by security and welfare staff. The day is divided into three shifts (morning, afternoon and nights) and a typical working pattern would be three mornings, three afternoons, one rest day, three nights, two rest days and the cycle would then be repeated. This gives 168 hours worked in 28 days. Additional rota rest days are then taken every 2½ weeks. Absence cover is provided in the 'set' manning complement.

The company believes that the main advantages of this pattern are that cover is carried on the set so that any product can be produced on the line at any time and that 'alternative hours' (overtime) only have to be worked to cover for high levels of sickness absence. The company also cites the following disadvantages:

- the need to carry cover even when workload does not demand it
- the high level of 'rota rest days' which cause constant disturbance
- sickness does not inconvenience other employees (one of managements' objectives stated above), so responsibility to maintain cover is not felt
- its inability to cope with a further reduction in the working week without implications for overtime
- difficulties in carrying out training and communications

The four set shiftworking pattern was used extensively in other

Pilkington plants and this pattern was not new at Greengate. Its use at Greengate is now being reviewed in the light of experience.

Five set shiftworking   The five set pattern is worked in the glass-making area. The times of the morning, afternoon and evening shifts are the same as those of the four set pattern, but the cycle has an important difference in the way cover is provided. At any one time, the five crews are deployed in the following way—one on mornings, one on afternoons, one on nights, a fourth on a rest day, and the fifth acting as a 'cover' shift. During the cover period, employees are either brought in on days from 8.00am to 4.00pm or have to be available to provide cover for any of the early, late or night shifts which require it.

The cycle runs as follows: three mornings, one rest day, three afternoons, three nights, two rest days, and then three days which are either consecutive rest days, or consecutive day turn or cover days. The three day turns or cover days occur every second cycle.

Management identify the following advantages and disadvantages of the five set shift pattern. First, the advantages:

- it is ideally suited to glass-making where the workload is relatively predictable and patterned
- the cover set is available for non time critical work, such as plant cleaning, assisting engineering and moving raw materials and also provides opportunities for communications and training
- it deals very effectively with planned absences
- short term sickness inconveniences the cover set, but they know when they are at risk
- employees like five day breaks

Some of the disadvantages found by the company are:

- it needs supervisory intervention to respond to short term sickness
- it could create restrictions on production planning
- the rota requires employees to work nine days out of 10

Six set shiftworking Greengate also runs a six set shift pattern where only one person works at a time and where the job must always be covered. Part of the shift cycle involves day work and additional day shifts to make up time, and so for certain periods on days, the job may be covered by two or three employees. This system operates for the engineering shift teams. The cycle is as follows: two days, two early shifts, one rest day, two afternoons, one rest day, two night shifts, two rest days, a pattern is repeated in the second cycle, except that the first rest day becomes a 'make up' day. Employees on this system are expected to provide all necessary cover for each other.

Looking at the pros and cons of the six set pattern, the company notes that it requires groups of six employees all motivated in the same way, but sees the following advantages:

- it puts pressures on individuals and teams to operate efficiently
- it operates without supervisory involvement
- it provides flexibility to use day turns and make up days to provide extra manpower (if the workload is appropriate), otherwise cover is spread evenly
- it will cater for a shorter working week
- it gives employees considerable flexibility

The following disadvantages have also been found:

- it needs supervisory intervention if all individuals do not contribute equally
- it needs intervention to cope with long term sickness
- if not monitored, it can result occasionally in having three men in when only one is required

Shift patterns and absence As a result of placing primary responsibility for covering for absenteeism on team members, the company reports the following typical levels of absence under the various shift patterns:

Shift system	%Absence
2 sets non continuous	4.68
4 sets continuous	5.6
5 sets continuous	2.7
6 sets continuous	1.6

Conclusions

Compared with its old sheet glass factory which employed 680 people to produce 1800 tonnes a week, the new plant employs 404 and produces 5000 tonnes per week. Output per person has gone up by a factor of five and even in comparison with other modern float glass plants, labour productivity is 30 per cent better.

The Greengate experiment is regarded as a major step forward at Pilkington, and many of the company's other plants are now following its lead. Productivity is high and sickness absence on the site averages three to four per cent.

Management believes that the successful introduction of new working practices at Greengate was due in large part to the two years of preparation by the management team. The team comprised the whole range of managers who would be running the plant, including personnel specialists.

The company believes that management must provide the lead if change is going to be accomplished, it must be clear in its objectives and the unions should be involved at an early stage. The unions at Pilkington initially resisted the setting up of the Greengate bargaining arrangements away from the traditionally centralized structure.

Careful selection of staff, especially of supervisors, played an essential part in Greengate's success. Flexible working practices demand a change in attitude from all those involved. Management reports that it took at least two years to change attitudes at Greengate and the process is still continuing. Managers and supervisors have to learn that flexibility requires intelligent application if it is going to work. For example, if employees are going to gain experience and skills across a wide range, supervisors must be prepared to allow all employees to do various different tasks and not always use those who are best at a particular job. If flexibility is to work, it has to be an absolute requirement for employees. They have to be committed to working flexibly to the limits of their abilities. It must not be open to them to opt out of the tasks if they are capable of doing them.

12 Sub-contracting at Rank Xerox Limited, Mitcheldean

Mitcheldean is the company's main UK site for the manufacture and assembly of photocopiers and duplicators. Since 1979 the workforce has been reduced from 4800 to around 1200. There are now 730 industrial employees and 470 supervisory, commercial, technical and management staff. There are four bargaining units for non management employees, incorporating seven trade unions, of which the largest are AUEW, EETPU and GMBATU. APEX and MATSA represent commercial staff, TASS technical staff and ASTMS' supervisors. Most employees work a 39 hour week.

The strategy

Before 1979 the plant produced a wide range of copiers and there was a large staff providing many support services. In order to reduce costs and increase efficiency the company decided to concentrate on three (subsequently two) main core areas of production at Mitcheldean:

- high volume of small copiers and the refurbishing of older, bigger machines
- the manufacture of fuser rolls for worldwide distribution
- acting as an international supply centre (this function has since been considerably reduced)

The strategy has been to concentrate the company's resources on the core productive activities and to reduce drastically the peripheral activities which had high overhead costs to the company. There has been some reduction in the number of staff employed in the production areas, but the major cutbacks have come in the indirect areas. This has been achieved both by elimination and amalgamation of work, and by sub-contracting.

There had always been some sub-contracting to cover peaks and troughs in activity, but in recent years a wide range of peripheral activities have been contracted by the company, including external transport, security, office cleaning, and internal mail. A number of other functions have been drastically reduced with much of the work being sub-contracted. The works engineering staff, for example, has been reduced from 200 to 31 with much of the work now being done by outside individuals and companies.

Although there were of necessity very large numbers of redundancies, the company's approach has been that, wherever possible, the employees whose jobs were being shed were encouraged to become self employed and offer their services back to the company. Where work was contracted to existing companies, Rank Xerox tried to negotiate with them to take on the workers formerly employed on the site.

Employees were given help and advice if they wanted to set up their own business and allowed to buy equipment on preferential terms. Some preference was given to them at the start if they tendered for work with the company, although in the long run they have had to compete on the open market.

Employees across a whole range of activities have set up in business and offered their services to the company. Three former members of the personnel department, for example, set themselves up as a training company and now not only provide training for Rank Xerox staff but for other companies as well. A former senior manager successfully tendered for the gardening contract on the site and another manager and a supervisor set up a firm which now does all the company's cleaning.

In addition, the company has used several of the buildings which became vacant on site to establish the Mitcheldean Enterprise Workshops (MEWS). The company spent £500,000 converting these buildings into starter units for new business and ex-employees have been encouraged to set up in business there by preferential rates. There is now 70 per cent occupancy of the workshops and, as more buildings become vacant, the company is negotiating to lease them to larger companies in order to provide work in the area. The Rank Xerox Business Park is also being developed to bring employment back to the site.

Example 1: external transport

Before 1983 the company provided all its own transport services, internal and external. An examination of the costs of providing external transport revealed that they were extremely uncompetitive, with Rank Xerox drivers' pay and allowances far above the average for the area. The company was also bearing the costs of an increasing legislative burden on this function, as well as the maintenance and replacement of vehicles. In addition, any disputes within the company could have led to disruption and stoppages, making it impossible to provide an efficient service for customers.

Management considered tenders from several companies and in 1983 decided to award the contract for external transport to National Carriers Limited. This was a three year contract, reviewed annually. The contract has recently been renewed. National Carriers agreed to employ all those redundant drivers who wished to join them and purchased the company's fleet of vehicles. It was agreed that Rank Xerox would continue to provide day to day supervision on the site and that the drivers would work exclusively for Rank Xerox.

There was no consultation either with the employees or unions before the announcement was made because of the possibility of industrial action. In the event the unions accepted the change and concentrated their efforts on other redundant employees who did not have offers of alternative employment.

Most of the drivers accepted the offer of a job with National Carriers, despite the reduced wages and conditions. They received redundancy pay from Rank Xerox and some hope of greater job security with a large transport firm.

For Rank Xerox the advantages of the change were immediate and have continued. They include:

- cost savings in the region of 30 per cent on a £600,000 budget
- improvements in efficiency and drivers' attitudes
- newer and better equipment

- no stoppages or disputes since 1983
- more flexibility to deal with peaks and troughs in activity
- a reduction in the number of supervisory staff from four to one
- no responsibility for legal requirements, maintenance and replacement of vehicles, holidays, absence, employment problems etc.

The only disadvantage management has found is that National Carriers' drivers are not permitted to load their own vehicles, but this is not seen as a major problem.

The company has also considered whether internal transport should also be sub-contracted, but at present it is felt that the relationship of these employees with the plant is so close that it would not be practicable. There has, however, been a considerable reduction in the numbers employed in this area.

Example 2: works engineering facilities

This department is responsible for maintenance across the whole range of the company's activities from cleaning to the servicing of equipment and the installation of new technology. It originally had a staff of around 200. This has now been reduced to 31, of which half are administrative, technical and supervisory staff and half are highly skilled mechanical and electrical tradesmen.

By 1983 redundancies had reduced the staff to 130. Ten jobs were saved the previous year through a productivity agreement which allowed for more flexible working practices and shift patterns. It was decided however to sub-contract progressively much of the work in this area, starting with the least skilled employees and working upwards. All that is left now is a small group of highly skilled and flexible craftsmen who are valuable to the company by virtue of their long years of training. These remaining employees are all on one grade.

Overall, since the exercise began, costs in the department have been reduced by around 20 per cent a year. The manager reports that the new system is working 'superbly'. There have been no demarcation disputes or stoppages, there is greater flexibility and peaks and troughs can easily be met. A great deal of effort was put into consultation and communication when the changes were introduced and this led to an understanding by employees of the need for change.

Cleaners In 1983 the company employed 36 cleaners on site, but some cleaning was already sub-contracted to an outside company. Management approached this company to see if it was prepared to take over the remaining cleaning and employ the existing Rank Xerox staff. The company agreed, but pay and conditions were considerably reduced and proved unattractive to ex-Rank Xerox staff who did not participate in the venture.

However two redundant Rank Xerox employees, a supervisor and a manager, formed their own company and successfully tendered to provide the cleaning done by Rank Xerox employees and to take them on. This company has now taken over all the cleaning on site.

Over the last two to three years the company estimates that 30 to 40 per cent has been saved on employment costs in this area. The contractors have also been found to provide a more efficient and flexible service. They have specialist equipment (eg for snow clearing) which the company had never been able to provide and they can call in extra staff if necessary. There is a two year fixed price contract with the company which covers materials and labour.

Civil trades There was a history of demarcation problems with the civil trades employees (carpenters, painters, builders, etc) which had led to considerable inefficiency. When these employees were made redundant, several of them were encouraged to become self employed and return to work for the company as sub-contractors. Demarcation disputes have since become a thing of the past. Greater flexibility has meant that the number of people required is less and costs have been reduced. These individuals have been able to make a living by working not only for Rank Xerox but also for outside customers.

Maintenance craftsmen Similarly several former employees in the higher skill ranges who were made redundant have returned to work on the site as sub-contractors. There were some uncertainties with the Inland Revenue over the status of electricians and fitters who wished to become self employed and return to work at the site. Although the Inland Revenue would give no firm ruling, the indications were that these individuals would not be regarded as self employed for tax purposes if they did more than 51 per cent of their work for one employer in the first six months. Protracted discussions between the individuals and the Inland Revenue led to delay and in the end these individuals either joined together to form their own companies or went to work for existing sub-contractors.

Now company policy is to use the 14 remaining skilled employees as first priority and then go to the former employees as sub-contractors. A contract base was set up on the edge of the site for them to work from. Although relationships were sensitive at the start, the new system is now accepted and former employees now work side by side with those still employed by the company. The new system has enabled the company to provide cover where and when it is needed at considerably reduced costs.

The future

Further major cutbacks in indirect staff are envisaged as the company continues to strive for cost competitiveness, although the company has for the first time in many years just started to take on new shop-floor employees, albeit on weekly contract terms which are more cost effective to the company and provide some security for current shop-floor employees. The concern now is to consolidate the improvements made and build on them. In the most recent annual negotiations, management achieved union agreement to a joint review of a wide range of topics, including grading structures, work patterns, flexibility, bargaining arrangements and the time spent on employee relations activities.

13 Annual hours and five crew shiftworking at Thames Board Limited

Thames Board is part of Unilever and makes high quality carton board at its Workington plant, which opened in 1967. Around 760 people are employed at the plant and there are eight separate bargaining groups: SOGAT, ATAES, AUEW Staff and four EETPU groups. Negotiations for hourly paid employees are at national level, for staff at local level. Since 1978 there has been very heavy capital investment at Workington and the plant is now totally computerized.

The company is part of the British Paper and Board Industry Federation (BPBIF). When the enabling agreement on annual hours (see p 298 ff) came into effect in 1982 the company decided to adopt the 'fallback' position of reducing weekly hours to 39.

New objectives

There was a four crew, three shift system at the plant and employees had worked 42 hours a week including two hours overtime. When hours were reduced, shiftworkers worked 41 hours and were given six days additional holiday which inevitably led to a further increase in overtime working.

By the end of 1983 there were several pressures on the business:

External—maintenance of production
       —competition from mills overseas, especially in Sweden and Finland
       —TUC objective of 35-hour week
Internal —monetary claims from unions
       —SOGAT wanted a reduction in the working week
       —AUEW and EETPU wanted increased differentials
       —union pressure for staff status
       —pressure to reduce overtime.

Overtime levels were very high. For SOGAT members overtime was peaking at 20 per cent, while among engineers it was up to 30 per cent.

Prior holiday arrangements led to lost production time and increased overtime. There was also a three week plant shutdown (two weeks in the summer, one at Christmas). When considering new working patterns, management established a number of key objectives, as follows:

- to achieve minimum dependence on overtime
- to achieve continuity of manning to enable the plant to be run throughout peak holiday times
- to improve basic pay relative to local industry
- to resolve grading and differential issues
- to reduce the cost of training resulting from having to provide high levels of overtime cover for holidays
- to achieve gains in productivity and manning levels equal to those of major competitors.

Three options were considered by management:

- continue with four crew working, but recruit extra staff and take hardline management action to reduce overtime
- continue with four crew working, but renegotiate holiday agreements and rationalize manning levels
- change to five crew working and an annual hours agreement.

The first option was rejected as too difficult and expensive, the second because it was too emotive. Management decided to try for the third option. A management team visited companies in Austria, Sweden and Finland to examine five crew working and annual hours contracts in operation.

By 1984 management was ready to start the consultation

process with the trades unions. A major breakthrough was achieved in the early stages when the unions decided to form a joint senior shop stewards committee to negotiate annual hours. Without this co-operation between the unions, it is doubtful whether the final agreement could have been achieved, as the company would have been faced with eight separate negotiations.

Introduction of annual hours

The BPBIF enabling agreement was taken as the base for negotiations which examined manning levels and working practices with a view to moving to five crew working and an annual hours contract. A seminar was held with the shop stewards, a national officer from SOGAT, the management team and a representative of the BPBIF.

In the negotiations management had several fundamental aims:

- one shut down a year at Christmas
- 39 hour week for five crew shift workers
- no overtime for holiday cover, but controlled overtime to cover sickness, machine shutdowns and training
- no increase in costs, ie the new pay bill and the cost of capital expenditure must not exceed the current pay bill

The unions' objectives were:

- no compulsory redundancies
- an increase in the basic rate
- a reduction in the working week
- an increase in holidays
- 100 per cent sick pay scheme (moving towards harmonization)
- compensation for loss of earnings through less overtime or downgrading
- floating days off

As the senior shop steward said "we didn't want the overtime, we just wanted the money".

The union representatives were not convinced by management's accounts of five crew working in the companies they had visited abroad. From the unions' point of view, the second major breakthrough was achieved when joint union-management study visits were arranged to see the company's foreign competitors. Not only were the union representatives able to see five crew working in operation for themselves, but representatives from both sides were thrown together for long periods of time and much fruitful unofficial negotiation took place.

By May 1984, the fundamental principles had been agreed and the unions had accepted that if their competitors had moved to annual hours they would have to do the same. Between May and November, there were detailed negotiations on manning and wage levels.

The final agreement allowed the company to move to five crew working with no increase in staff numbers because of increased flexibility and the combination of jobs. Thirty new jobs were created, however, because of a move to three shift working in the dispatch department.

Under the new rota shift, workers get blocks of 10 days off nine times during the year and one summer break of 20 days. In addition there are 48 'floating hours' which can be taken at any time. At the employees' request, two shifts are worked 'back to back' ie employees work the morning shift and return for the night shift. Although management was not in favour of this, the employees said they were used to this system and wanted it to continue. Management has agreed to try not to call employees in to work overtime on their 10 day breaks except in emergencies.

On pay, it was decided to go for a percentage increase plus an efficiency supplement in order to maintain differentials. An estimate of predictable overtime pay, which would be reduced by five crew working, was made. This was subtracted from P60 earnings and a percentage of the difference paid.

A joint management-union committee was established to monitor sickness absence, in the hope that pressure from workmates would prevent persistent absence. In the event, since annual hours were introduced, sickness absence has increased from two to three per cent.

The agreement was finally approved by a majority of 62 per cent of the workforce.

Conclusions

The process of researching and negotiating the new arrangements took about 18 months to complete. A very great effort was made to communicate with the workforce. The new arrangements were often difficult for employees to understand and had to be explained several times.

Of special importance in the communication process were:

- that all communications with the unions were in writing
- presentations were made to groups of employees by department and section
- a final presentation was made to the whole workforce
- trade unions' presenters were used, basing their presentation on a text written jointly with management.

For the company the new arrangements have several advantages:

- no annual shutdown
- overtime cut in half, it is now 13–16 per cent and there are plans for further reductions
- competitive manning levels
- a stabilized holiday system
- all pay claims resolved
- greater flexibility
- the joint sick pay panel

The senior shop steward reported that the annual hours system is "the best thing that ever happened to the employees". Although the agreement was only accepted by a small majority, there is now no one who wants to change it. For the unions the advantages are:

- increase in pay
- no redundancies
- 48 floating hours
- increase of 30 in workforce
- 100 per cent sick pay scheme
- reduced working hours, and a further reduction to 38 hours expected in 1986
- increase in time off

A new rapport has been established between the management and the workforce and the agreement is seen as providing the basis for further improvements in the working arrangements at the plant.

MEMORANDUM OF AGREEMENT

BETWEEN

THE BRITISH PAPER AND BOARD INDUSTRY FEDERATION

AND

THE SOCIETY OF GRAPHICAL AND ALLIED TRADES

THE TRANSPORT AND GENERAL WORKERS UNION

GENERAL AND MUNICIPAL WORKERS UNION

Dated: 5th February 1982

SUBJECT: Reduced working time.

It is hereby mutually agreed as follows:

INTRODUCTION

1. That this agreement provides guidelines for negotiations at local level to achieve a reduction in working time coupled with the adoption of new systems of work and using the annual hours concept with a fall-back arrangement of reduced hours at national level for those mills not making greater changes by locally using these guidelines.

2. At present the hours worked per year are made up of:

    (a) Basic hours (based on a 40 hour week and five weeks holiday)

    (b) Contractual overtime (to give 42 hours for the four shift cycle. 44 hours for the three shift cycle)

    (c) Essential overtime to cover for staggered holidays, break-downs, maintenance etc.

    (d) Casual overtime for absence due to sickness, etc.

Negotiations on reduced working time need to achieve an actual reduction (not more hours at overtime rates) by not only reducing basic hours, but also reducing to a minimum contractual overtime and overtime for holiday cover. To achieve this without an unacceptable increase in production costs, or a large reduction in employees' earnings will require major changes in working practices and rotas, details of which can only be worked out and agreed at local level.

1. Therefore this agreement provides:

   (a) Nationally agreed guidelines for the introduction into a mill of the annual hours concept of working time by local negotiations (paragraph 4 to 10) and,

   (b) A fall-back arrangement of reduced hours at national level for those mills not making greater changes locally using the annual hours approach (paragraphs 31 and 32).

Part (a) setting out guidelines for annual hours is *not compulsory* on employees or companies, but the reduced hours in (b) *will apply* to all mills who have not achieved the same or greater reduction in hours by local negotiations under (a).

GUIDELINES FOR THE INTRODUCTION INTO A MILL OF THE ANNUAL HOURS CONCEPT OF WORKING TIME.

Conditions and Changes Necessary

4. The parties to this Agreement emphasize that:

   (a) Achievement of more leisure time must not be at the expense of mills competitive positions such as would only lead to more redundancies and mill closures than may otherwise occur. Furthermore the availability of investment capital derived from profits is essential to future viability.

   (b) A substantive mill agreement when brought into operation must mean an actual reduction in working hours, and not merely payment of more hours at overtime rates.

   (c) Production hours must be maintained or increased, which may mean less shut time at weekends and for holidays.

   (d) The changes must be achieved with no increase in unit cost of production.

5. Successful achievement of the changes envisaged in this agreement is dependent upon the conditions at the mill being right when they are introduced. These conditions include *either.*

(a) That the mill is operating on a profitable basis, has the prospect of continuing to operate profitably after the changes, and the prospect of achieving an acceptable return on capital to finance necessary future investment; *or*

(b) the company is satisfied that the changes will lead to the above conditions being met

and

(c) that conditions are right for overtime as a means of

	1981	1982	1983 Additional this August
		(5 wks hol)	(47 hours)
Continuous	1931	1914	1867
Semi-continuous	2023	2005	1958
Day	1839	1823	1776

(d) This reduction in working time without loss of pay must be achieved with minimum damage to a company's competitiveness. Therefore under this part of the agreement managements have the right to maintain production by retaining existing mill operating weeks, to continue where necessary existing day and shift rotas and requirements for shift cover, and to roster holidays or take other measures designed to ensure no loss of production and minimum cost.

(e) Therefore the reduction in working time in each year will be implemented in one or more of the following ways; the choice being made by management after consultation with their employees' representatives:

(i) One 8 hour shift off for each 8 weeks worked, payment for which will be made from the bank of 47 hours pay provided under sub paragraph (b) above of this Agreement. Such time off to be rostered as necessary.

(ii) In the case of some dayworkers it may be possible for the hours worked each day or week to be reduced by an appropriate period with payments for that period being made from the bank of hours referred to in sub-paragraph (b) above.

(iii) Where due to market requirements or for other reasons the production hours are not required the time off may be given by a mill shut period.

(f) In this way all employees would have the equivalent of an hour per week reduction in working time. No change in hourly basic rates or hours ranking for overtime premia would be required and at this stage no change in shift rotas.

(g) where time off is given against the banked hours the job will only be covered by overtime when all alternative means of cover have been exhausted. Production to be reduced or eliminated (though some overtime will still be necessary to cover for sickness and other absence, and unforeseen maintenance requirements).

Annual Hours Agreement

6. The increased productivity which must accompany any increases in leisure time can only be achieved if accompanied by agreed fundamental changes in current work practices. The changes necessary will be determined at mill level by the employer after consultation with his employees and form part of the local negotiations on the introduction of the annual hours system.

Annual Hours System

7. Under the present system, shift rotas assume that employees will be available for work throughout the year. This means that holidays have to be covered by the remaining employees working overtime, by use of spares or by the mill shutting. The Annual Hours system specifies only the actual hours that an employee is required to be at work (including any contractual overtime incorporated), and the rotas and crewing are designed according to the production hours required.

8. The Annual Hours System requires identification separately of (a) production requirements, if possible for the year, and (b) the number of hours per year that the employee is available to work after taking into account the length of the nominal working week and days of holiday in respect of annual and public holidays. The shift system and crewing arrangements are then designed to meet these requirements.

9. Production hours have to be decided by the company having regard to market, commercial and technical requirements.

10. Employee hours are decided by agreement with the employees in accordance with the provisions of this Agreement.

11.   The shift system and crewing arrangements will be organised with minimum use of overtime either as a means of production or to cover for colleagues on holiday. Casual overtime will still be necessary to cover for unforeseen events such as absence, sickness etc.

12.   With the full implementation of the Annual Hours System it is necessary to agree:

(a)   The *Basic Annual Hours*

(b)   The *Total Hours* worked, to be built into the agreed rota, reserve shifts etc.

13.   The *Basic Annual Hours* will be the minimum hours to be worked per year by each employee whether on daywork or a shift system after taking into account all annual and other holidays. Hours outside the Basic Annual Hours specified will by definition be overtime.

14.   However to meet local circumstances and to ensure cover for the production hours required with the shift system chosen locally, it will sometimes be necessary for some additional hours to be worked on a contractual basis. These will be paid as overtime and together with the Basic Annual Hours will form the *Total Hours* worked to be built into the agreed rota.

15.   An example of this in operation is shown in the Points for Guidance.

Shift Rotas

16.   The number of crews required, the extent and use of spares, working out the most effective use of manpower, the actual rota chosen and the extent of such overtime working as is required, are matters for determination at mill level in discussion with the recognised trade unions. Examples of rotas and the principles involved in designing a suitable rota are set out in Points for Guidance to this Agreement. The principles of the Agreement apply to maintenance and process employees although their rotas may of course differ. Similarly the principles apply to both day and shift employees although daywork arrangements will inevitably be simpler.

Rota Cards

17.   Shift and perhaps some day rotas are likely to be based on a long cycle, in which case it will be necessary once a year for each employee to be given a card showing his rostered hours for the twelve months ahead. This will enable him to see when (a) there is a mill shut period (b) rostered holiday weeks, and (c) he has substantial periods with no scheduled working shifts, so that he will arrange the remainder of his holidays during these periods.

18. The card should also show the number of hours, if any, which are not rostered but which are required to be worked during the year in order to make up the person's annual hours (See Points for Guidance).

Payment for Hours Worked

19. The design of shift rotas and payment systems shall be within the following principles:

    (a) The management decide the number of production hours in the year. (See para. 9.)

    (b) Basic Annual employee hours will be decided by agreement with the employee taking into account the provisions of this Agreement. (See para. 10.)

    (c) If less than the agreed basic annual hours per person per year are built into the rota the balance will be banked and worked during the year to cover for absence either as reserve shifts or by 12 hour shift cover.

    (d) If in excess of the agreed basic annual hours per person are built into the rota the balance will be contractual overtime hours and paid at time and a half. Such hours should be kept to a minimum.

    (e) Rostered hours, and reserve shifts or banked hours under (c), worked between midnight Saturday and midnight Sunday shall be paid at double time. (But see para. 20).

    (f) Rostered hours, and reserve shifts or banked hours under (c), worked between 6 a.m. Saturday and midnight Saturday and midnight Sunday and 6 a.m. Monday shall be paid at time and a half. (But see para. 20).

    (g) All other rostered hours and reserve shifts are at plain time, except as provided in sub-paragraph (d) and (h).

    (h) Where the rota requires work to be done on any of the eight additional days holiday with pay in respect of public holidays, provided in the National Agreement, such hours worked will be paid at double time. (The time off is assured because these days are taken into account already by the calculation of the annual hours).

    (j) The agreed basic annual hours are the minimum number of hours to be worked per year after deducting all holiday entitlement, and therefore all holidays must be taken outside the hours rostered to be worked.

    (k) Payment for hours worked additional to rostered hours in order to cover for absence caused by sickness and other reasons, where they are not reserve shifts, will be at the appropriate premium of time and a half or double time according to when worked, and would be related to the individual's hourly rate as at present.

(l)   Overtime only becomes payable after the hours contained in the rota for each pay period, including any required reserve shifts, have been worked.

20.   There may be some variation in the periods specified in (e) and (f) provided the principle is observed of 24 hours to be paid at double time and 24 hours at time and a half.

Holidays and Mill Shuts

21.   In cases where the mill is planned to be shut for a period during the year ahead to meet maintenance or other requirements, the employees annual hours will be rostered over the remainder of the year, except of course where they are required to be present during the shut period in question.

22.   Whatever an individual's yearly rota pattern it must be designed in such a way that it provides every employee with two consecutive weeks (14 calendar days) between 1st June and 30th September when there are no scheduled working shifts. This enables him to be away from the mill on holiday for at least two consecutive weeks without interruption. This will normally be met by rostered 0 weeks, i.e. this break will be on a scheduled basis. See Points for Guidance.

23.   The new rota will be published annually by no later than 31st October for the following year's production needs having regard to market and/or maintenance requirements. Any changes will continue to be within the principles laid down in this agreement.

Absence Cover

24.   With increased leisure time, more complex shift rotas, and minimum manning levels, any absenteeism can be extremely disruptive both to production and to other employees. The parties agree therefore that it is vital to ensure that absence from scheduled working shifts, for whatever reason, is kept to a minimum.

25.   Overtime cover for colleagues on holiday can be eliminated by suitably designed rotas under the annual hours system, but the obligation to work overtime where necessary to cover for absence due to sickness or other reasons, and to cover maintenance requirements will continue.

26.   However where practical any reserves or banked shifts or spares available will be worked before use is made of overtime.

Pay on an Equalised Basis

27.   To avoid fluctuation week by week, and having regard to the complexities of a lengthy rota, it may be desirable for pay to be calculated on an annual basis although, of course, continue to be paid at short intervals. A suggested equalised pay scheme is set out in the Points for Guidance.

Credit Transfer

28.   For security and administrative reasons it is strongly recommended that payment be made by credit transfer.

Definitions

29.   With the design of rotas around the annual hours concept the present four shift, three shift, double day shift, and day work systems will no longer be as easily identifiable. Therefore the following definitions will apply:

Continuous operation, defined as rotas spread over twenty four hours per day seven days per week in order to give a regular 168 hours per week production cover. (Currently 4 crew but in future could for example be 4, $4\frac{1}{2}$ or 5 crew).

Semi-continuous operation, defined as rotas spread over 24 hours per day but less than seven days per week in order to give production cover of less than 168 hours per week on a regular basis. (Currently 3 crew but in future could for example be 3, $3\frac{1}{2}$ or 4 crews).

Discontinuous operation, defined as rotas spread over at least 16 hours per day but giving cover for less than 24 hours of production per day. (Currently Double Day Shift.)

Day Work, systems based on one shift per day normally worked between the hours of 6 a.m. and 6 p.m.

Points for Guidance

30.   Detailed notes with examples are set out in Annex A and show:

(a)   Calculation of employees' Basic Annual Hours.
(b)   Calculation of Production Hours required.
(c)   Calculation of crews required and practical options available.
(d)   Design of basic rotas.
(e)   Implications in relation to holiday etc.
(f)   Equalised Pay in detail.

MILLS NOT USING THE ANNUAL HOURS APPROACH

31.   Most of the industry will not be in a position within the next year or two to adopt the major changes envisaged in the Annual Hours approach set out in this Agreement.

32.   In such cases, i.e. where for whatever reason an annual hours agreement has not been reached locally, the following reduction in working time will operate from the beginning of the first full pay period in January 1983:

   (a)   A reduction of 47 hours worked per year, per employee, subject to the conditions set out below.

   (b)   In order to implement this reduction in working time without loss of pay each employee covered by this agreement shall have a banked entitlement to 47 hours of time off at his hourly basic rate. Nominally this will accrue from 1st January 1983 at 1 hour per week worked. The method of taking the time off and payment is detailed below.

   (c)   This, together with the 5 weeks holiday agreed for introduction in 1982, will result in the following development in minimum annual hours worked under the National Agreements:

MATTERS ARISING UNDER THIS AGREEMENT

33.   Any issues arising under this agreement and local agreements derived therefrom shall be dealt with under the normal Provisions for Avoiding Disputes between the parties.

34.   Matters not specifically covered by this agreement will continue to be governed by existing National Agreements.

DATE OF OPERATION

35.   The provisions of this Agreement come into operation with effect from the beginning of the first full pay period in January 1983.

36.   However detailed discussions at mill level on the arrangements for implementation will need to take place during 1982.

Signed for and on behalf of:

THE BRITISH PAPER AND BOARD INDUSTRY
FEDERATION   . . . .

THE SOCIETY OF GRAPHICAL AND ALLIED TRADES . . . .

THE TRANSPORT AND GENERAL WORKERS UNION . . . .

GENERAL AND MUNICIPAL WORKERS UNION   . . . .

DATED: . . . .

POINTS FOR GUIDANCE
TO THE ANNUAL HOURS SECTION
(Paras 4 to 30)

CURRENT EMPLOYEE ANNUAL HOURS

1. To transfer from the present system it is necessary to calculate the existing annual hours worked based on the present working week and holiday entitlement. This gives us the starting point by indicating how many hours are available to be built into a total under the present system after taking out the entitlement to holidays.

2. For example, under the *existing* national agreement (as at December 1981) the minimum annual hours will be:

(a)	Weeks per year	52.179
	(i) Take out weeks of annual holiday	4.6
	(ii) Take out eight public holidays (expressed in weekly terms)	1.6
	Leaving weeks to be worked	45.979
	Multiply result by number of hours worked per week	×40
		1839 hours per year

    (b)   Comparable figure, continuous (42 hrs) 1931

    (c)   Comparable figure, semi-cont (44 hrs) 2023

3. The relevant figures for 1982 and 1983 are given in paragraph 32 of the Agreement.

4. The actual hours to be built into a rota on the new system under this agreement would of course be determined locally having regard to mill circumstances, the extent of changes being made etc.

CALCULATION OF PRODUCTION HOURS

5. The company take their forecast sales for the year and make adjustments to allow for broke, downtime, and taking into account the capacity of the making machine in tonnes per hour, are able to calculate the production hours required per year.

6. This in turn will determine the necessary mill operating week and duration of mill shut.

7. For example if production requirements in a year is 24,000 tonnes and the machine capacity is 2.81 tonnes per hour, the production hours required will be 8,541.

8. To achieve this it would be necessary to run 168 hours per week for 356 days per year leaving 9 days of shut.

CREWS REQUIRED

9. The theoretical number of crews required can be calculated by dividing the number of hours to be worked by each employee into the number of production hours.

10. Continuing the example
in paras 2 and 7 above: $\dfrac{8541 \text{ prodn. hrs.}}{1839 \text{ employee hrs.}} = 4.64 \text{ crews}$

11. Under the present system 4 crews would operate with the balance made up by way of overtime or in some cases spares.

12. Under the proposed annual hours approach the objective would be to minimise overtime by using $4\frac{1}{2}$ or 5 crews and eliminating not only the overtime necessary for holiday cover, but where possible contractual overtime. Suppose we take 5 crews.

BASIC ROTA

13. The basic rota is then designed around the agreed annual hours so that all rostered shifts are shifts to be actually worked because holidays have already been taken into account in employee hours and are taken during the intervening periods between working shifts.

14. A typical five crew basic rota would be as follows:

Week	M	Tu	W	Th	F	Sa	Su
1	a	a	a	a	a	–	–
2	–	–	n	n	n	N	N
3	n	n	–	–	m	M	M
4	m	m	m	m	–	–	–
0	–	–	–	–	–	–	–

15. Such a rota if accompanied by 9 days of shut at Christmas would result in 1710 rostered hours worked leaving 129 hours (approx. 16 shifts) to be worked on reserve to make up the contractual hours, in this example of 1839.

16. The 16 reserve shifts may be built into the rota as cover during some of the '0' weeks or may be a bank of time to be worked to cover for absence during the year. Because the hours are part of the basic annual hours they are not overtime hours and will not be at premium rates unless they are used on a Saturday or Sunday.

ANNUAL ROTA

17. The basic rota is then incorporated into the complete rota for a year, an extract from which is as follows:

WEEK

Summer Holiday Period

		16	17	18	19	20	21	22	23	24	25	26	27	28	29	30	31	32	33	34	35	36	37
	A	0	1	2	3	4	0	1	2	3	4	0	0	2	3	4	1	1	2	3	4	0	1
	B	4	0	1	2	3	4	0	1	2	3	4	1	1	2	3	4	0	0	2	3	4	0
CREW	C	3	4	0	1	2	3	4	0	1	2	3	4	0	0	2	3	4	1	1	2	3	4
	D	2	3	4	0	1	2	3	4	0	0	2	3	4	1	1	2	3	4	0	1	2	3
	E	1	2	3	4	0	1	2	3	4	1	1	2	3	4	0	0	2	3	4	0	1	2

18. The 'boxed' 0 weeks are ensuring each person has 2 consecutive weeks when he will not be required to be at work and therefore can take his summer holiday. The rest of his holidays are taken in other '0' weeks occurring during the year.

19. These aspects are illustrated more fully in the worked examples (to be added).

EQUALISED PAY

20. By the nature of the rota the period to be worked from week to week varies considerably and there are a considerable number of weeks in the course of the year when no shifts are scheduled to be worked. Therefore equalisation of pay becomes desirable.

21. It is a matter for local agreement whether the payment is then made weekly, fortnightly, monthly or four weekly although monthly is recommended.

22. Holiday pay may no longer need to be identified separately, and the P60 formula could be largely irrelevant.

23.	The equalised payment thus established would apply throughout the year until such time as there was a change in one of the factors e.g. a national wage increase. Adjustments for each pay period would still be necessary to cover payment for overtime, or any reduced time through absenteeism or lay off, unless some form of banking system is used.

24.	The treatment of sickness pay would be dependent on the requirements of a mill's sick pay scheme.

25.	In some cases there will be bonus schemes in operation and it would be for local consideration how they should be applied.

26.	This can more easily be achieved by taking the complete rota for the year and working out the number of worked hours and paid hours the latter being higher to take into account shifts that fall on Saturdays or Sundays and therefore ranking for premium, or for other reasons are paid on an enhanced basis (see Para. 19 of the Agreement).

27.	Using a current situation based on a typical 4 crew rota, the 1931 hours worked per year would be approximately 2345 paid hours.

28.	If his rate were £2.50 an hour the total pay for all the shifts worked during the year would be £5,862.50 (2345×£2.5).

29.	This pay relates to an average of 45.979 weeks worked (see calculation of the annual hours) i.e. £127.50 per week.

30.	However the £5,862 does not include holiday pay so we have to add to that 6.2 weeks of holiday (4.6 weeks annual plus 1.6 weeks public holidays) at £127.50 per week namely £79.50 making a total £6,653 per year.

31.	This is equalised at regular intervals throughout the year.

32.	eg. if payment is made *monthly* it equals $\dfrac{6653}{12}$ =£554.42

if payment is made *weekly* it equals $\dfrac{6653}{52.179}$ =£127.50

if payment is made four weekly= $\dfrac{6653}{13}$ =£511.77

Absence and Overtime

33.	There are some circumstances in which this regular payment will require to be adjusted.

34.	For example let us assume the person is paid monthly and is receiving £554 a month. Suppose during the month he worked three 12 hour shifts instead of 8 hour shifts in order to cover for the absence of a colleague away sick. He would receive an *additional*

18 hours pay at £2.50 per hour equals £45 to cover the overtime work.

35.   Similarly if he were absent without leave for example on one Saturday shift during the period his monthly payment would be reduced by £30 (8 hours at time and a half, because it is Saturday, × his rate).

36.   Other reasons calling for adjustment of the weekly payment could be: if he was required to come in on what had locally been agreed as a public holiday, assuming the premium for such work had not been included already in the total paid hours for the roster; in the event of lay off in accordance with the provisions of the national agreement; if absent sick in accordance with the company sick pay scheme.

FURTHER GUIDANCE

37.   Further detailed guidance and examples will be issued in due course.

14 High productivity work patterns at the Wessex Water Authority

The Wessex Water Authority, with a head office in Bristol, has a responsibility for the collection, treatment and distribution of drinking water; collection, treatment and disposal of sewage; control and maintenance of mains rivers; water quality and water-related recreation facilities.

In recent years, the Authority has increasingly taken the view that much of its services (therefore much of the demands on its workforce) fall outside the traditional working week and normal working hours. These demands, which were not new, had been met over the years by overtime at expensive hourly rates. The trade unions indicated that they would continue to seek the traditional solution and demanded high compensation payments for working outside those normal working hours (ie overtime and shift *premia*, unsocial hours payment etc). Wessex was looking to maximize the use of working hours and achieve the maximum flexibility, but it believed that the flexible approach provided its own reward for the employee (for example, working on fewer days and longer off duty breaks) and that compensating payment should be fairly small and should apply only to the unsocial element of the working time. Furthermore, the salary should recognize demands on flexibility.

An investigation into the demands on the workforce, and the means by which the greatest effectiveness could be obtained in the use of that workforce, indicated that there were certain areas where the benefits gained from flexible work patterns would be greater than others. It also revealed that some groups of employees would find the revision of their work time patterns more acceptable than some of their colleagues. As a result of that investigation, it was decided that the working groups in which the most benefit may be obtained and the proposals most easily accepted were as follows:

- *land drainage—maintenance operatives*: these workers are responsible for keeping main river water courses and the associated constructions free running, clear of obstruction and clean and attractive
- *tanker drivers and some associated sewage works operatives*: these employees are responsible for ensuring that the sewage treatment works operate effectively and efficiently and that the sludge is transported to various disposal points
- *central laboratory services*: this involves all activities related to collecting, analysing and reporting on samples from all water services

The remainder of the case study describes how flexible work patterns, 'high productivity work patterns' as they are termed by the Authority, were applied in these functions.

Example 1: land drainage

The special problem of the land drainage operation is that most of the workload (ie routine clearing work) is related to the growth of river weed and riverside trees, shrubs and grass. This means that during the growing seasons there is a lot of work to be done and demands on the labour force are high. The work is almost all out of doors and there is plenty of daylight in which to get the work done, but to make the best use of the daylight, it has meant paying overtime *premia* or employing additional labour for these peak periods. The labour resourcing is not helped by a natural desire of the workers to take much of their leave entitlement during the busiest period because that happens to coincide with the warmer summer days. The reverse side of the problem is that during the winter period, managers have limited work available, since the working hours (daylight hours) are severely restricted and few workers are anxious to take much of their annual leave allocation during this time. At this time, such tasks as lubrication, the painting and repair of plant and equipment and installations can be done, but there is only a limited amount of this type of work available and storms and floods often provide a welcome relief for the workers involved in the tedious winter maintenance routines.

These problems appeared to be best tackled through the introduction of flexible work patterns. In consultation with the managers, a pattern of work was produced which gave a variable start and finish over the year, so that during the summer the workers would cover up to a 10 hour working day and in the darkest winter months a minimum of seven hours per day. The variable work pattern was designed to average 38 hours per week over the year, this being the contractual hours per week. Discussions were opened with the trade unions and after the negotiations were completed, the company and unions arrived at a pattern of four working days of $9\frac{1}{2}$ hours equalling 38 hours during the British Summer Time period and 38 hours spread over five days when Greenwich Meantime was in operation in the winter, as follows. In summer, a four day week is worked on a fixed basis, either Mondays to Thursdays or Tuesdays to Fridays to maintain full five day cover. The hours are 7.30am to 5.30pm, with a 30 minute break for lunch. In winter, all the men work a five day pattern 7.30am to 4.15pm, with a 30 minute lunch break, Mondays to Thursdays and 7.30am to 12.30pm on Fridays. Additional productivity improvements were obtained by reaching an agreement to report on and off duty on the site, rather than at the depot. This removed the travel element from valuable daylight hours.

This pattern of work has been operating for two full seasons and has worked well. The pattern is voted on by both management and men annually and has so far continued to receive their support. The main advantages of the scheme have been:

- it has done away with the need for depot reporting, giving considerable extra working time at the working location
- it has improved utilization of plant, vehicles and equipment
- machines can be serviced out of hours so there is no downtime
- it has proved popular with the men
- it has raised the possibility of disposing of two depots now that the men no longer need to report to them

One problem arose over the definition of a 'day' for leave purposes, since daily hours were different in summer and winter, but this was resolved by agreement. Leave entitlement has been expressed as 1600 hours per year (20 days at a normal eight hour day) and is booked according to the hours that would have been worked on the day or days being taken, ie 9½ hours per day in the summer, 8½ hours per day Mondays to Thursdays in the winter (five hours on Fridays).

Example 2: sludge tanker drivers and sewage treatment work operatives

The tanker drivers originally worked normal hours of duty from Mondays to Fridays doing any deliveries that were required outside the normal working week on a weekend or evenings at overtime rates. The introduction of a staggered work pattern to these operatives (see rota below) proposed that the men would work a 40 hour week (38 hours plus two hours at overtime premium) on the basis of four days between Mondays and Saturdays at 10 hours per day. There were substantial savings on the cost of the equipment (notably, a reduction in the number of road tankers that were required) and there were two men fewer employed in the new working patterns. The net savings were about £35,000 per annum and the benefits of the new pattern included:

- a small decrease in wages cost
- all vehicles on the road, giving more cover
- some spare hours available for additional work if required

The workers in the sewage treatment works, who had previously been on a three shift round the clock system, were initially reduced to a two shift system (a morning and late shift over the whole week). However, the remuneration package for shift systems was expensive by comparison with the flexible day working which was subsequently introduced. The new pattern enabled complete cover on every day of the week, with 10 hours working each day, by rotating the staff on the basis of four days work out of seven. There was no substantial overtime requirement, other than the two hours above their contractual 38 hour week. As a result of the scheme, payroll costs were reduced by one-third compared with the previous system of alternate shift working.

SLUDGE TANKER DRIVERS
Staggered work pattern

MAN	*W/E*	T	F	S	S	M	Tu	W	*W/E*	T	F	S	S	M	Tu	W	*W/E*	T	F	S	S	M	Tu	W	*W/E*	T	F	S	S	M	Tu	W
A		X	X	X	R	X	X	R		R	X	X	R	X	X	R		X	R	R	R	X	X	X		X	⊗	⊗	R	R	R	X
B		R	X	X	R	X	X	X		X	R	R	R	X	X	X		X	⊗	⊗	R	R	R	X		X	X	X	R	X	X	R
C		X	R	R	R	X	X	X		X	⊗	⊗	R	R	R	X		X	X	X	R	X	X	R		R	X	X	R	X	X	X
D		X	⊗	⊗	R	R	R	X		X	X	X	R	X	X	X		R	X	X	R	X	X	X		X	R	R	R	X	X	X

X = Working day
R = Rest day
⊗ = Additional day's duty

Example 3: central laboratory services

The laboratory services manager was faced with a number of problems relating to the provision of a laboratory service to the Authority. He was in the process of centralizing a number of smaller laboratories into one central laboratory and at the same time he had to provide an analytical service to the operational managers across a very wide geographical area over seven days each week. He recognized that the use of shiftworking and/or overtime was likely to be expensive and, after considering several options, he turned to an extended hours work pattern to provide the service for his client departments. The employees concerned are non manual technicians used to very formalized work patterns and contracted to work 37 hours per week on a salaried basis. The thought of variable work patterns was alien both to the employees and to their trade union and at first they opposed the proposals. However, after what turned out to be fairly sensitive negotiations with the employees and their representatives, an agreement was reached for the staff concerned to operate a five week cycle in which they would operate $9\frac{1}{4}$ hours of duty which, with refreshment breaks, covered 10 hours attendance at the laboratory. This arrangement ensured that the laboratory was able to provide service from 8.30am to 7.30pm on week days and 8.30am to 6.30pm on weekends and on bank holidays (for further details, see rota on p 320). The changes to the workings of the laboratories which included the revised working hours, resulted in a reduction in the cost of analysing a sample by almost half in the year 1985/86 compared with 1983/84.

Conclusions

The above has described the application of four different variable working pattern schemes for employees in a variety of work functions within an Authority responsible for water services. Benefits have been identified during the relatively short time that these revised patterns have been in operation and the benefits which accrued, both to employees and to the Authority, are likely to continue. However, the full advantages of variable work patterns have not been fully explored. There are still other areas of employment which require investigation and other

forms of distributed work patterns. Averaging of hours over a
working year will continue to be explored to the advantage of
both the workers and the efficiency of the system. There are also
areas of work such as accounts processing and collection which
have seasonal peaks once or twice a year and work patterns
could and should be adapted to meet these peak demands on
staffing.

In preparing such a scheme, it is important to identify the
workload in relation to the day, week, month, or year, to look at
the staffing requirements over the longest possible period and to
identify the peaks and troughs over that period. Having established the workload in relation to the manpower requirements, it
is then necessary to consult with the staff involved and identify
both the advantages to the employees and to the organization. In
almost every area there will be advantages to both, and negotiations will follow from there. However, the most important factor
is to avoid being bound by traditional agreements or practices
which are not relevant to the workloads.

WESSEX WATER AUTHORITY REGIONAL LABORATORY EXTENDED HOURS ARRANGEMENT

INTRODUCTION

1.1 A work rota and remuneration package has been determined and agreed for certain designated staff at the Authority's Regional Laboratory, Saltford.

1.2 The arrangement will enable the Authority to obtain more effective and economic benefit of plant and equipment at the laboratory.

1.3 This arrangement will apply until or unless superseded by any agreed alternative.

2. PRINCIPLES

2.1 Rota is on a 5 week cycle.

2.2 In each 5 week cycle a person works 18 weekdays and 2 weekend days.

2.3 Weekdays are 10 hours attendance $9\frac{1}{4}$ hours working

2.4 Weekend days are 10 hours attandance $9\frac{1}{4}$ hours working (paid at enhanced rate)

2.5 In any 5 week period a person works $20 \times 9\frac{1}{4}$ hrs=185 hrs ie 37 hour average week

3. WORKING HOURS

3.1 It is necessary for the laboratory to operate until at least 7.30 pm. However after 6.30 pm there is only need for 1 senior and 3 other staff to be in attendance. Also at weekends and Bank Holiday times (excluding Christmas and Boxing Days) there is a need for 1 senior+3 other staff to be in attendance.

3.2 The core work period will be from 8.30 am to 6.30 pm. However it will be necessary for staff to provide cover on a rotating basis to ensure that there is at least the minimum staff requirement on duty until 7.30 pm weekdays and 8.30 am to 6.30 pm at weekends and Bank Holidays. This cover to be provided as a part of the normal day work arrangements for all laboratory staff.

Laboratory Rota

ROTA repeated in blocks of 5 to make up to 20 staff

x x x x x   Late Start and Finish

15 Flexible 'committed hours' working at Whitbread, Romsey

Background

Whitbread, Romsey currently employs 226 people of which 145 are members of the TGWU; office workers are represented by the ACTSS. The TGWU has a closed shop for the former manual group.

During the 1970s, the plant had a reputation as one of the more militant in the Whitbread group and there were some fears that it would close. There were very high levels of overtime, with many employees earning more in overtime pay than on the basic rate. Employees were averaging 15 to 20 hours overtime a week, with some working up to 30 hours; overtime was 'manufactured' through various working practices and was not necessary.

The nature of the work at Romsey means that there are fluctuations in activity which are fairly predictable throughout the year. Peaks occur at Christmas, Easter and during the summer holidays. Working hours therefore have to be flexible.

Negotiations

Management's aim in negotiating the Hours Commitment Scheme was to meet the employees' long term aspirations for staff status. This was based on a philosophy that all employees should be treated equally and all involved in working together.

When the idea was first raised in Autumn 1982, the unions were suspicious. They expected management to have proposals to put to them and the shop stewards were surprised when management said there were no detailed plans, but suggested a joint approach to the problem. A small group was set up which spent five months of concentrated effort examining the working patterns and pay of each individual in the plant for the previous year. Full time union officials were not involved in the negotiations, but they were kept informed of progress and approved the final outcome.

Management decided to be entirely open with the union representatives, and all relevant information was made available to them. The union reps did much of the work themselves, estimating what the committed hours in each unit should be and calculating the appropriate salary level. This detailed examination of work showed several unexpected results; for example, the group discovered that some employees were taking their holiday pay but not taking the time off.

The financial settlement was not discussed until the final stages of the negotiations, the group first concentrating on achieving agreement on the new concepts involved in the scheme. Much of the time was spent on argument and debate. The unions liked the idea of salaried status, but they were suspicious that their members might be taken advantage of. Their main concern was that groups of employees might suffer financially when they moved to an annual salary. They recognized that some individuals would have to lose out because the average income of the group (including overtime) would have to be taken as the new salary level. They were also concerned about management's proposals for increased flexibility, but when they understood that the greater flexibility did not mean that jobs would be lost, they were able to accept more flexible working practices.

The union reps explained the new scheme to each unit individually, and employees were given time to consider the proposals before they voted on it. The final agreement was accepted in a ballot by 123 votes to 28.

The Hours Commitment Scheme

The concept of the Hours Commitment Scheme is to harmonize terms and conditions for all hourly paid and monthly paid staff, excluding managers, at Whitbread, Romsey. The groups of employees covered include drivers, craftsmen, warehouse and production operators, clerical, secretarial and technical staff.

The main feature of the scheme is that all employees receive a salary based on grade and the number of annual average weekly committed hours of work. Each individual has a commitment to work up to a defined daily maximum number of hours and, in some cases, a commitment to weekend working. There is no overtime, nor are there overtime rates, bonuses, allowances or tea breaks. The only fixed additions to salary are shift pay and charge-hand pay.

An individual's salary is based on job grade and annual average weekly committed hours and determined from a salary matrix (see box on p 332). All salaries are paid monthly, in arrears, by credit transfer into a bank account of the individual's nomination.

The basis of the Scheme is the need for individuals/sections to commit themselves to being available to work a number of average hours over a 12 month period, as determined by the needs of the business. Linked to this is the commitment to achieve the daily workload in each section. The arrangements applying to weekdays and weekends are as follows.

Weekdays   Each individual is committed to a daily maximum number of working hours with minimum hours as shown in the table below for each section. Individuals are not committed to work more than their daily maximum hours, but must attend for their committed daily minimum hours.

Each section/individual must complete the required workload on each day. When all required work is completed to the satisfaction of the departmental manager, the individual may go home provided he has attended for his minimum hours. In certain sections, it is possible for the majority of individuals in the section to go home, provided satisfactory arrangements have been made for the required work to be completed. Variations in actual hours from the average, weekly committed hours in any one week cannot be carried forward into subsequent weeks to change minimum/maximum committed hours in subsequent weeks.

Weekends Each individual is committed to a specified annual number of Saturdays, and in some cases, Sundays, with a respective annual total hours commitment, as shown in the boxes on pp 330 and 331. The programmed maximum number of hours worked on any committed Saturday/Sunday will not exceed the individual's daily committed maximum levels.

Excess hours Excess hours are those hours worked above the daily maximum commitment and those worked above committed weekend hours for the individual. If an individual agrees to work time in excess of his daily maximum hours, he is entitled to Time Off in Lieu (TOIL) and the following arrangements for TOIL apply:

- *Monday to Friday*: excess time counts as flat rate for TOIL (one hour of TOIL for one excess hour worked or 15 minutes of TOIL for 15 minutes excess worked)
- *Saturday and Sunday*: excess time worked on Saturday/ Sunday is increased by 25% for TOIL ($1\frac{1}{4}$ hours TOIL for one excess hour worked or 19 minutes of TOIL for 15 minutes excess worked)
- *bank holidays*: excess time worked on a bank holiday is increased by 75% ($1\frac{3}{4}$ hours TOIL for one excess hour worked or 27 minutes for 15 minutes excess worked)

Part hours are accumulated at the appropriate rate and rounded to the nearest minute.

Monitoring and review The introduction and continued operation of the Hours Commitment Scheme is monitored by an agreed review procedure. The review is undertaken by members of the negotiating teams and, where necessary, involves departmental management and the steward/representative. The review includes consideration, both quarterly and cumulative, up to one year of:

- maximum hours ⎫
- average hours ⎬ for individuals
- minimum hours ⎭
- departmental/section average hours
- departmental workload
- movement out of section/department
- excess hours
- weekend working
- sickness/holiday effect
- the effect of changes in plant, equipment, technology, operating procedures and working methods

The purpose of the review is to highlight permanent trends and determine appropriate action. Review meetings take place during the months of April, July, October and January.

Results The main outcome is that employees are now working shorter hours for the same earnings. Productivity increased dramatically when the Scheme was introduced and has been sustained since.

However, the most important result emphasized by both union reps and management was the new atmosphere of honesty and trust which resulted from their joint co-operation in developing and introducing the Scheme. This new climate has eased the burdens on both sides and means they spend less time on negotiations, dealing with disputes etc.

How far this atmosphere has penetrated through to the rest of the workforce is difficult to judge. The shop stewards and manager involved in negotiating the Scheme recognize that, although their attitudes have changed, it will take much longer for their colleagues (managers as well as other employees) to accept fully the new approach. However, the Hours Commitment Scheme is now fully accepted at Romsey and most employees regard the results as beneficial. For employees the main advantage of the scheme are:

- staff status
- a stable income
- shorter working hours—job and finish now applies to all tasks; in the warehouse, for example, the 12 hour day has been reduced to nine

- better sick and holiday pay
- higher pensions (and contributions)
- more job security

For the company the main advantage is that employees are committed to finishing their allocated day's work on the day. There are no changes in the way the work was scheduled when the scheme was introduced, but employees are now motivated to complete their work as soon as possible. Other advantages are:

- more responsibility and commitment from the workforce
- higher productivity
- greater flexibility
- reduced overheads because of shorter working hours
- tea breaks abolished
- labour costs can be accurately predicted
- less need to use contractors

Both management and unions are pleased that the better performance of employees has meant that the number of contractors brought in to cover peaks has been considerably reduced. Management would prefer not to use contractors because the company does not have the same control over them as over its own employees. Use of contractors is costly and not regarded as improving the company's (or the manager's) image. The unions want to see their jobs protected, not threatened by outside contractors.

Some aspects of the scheme have caused concern among the employees. For example, some of them have found it difficult to get used to receiving monthly pay by credit transfer. Employees were also concerned that they would be taken advantage of by management insisting that they work their maximum hours all the time. In fact, this has not happened and the 'job and finish' principle has meant that working hours have reduced. Employees very rarely have to work more than their committed hours and the 'time off in lieu' provisions have been used on only a handful of occasions since 1983. The original estimate of committed hours turned out to be accurate in all but one unit where the agreement has been amended to increase committed hours by $2\frac{1}{2}$ hours a week, with a corresponding increase in salary.

The flexible hours scheme has been applied to shiftworkers by an informal agreement that the early shift will normally work minimum hours and the late shift works the maximum if necessary.

A few employees have tried to 'take advantage' of the more generous sick pay benefits, but this has been kept under control by a joint union-management approach.

For former monthly paid staff employees, who are also included in the Scheme, the main change was that for the first time they had to 'clock'. They also lost the opportunity to receive 'merit' increases under the new pay structure.

Management and union representatives report that the introduction of such a scheme is only possible if both sides are committed to making it work. They thought it could be adapted to other working situations, but only if an atmosphere of honesty and trust was established.

DEPARTMENTAL COMMITTED WORKING HOURS

Grade	Department	Av hours	Min hours	Max hours
A	Vehicle fitters	42.5	37.5	47.5
A	Electricians	47.5	40	55
A	Builders/carpenters	42.5	37.5	47.5
A	Engineering fitters	45	37.5	52.5
B	CD driver	50	40	60
B	Transfer driver	50	40	60
C	CD mate	50	40	60
C	Storage/handling	47.5	40	55
C	Processing	45	37.5	52.5
C	Engineer storeman	40	35	45
C	Vehicle W/S storeman	42.5	37.5	47.5
C	CD van driver	47.5	40	55
C	Plant services op	47.5	40	55
D	Container racking	47.5	40	55
D	General hand	42.5	37.5	47.5
E	M/T sorter and yard cleaner	47.5	40	55
	Apprentices	42.5	37.5	47.5

DEPARTMENTAL COMMITTED WORKING HOURS

Grade	Department	Av hours	Min hours	Max hours
A	Site nurse	42.5	42.5	42.5
B	Distribution admin/co-ordinator	45	37.5	52.5
B	C/S standby technicians	40	35	45
B	Assistant area managers	40	35	45
B	Cellar service technicians	37.5	35	40
B	Site services administrator	37.5	35	40
C	Distribution admin assistant	40	35	45
	Sen sec—inns	40	35	45
C	Sen sec—exec team/inns	37.5	35	40
C	sen sec—production	35	35	35
C	Senior production clerk	37.5	35	40
C	Cellar service planner	37.5	35	40
C	Cellar service storeman	37.5	35	40
C	C/S workshop technician	37.5	35	40
C	C/S secretary/admin clerk	37.5	35	40
C	Trade administrator—inns	37.5	35	40
C	Cash call supervisor	35	35	35
D	Depot stock/admin clerk	40	35	45
D	Laboratory assistant	37.5	35	40
D	Production clerks	37.5	35	40
D	C/S assistant planner	37.5	35	40
D	Site services assistant	35	35	35
D	Micro processing/audit clerk	35	35	35
D	Secretary/clerk—inns	35	35	35
D	Clerk/typist p/t	20	20	20
E	Laboratory stewardess	40	40	40
E	General clerical/reception/switchboard p/t	21	21	21
E	C/S micro operator p/t	21	21	21

MAXIMUM AND MINIMUM WEEKLY/DAILY COMMITMENT HOURS

The following table sets out for each level of annual average weekly hours commitment the weekly and daily maximum and minimum hours.

Weekly hours			Daily hours	
Av	Min	Max	Min	Max
35	35	35	7	7
$37\frac{1}{2}$	35	40	7	8
40	35	45	7	9
$42\frac{1}{2}$	$37\frac{1}{2}$	$47\frac{1}{2}$	$7\frac{1}{2}$	$9\frac{1}{2}$
45	$37\frac{1}{2}$	$52\frac{1}{2}$	$7\frac{1}{2}$	$10\frac{1}{2}$
$47\frac{1}{2}$	40	55	8	11
50	40	60	8	12*

* This must be within the legal limit

Weekend work does not count toward actual hours for calculation of the weekly maximum in the week it occurs. Weekend work will count towards the annual and quarterly calculation of hours worked.

WEEKEND WORKING

This schedule represents the commitment to weekend attendance for each individual in the respective sections,

Section	Committed no of Saturdays per year	Committed total Saturday hours per year	Committed no of Sundays per year	Committed total Sunday hours per year
Processing	8	46	2	10
Customer delivery	6	44	—	—
Storage/handling	14	56	—	—
Transfer drivers	8	60	—	—
Kegging	8	39	—	—
Engineers storeman	5	20	—	—
Builders/ carpenters	21	84	3	$13\frac{1}{2}$
Maintenance fitters	17	100	6	36
Maintenance electricians	15	74	4	22
Plant service operators	21	124	8	44
Site cleaner	5	20	—	—
Vehicle fitters	21	84	—	—
Vehicle general hand	11	44	—	—
Vehicle storeman	21	84	—	—
Advert storeman	14	56	—	—
Apprentices	6	24	—	—

No minimum or average weekend days or hours have been defined and individuals will be required to work up to the total number of weekend attendances or hours, whichever is reached first. Once attendances or hours have been exceeded then the weekend excess hours provisions will apply.

WEEKEND WORKING

This schedule represents the commitment to weekend attendance for each individual in the respective occtions.

Department /group	Personnel/job group	Committed number of Saturdays per year	Committed total Saturday hours per year
All 35 hour commitment staff		—	—
Distribution	Admin assistant	12	48
admin	Bonus clerk	8	32
	Stock control	8	32
	All other distribution admin	3	12
Assistant area	*managers*	14	82
Surveyors/			
draughtsmen		3	12
Finance/	MD's secretary	8	39
admin	Senior secretaries	3	12
	Site nurse	1	4
	Site services' admin	3	20
	Surveyor's clerk	37	148
	Trade admin asst	1	4
	Reception	1	4
Production	Production clerks	7	28
	Engineer's sec/clerk	3	12
	Laboratory steward	3	12
	Laboratory asst	8	46
Cellar	IoW technician	27	108
service	Other 40 hr standby staff	14	56
	Workshop technicians	14	56
	Storekeeper	14	56
	All other cellar staff	3	12

No minimum or average weekend days or hours have been defined and individuals will be required to work up to the total number of weekend attendances or hours, which ever is reached first. Once attendances or hours have been exceeded then the weekend excess hours provisions will apply.

EXAMPLE OF ANNUAL SALARIES FOR GRADE AND AVERAGE HOUR COMMITMENT*

Average Weekly/Committed Hours

Grade	35	37.5	40	42.5	45	47.5	50
A	—	—	8400	—	—	—	—
B	—	—	7600	—	—	—	—
C	—	—	6800	—	—	—	—
D	5100	5600	6100	6400	6900	7400	8000
E	—	—	5500	—	—	—	—
F	—	—	—	—	—	—	—

Salary is paid one month in arrears by 12 equal instalments.

* 1985 rates.

16 Temporary employment and sub-contracting at Xidex (UK) Limited

The Xidex Corporation is an American company which is the world's largest producer of computer magnetic media and microfilm. In December 1985 it acquired the Brynmawr plant previously owned by another US company, Control Data, which had been producing computer tapes and disks there for the previous 12 years.

Nearly 1000 people are employed at Brynmawr. There are 215 monthly staff, 593 full time production workers and 182 'supplemental' production employees, most of whom work 30 hours a week. This is a single status company with all full time employees working a 37½ hour week. Most of the production workers are semi skilled and 51 per cent of the workforce is female. The EETPU is the only recognized union and has full negotiating rights for the production workers.

The recent change in ownership has not had, and is not expected to have, an impact on working patterns.

The background

When Control Data took over the plant in 1974 it adopted a typically American approach, which at the time was unusual in Britain. Many of its personnel policies can be seen as precursors of the changes now being introduced in many other companies. Not only were terms and conditions the same for staff and production workers, but restrictive practices were 'unknown' at Brynmawr where flexible manning has always been the policy. From the beginning it was decided to concentrate on the 'core' activity of manufacturing. Peripheral activities, such as catering, cleaning and security have been sub-contracted since 1974. An 'open' management style was another characteristic.

One of the main objectives of personnel policy has been to maximize the job security of the 'core' production workers. Unemployment in the area is around 30 per cent and one of management's main concerns has been to provide stability of employment for its long serving employees.

For the first 10 years or so, the company expanded rapidly. The workforce grew from 150 in 1974 to over 1000 in the early 1980s, but the volatile nature of the market for the company's products became of increasing concern and in 1980 management at Brynmawr decided to adopt the policy of 'supplemental' employment which had already been developed by its parent company in the United States. This policy was designed to maintain flexibility and provide a buffer for the workforce in the face of volatile market conditions. It is a management policy, not negotiated with the union, although the principles are outlined in agreements with the union.

The introduction of the policy coincided with the expansion of the workforce from 500 to 850. 'Supplemental' staff were initially employed on three month contracts before transfer to the permanent staff.

Later a system of 10 month contracts was applied to all new production employees, whether they were employed as part of the expansion or to replace existing staff. The 10 month period was chosen to avoid complications with employment legislation. At the end of the 10 month contract period, if market conditions permitted, the employee would normally be transferred to the permanent staff.

While output was increasing and the workforce expanding, the 10 month contract system worked well. However, in 1984 a downturn in output was forecast and it was decided to terminate the employment of those coming to the end of their 10 month contracts. The result was that employees who had been with the company for 10 months had to leave, while those at the beginning of their 10 month contract stayed on with the company, still with some hope of permanent employment if market conditions improved.

This decision led to protests from employees and a demand for a 'last in, first out' policy to be applied. Management refused to accede to this request, but it did agree to a review of the supplemental employment policy.

The result of this review was that supplemental employees continued to be employed on 10 month contracts, but in future they would only work 30 hours a week (four days). They would be clearly identified as part time and therefore different from full time permanent employees.

The current policy

In early 1985 however a further decline in the market led to another re-examination of the policy. Further cutbacks in the workforce became necessary, 10 month contracts were abolished and it was decided that supplemental staff would be employed on contract, only as and when required. The contracts would be of varying lengths, depending on market requirements. Supplemental staff would continue to be employed for 30 hours a week in order to differentiate between them and full time permanent employees. The 30 hour week has the additional advantage of providing work for a greater number of people than full time employment. Normally management is able to predict labour requirements about two months in advance and can call in the required number of supplemental employees. The new policy is based on several 'rings of defence'. For the 'core' workforce (see figure 9, p 158).

This policy only applies to production workers as volatile market conditions do not have the same immediate impact on technical, clerical and management staff.

All supplemental employees have experience of working on the site and can therefore be slotted in to the workforce with ease when they are required. They receive the same rates of pay as full time permanent staff, and accrue holiday entitlement pro-rata. They receive all other benefits, but they are not allowed to join the company pension scheme or receive company sick pay.

On the edge of the rings of defence are 68 *stand by* operatives whose employment had previously been terminated by the company. Management keeps a list of the names of these people and they are called in and laid off, as and when required. They are all employed on short term contracts.

The next ring consists of *30 hour supplementals* who are regular rather than permanent employees, working a four day

week, normally Monday to Thursday or Tuesday to Friday. Like
the stand by operatives they are employed on short term contracts and their employment can be terminated with a week's
notice.

The next ring consists of *37½ hour supplementals*. These are
employees who were employed on 10 month contracts when the
new system was introduced. They will disappear over time but
are being kept on until there is an opportunity to provide them
with permanent employment.

Sub-contractors provide the final ring of defence. They
include cleaning, catering and security staff as well as distribution and building workers. If business turned down to the extent
that core workers' jobs were threatened, management would be
able to use production employees to do in house some of the work
traditionally done by sub-contractors (subject to contractual
requirements).

In November 1985 it was agreed that supplemental
employees should constitute no more than 20 per cent of the
workforce. Once the 20 per cent trigger is reached further
permanent staff will be employed from among the supplementals. The current number of supplementals employed is around
16 per cent.

Index